The International Conference on Business History 8

THE TEXTILE INDUSTRY AND ITS BUSINESS CLIMATE

Proceedings of the Fuji Conference

edited by
AKIO OKOCHI
SHIN-ICHI YONEKAWA

UNIVERSITY OF TOKYO PRESS

382.4
I611t

83-3262

THE TEXTILE INDUSTRY AND ITS BUSINESS CLIMATE

ORGANIZING COMMITTEE FOR THE SECOND SERIES
INTERNATIONAL CONFERENCE ON BUSINESS HISTORY
1979–1983

Chairman:	Okochi, Akio	(University of Tokyo)
Treasurer:	Watanabe, Hisashi	(Kyoto University)
Secretary:	Yuzawa, Takeshi	(Gakushuin University)
	Daito, Eisuke	(Tohoku University)
	Hara, Terushi	(Waseda University)
	Ishikawa, Kenjiro	(Doshisha University)
	Kita, Masami	(Soka University)
	Miyamoto, Matao	(Osaka University)
	Udagawa, Masaru	(Hosei University)
Advisory Board:	Nakagawa, Keiichiro	(University of Tokyo)
	Kobayashi, Kesaji	(Ryukoku University)
	Morikawa, Hidemasa	(Hosei University)
	Yasuoka, Shigeaki	(Doshisha University)
	Yonekawa, Shin-ichi	(Hitotsubashi University)

Participants

Project Leader for the Third Meeting:
Yonekawa, Shin-ichi (Hitotsubashi University)

Adelmann, Gerhard
(University of Bonn)
Choi, Jong-Tae
(Seoul National University)
Daito, Eisuke
(Tohoku University)
Farnie, Douglas A.
(University of Manchester)
Hara Terushi
(Waseda University)
Ishikawa, Kenjiro
(Doshisha University)
Kawabe, Nobuo
(Waseda University)
Kita, Masami
(Soka University)
Kuwahara, Tetsuya
(Kyoto Sangyo University)
Miyamoto, Matao
(Osaka University)

Nakagawa, Keiichiro
(University of Tokyo)
Oates, Mary J.
(Regis College)
Okochi, Akio
(University of Tokyo)
Takamura, Naosuke
(University of Tokyo)
Tripathi, Dwijendra
(Indian Institute of Management)
Udagawa, Masaru
(Hosei University)
Watanabe, Hisashi
(Kyoto University)
Wortzel, Heidi Vernon
(Northeastern University)
Yuzawa, Takeshi
(Gakushuin University)

CONTENTS

Preface .... (A. Okochi).. ix
Introduction .... (S. Yonekawa).. xi

The Growth of Cotton Spinning Firms: A Comparative
  Study .... (S. Yonekawa).. 1
  Comments 1 .... (D. Tripathi).. 39
  Comments 2 .... (K. Nakagawa).. 42
The Structure of the British Cotton Industry, 1846–1914
  .... (D. A. Farnie).. 45
  Comments 1 .... (H. Vernon Wortzel).. 87
  Comments 2 .... (N. Takamura).. 89
The Business Climate of the German Cotton Industry,
  1850–1914 .... (G. Adelmann).. 93
  Comments 1 .... (M. J. Oates)..124
  Comments 2........................ (H. Watanabe)..126
  Reply to the Comments .... (G. Adelmann)..135
The Business Strategy of Japanese Cotton Spinners:
  Overseas Operations 1890 to 1931 ..... (T. Kuwahara)..139
  Comments 1 .... (J.-T. Choi)..167
  Comments 2 .... (M. Miyamoto)..169
Innovations in the Indian Textile Industry:
  The Formative Years .... (D. Tripathi)..175
  Comments 1 .... (D. A. Farnie)..194
  Comments 2 .... (S. Yonekawa)..195
Changing Patterns of Management in the Lowell
  Mills .... (H. Vernon Wortzel)..199
  Comments 1 .... (S. Yonekawa)..221
  Comments 2 .... (T. Yuzawa)..223

Locational Patterns of Southern Textile Mills,
    1880–1920 ....(M. J. Oates)..227
    Comments 1 ....(N. Takamura)..244
    Comments 2 ....(M. Kita)..246
Business Climate and Industrialization of the Korean
    Fiber Industry.......................(J.-T. Choi)..249
    Comments 1 ....(G. Adelmann)..270
    Comments 2 ....(E. Daito)..273
Japanese Cotton Spinning Industry during the Pre-
    World War I Period..................(N. Takamura)..277

Concluding Remarks ....(S. Yonekawa)..287

Index...293

PREFACE

The third meeting of the Second Series International Conference on Business History was held on January 5–8, 1981, at the Fuji Education Center, Shizuoka, Japan, under the auspices of the Business History Society of Japan.

The central theme for the third meeting was the cotton industry and its business climate. Initially the Organizing Committee planned an investigation into business climate in an international comparative way. Business climate here means the human and natural environmental factors surrounding an enterprise; it is a prerequisite to business activities, along with economic and technological factors. It differs from nation to nation, from time to time, and even from industry to industry. For the purpose of an international comparison, therefore, it is necessary to limit our scope to the same period and to the same industry. The cotton industry was chosen for our investigation because it was a leading industry in several nations in the course of their industrialization.

Accordingly, the Organizing Committee asked Professor Shin-'ichi Yonekawa, a leading specialist in the history of the cotton industry, to accept the role of Project Leader. Professor Yonekawa, in co-operation with the Organizing Committee, designed and organized the third meeting.

The following proceedings are a record of the meeting. On behalf of the Organizing Committee, I would like to express my sincere thanks to Professor Yonekawa for his effort in editing these Proceedings and preparing a summary of the discussions. I would also like to thank the Taniguchi Foundation for its generous support of

ix

both the meeting and the publication of this book. We also wish to express our warm thanks to Ms. S. Schmidt and Mr. W. Izumi of University of Tokyo Press for all their labors in editing and producing this volume.

February 1982

Akio Okochi
General Editor and Chairman
of the Organizing Committee
for the International Conference on Business History

INTRODUCTION

The textile—above all the cotton—industry was a lever of industrialization. Its material, cotton, was easy to transfer; its cheapness made it easy to find markets for the goods in the area where they were manufactured; the industry could create employment, as it was labor-intensive; as a consequence it could expect support for its establishment and development from government and community. Cotton goods have been one of the world's most widely traded goods up to now. Since the late nineteenth century, the cotton goods trade has been most competitive, especially in Asian markets. These facts tell us that comparative study of cotton spinning and weaving enterprises would be most fruitful.

This book contains the papers presented at the Fuji Conference on Business History and the discussions based on them. The focus of many of the papers was wider than business history in the narrow sense of the words, taking a wider approach than the discussion of individual enterprises.

D. A. Farnie's M.A. thesis was extremely informative on English cotton firms,* having content rather different from his later published work.** In his paper for this conference he gives us his analysis of the decline of England's cotton industry, although he does not refer to W. Lazonick's recent stimulating papers.***

The German textile industry has occupied a unique position up to now. G. Adelmann, who was engaged in an enterprise history of the German cotton industry,**** gives an overview of the devel-

---

* D. A. Farnie, English Cotton Industry, 1850–1896 (unpublished M. A. thesis, University of Manchester, 1953).
** D. A. Farnie, The English Cotton Industry and the World Market, 1815–1896, 1979.
*** W. Lazonick, Industrial Relations and Technological Change: The Case of the Self-acting Mule, Cambridge Journal of Economics, 1979; the same, Competition, Specialization, and Industrial Decline, Journal of Economic History, 1981.
**** G. Adelmann, Die Grundung der Aktiongesellschaft "Gladbacher Spinnerei und Weberei" in Spiegel der Geschichte: Festgabe für Max Braubach, 1964.

opment of the industry and its contribution to the national economy.

Second only to Great Britain in spindleage at the time considered here, the U.S.A. is an attractive country for a comparative study of the industry, as it contained two regions engaged in cotton spinning and weaving in which business climates differed markedly. H. V. Wortzel's and M. Oates's papers supply us with the industry's developments in those two regions, with special reference to business climates; both papers were developed from the authors' Ph.D. theses.*

India and Korea had common histories in that they were colonies, of Great Britain and Japan, respectively. India's spindleage has increased consistently, even since the Second World War. In his paper D. Tripathi shows us Indian entrepreneurship during the formative period of the cotton industry. On the other hand, in Korea where the development of the textile industry began in earnest only after the Second World War, cotton did not play an important part in the textile industry, as J. Choi shows in his paper. As for Japan, N. Takamura gives an overview of the formation and development of the cotton industry at large,** while T. Kuwabara's paper analyzes the overseas strategies of major Japanese spinning firms which were growing into big businesses after the First World War. Last, S. Yonekawa's paper presents a comparative study with special reference to the growth of spinning firms. Throughout the discussion attention was often paid to A. D. Chandler, Jr.'s impressive works, and Yonekawa's paper is also conscious of them.*** The editor regrets that the paper presented by K. Ishikawa was incomplete, so it could not included in this proceedings.

Shin-ichi Yonekawa

---

* H. V. Wortzel, Lowell; The Corporation and the City, 1859–1874 (unpublished Ph. D. thesis); M. J. Oates, The Role of the Cotton Textile Industry in the Economic Development of the American Southeast, 1975.

** His Nippon Bosekigyoshi Josetsu (A History of Cotton Industry in Japan, 2 vols., 1971) is a standard work in this field.

*** Conf. S. Yonekawa, A Century of Cotton Spinning Firms in Japan, The Japan Society of London, Bulletin 93–4, 1981.

The Growth of Cotton Spinning Firms: A Comparative Study

Shin-ichi Yonekawa
Hitotsubashi University

I.

The ultimate aim of an international conference on business history is comparative study. In the case of the present meeting, the comparative study of textile firms, especially of cotton spinning firms, was felt to be a fruitful topic, for reasons which I will outline below.

(1) In discussing cotton spinning firms in historical perspective, we can expect some merits that cannot be derived from the study of another industry. Firstly, although the cotton textile industry is still an important industry in developing countries, it has been quite rare in the study of business history to pay attention to these countries, although such study would be useful. The Japanese cotton industry, for example, started after those in Western countries and India, subsequently caught up with them, and is now struggling for existence in stiff competition with the industries of developing countries. After one century, the history of the Japanese cotton industry can be considered the history of "catching up" with Western countries and of subsequently being "caught up with" by developing countries. One can thus expect business historians to derive a number of fruitful suggestions from this study. Secondly, in the case of comparative business history, there might be some apprehension that the firms observed are selected by chance or that the number of firms studied is too small. However, the countries mentioned here have so many cotton industry firms that a picture of the typical management can be deduced from examining

1

a number of firms operating at the time considered. As a matter of fact, quite a number of large cotton spinning firms existing on the eve of World War II were established in the latter half of the last century, especially in the 1870s or 1880s, as will be mentioned later. This is due to the prevalence of public companies resulting from the enactment of company acts in each country.

(2)   It will be noticed that I have been using the term "firms." It is proper in a study of business history to pay attention to individual firms initially and then, in the course of the study, to observe the industry as a whole. This does not deny the significance of a macro-approach where attention is focused not on specific firms but on aggregates, but at the same time it is also true that a business history based on an analysis of individual firms gives a new perspective. As an example, the industrial structure of a country where several large firms control a big share of the market is sure to be different from that of a country where this is not the case, even though both countries may operate with the same spindleage figure. No less important is the fact that even if the market share is equal in two countries, the industrial structures will differ considerably if the ranking of the largest firms is stable over time in one country but not in the other.

Although historical study does not have direct policy implications, past history shows that developing countries have been more competitive in the industry than developed ones. It might be said, judging from the international division of labor, that advanced countries would be better off abandoning the industry for more sophisticated fields; however, this is a question of a different dimension. Even if we admit that some industries in advanced countries will decline in the course of time, this does not necessarily mean that all firms in that industry will decline correspondingly. Rather, under such adverse circumstances one competitive firm may emerge through the absorption of several small firms. The fate of an industry is not necessarily tantamount to that of its constituent firms; even if an industry should disappear, some of the firms constituting it could survive by diversification into other fields. Kanegafuchi, one of Japan's largest cotton spinning companies before World War II, has been gaining profits in the past several years mainly from its cosmetics division. Scholars interested in the growth of firms will find such a metamorphosis significant.

(3)   The term "business climate" has been selected as the theme of this conference. This may mean "business environment" from top management's viewpoint. For the business historian it means not only the conditions of available production factors, but also something more than these impersonal elements. Above all the historian will take an interest in the human elements: in the entrepreneur more than in capital and in the worker more than in wages; in the motives of these economic actors and their underlying social values.

With this in mind, I have thought it useful in this paper to distinguish between the "innovator" and the "follower" on which J. Schumpeter has put emphasis, although the "innovative firm" and the "imitative firm" would be better alternatives during the period considered. The presumption here is as follows: the vital ability to maintain industrial dynamism and competitiveness depends largely upon whether or not a few innovative firms appear, and how quickly other firms respond to them. If the response is very slow, the next question to ask is what the limiting factors are.

(4)   Innovative firms are not necessarily those which are large right from the beginning; they become large if they remain innovative for a long time. On the other hand, as large firms enjoy a high market share, their inherent capacity for being innovative is also greater than that of small firms. The consequence is that in the case of an industry such as the textile industry where a number of small firms exist, special attention ought to be paid to the managerial behavior of the upper-ranking firms.

The aspects of business management chosen for observation under the conference theme of "Business Climate and Industrialization" may differ according to the individual scholars' interests. In this paper, the growth, both horizontal and vertical, of cotton spinning firms will be observed so that the patterns in each country will be made clear. Obviously the author is aware of Prof. A. D. Chandler, Jr.'s proposition that integration played an important role in the development of consumer goods industries, although Chandler has not mentioned much about the industry of this period in his

TABLE 1. The Ten Largest Cotton Spinning Firms in the 1880s.

U.K.* (1884)		U.S.A.** (1886)		India*** (1882)		Japan (1892)	
Firm	Spindles +looms	Firm	Spindles +looms	Firm	Spindles +looms	Firm	Spindles +looms
J. Mayall (1)	420,000	Harmony (1)	275,000 +6,200	Maneckji Petit (1)	110,640 +1,954	Osaka (1)	60,391 +333
Crosses & Winkworth (2)	326,090	Wamsutta (2)	203,000 +4,500	New Dhurmsey (2)	94,108 +1,288	Settsu (2)	35,328
Musgrave (3)	257,714	Amoskeag (3)	170,000 +6,000	Oriental (3)	87,238 +1,288	Mie (3)	30,672
Sidebottom (4)	293,000 +4,700	Merrimack (4)	156,480 +4,462	Sassoon S. & W. (4)	50,220 +800	Kanegafuchi (4)	30,528
J & J Hayes (5)	229,880	Lonsdale (5)	151,824 +2,878	Western India (5)	37,392	Naniwa (5)	30,280
J. Wood (6)	204,000 +3,360	Boott (6)	142,080 +3,987	Hindostan (6)	36,840 +400	Hirano (6)	26,680
G. Mayall (7)	200,000	Pacific (7)	136,000 +2,500	M. Gokuldas (7)	34,336 +471	Kanakin (7)	19,906 +50
T. Taylor (8)	182,000	Dwright (8)	120,000 +3,200	Anglo-Indian (8)	31,680	Tenma (8)	16,388
J. Marsden (9)	182,000	Great Falls (9)	120,000 +2,600	New Great Eastern (9)	30,664 +685	Owari (9)	15,328
Middleton & Tonge (10)	177,660	Massachusetts (10)	119,528 +3,658	Mazagon (10)	30,096 +360	Senshu (10)	15,136

* Tables 1–6 do not contain J.P. Coats and English Sewing.

** Data for 1884 are not available. Tables 1–6 do not contain subsidiaries of J. P. Coats and English Sewing.

*** Data for 1884 are not available in India.

India

(1) Founded in 1860. Established firm operating three units at this time.
(2) Large but unsuccessful firm. Closed in 1887.
(3) Founded as the first public company in 1858. Closed in 1903.
(4) Founded in 1847.
(5) Founded in 1880 and survived to 1920s.
(6) Founded in 1873 and survived until 1920s.
(7) Founded in 1870. One of the companies with the best performances.
(8) Registered in London in 1876 and closed in 1890s.
(9) Founded in 1860 and reorganized in the middle of 1870s.
(10) Founded in 1874 and closed at the turn of the last century.

Japan

(1), (3) Amalgamated in 1914 to form Toyo S.C.
(2) Amalgamated with Amagasaki to form Dainippon C.S. in 1918.
(4) Firm most energetic in absorbing a number of small firms.
(5) Reorganized in 1899 and absorbed by Mie in 1906.
(6) Absorbed by Settsu in 1902.
(7) Absorbed by Osaka in 1906.
(8) Amalgamated with Asahi to form Osakagodo.
(9) Absorbed by Mie in 1905.
(10) Founded in 1889 and absorbed by Kishiwada in 1903.

U.K.

(1) Wound up after reorganization of 1894.
(2) A long-established company which came into being through amalgamation in 1875 and later became a public company.
(3), (8), (9) Amalgamated to form F.C.S.D.A. in 1898.
(4) Wound up in 1901.
(5) Converted to a private company in 1881 and remained so up to the time of its closing in the 1930s.
(6) Reorganized as a private company in 1891 and afterward became public.
(7) Wound up in 1903.
(10) Only public company among the ten and one of the earliest, founded in 1861 and closed in 1894.

U.S.A.

(1) Founded in Cohoes, N.Y., in 1851.
(2) The largest firm in New Bedford, established 1847.
(3) Founded in Manchester, N.H., in 1841.
(4) The oldest firm in Lowell, established in 1822.
(5) Founded in Lonsdale, R.I., in 1834.
(6) Founded in Lowell in 1836.
(7) An established firm in Lawrence since 1852.
(8) Founded in Chicopee, Mass, in 1841.
(9) Founded in Great Falls, N.H., in 1823.
(10) Founded in Lowell in 1840.

TABLE 2 The Ten Largest Cotton Spinning Firms in 1897.

U.K.		U.S.A.		India		Japan	
Firm	Spindles	Firm	Spindles	Firm	Spindles	Firm	Spindles
J. Mayall	444,000	B. B. R. & Knight (1)	388,862 +10,016	Maneckji Petit	131,132 +1,253	Kanegafuchi	81,778
Crosses & Winkworth	325,430	Amoskeag	290,000 +10,000	J. Sassoon (1)	90,096 +1,718	Mie	56,784 +400
Musgrave	320,000 +620	Fall River (2)	285,000 +7,500	Empress (2)	76,684	Osaka	52,297 +557
Sidebottom	293,000 +4,700	Harmony	275,000 +6,557	Victoria (3)	71,293 +126	Nippon (1)	40,194
Howe Bridge (1)	250,000	Wamsutta	219,216 +4,346	Bowrem (4)	65,148	Settsu	38,016
Ryners (2)	230,000 +1,620	Lonsdale	181,370 +3,717	Oriental	64,012 +1,140	Owari	30,340
J. Wood	221,000 +3,385	Pacific	180,000 +6,660	Bengal (5)	62,972	Amagasaki (2)	29,873
Horrockses & Crewdson (3)	220,000 +8,312	Merrimack	158,976 +4,502	Dunbar (6)	60,880	Hirano	27,616
J. & J. Hayes	216,518	Berkshire (3)	156,292 +3,700	Sassoon	53,624 +1,140	Kanakin (3)	26,096 +459
Barlow & Jones (4)	210,000 +1,300	Boott	152,992 +4,215	Swadeshi (7)	50,780 +1,025	Naniwa (4)	25,953

India

(1) Founded in Bombay with the largest mill in India in 1895.

(2) Founded in Bombay in 1883, and closed in 1915.

(3) Founded in Cawnpore.

(4) Founded in Calcutta.

(5) Registered in London in 1873 and operated in Calcutta.

(6) Founded in 1896 and operated near Calcutta.

(7) Founded in 1887 by N.J. Tata who bought closed Dhurmsey mills.

Japan

(1) Absorbed by Amagasaki in 1916.

(2) Amalgamated with Settsu to form Dai-nippon C.S. Co. in 1918.

(3) Absorbed by Osaka in 1906.

(4) Absorbed by Mie in 1905.

U.K.

(1) Founded in Bolton in 1867. An exceptionally energetic public company.

(2) Converted to a private company in 1891. Closed in 1912.

(3) Established process-integrated firm. Born in Preston and amalgamated with Crewdson in 1887.

(4) Established full integrated firm in Manchester. Converted to private company in 1900 and afterward became public.

U.S.A.

(1) Full integrated firm, originated in Providence, R.I. Partnership.

(2) Began to operate in Fall River in 1890.

(3) Organized in Adams, Mass. in 1889.

Table 3　The Ten Largest Cotton Spinning Firms in 1913.

U.K.		U.S.A.		India		Japan	
Firm	Spindles	Firm	Spindles	Firm	Spindles	Firm	Spindles
F. C. S. D. A.*	3,243,674	Amoskeag**	790,000 +24,400	Moneckji Petit	148,388 +5,043	Kanegafuchi (1)	465,524 +4,783
Crosses & Winkworth	364,000	Union Mills (1)	540,000	Madura (1)	106,536	Mie (2)	283,522 +5,330
Iwell Bank (1)	326,160	Fall River	458,288 +13,767	Victoria	106,000 +1,400	Fugigasu (3)	245,688 +979
Howe Bridge	316,000	Pacific**	404,360 +10,468	J. Sassoon	103,816 +2,079	Nippon (4)	173,412
Bolton Union (2)	290,478	B. B. R. & Knight	358,519 +9,323	Campore (2)	102,504 +962	Osakagodo (5)	163,252 +400
Times (3)	264,144	Parker (2)	289,652 +6,406	Central India (3)	100,352 +2,264	Settsu (6)	157,174
Broadstone (4)	262,504	Massachusetts	273,088 +8,238	Century (4)	92,016 +3,093	Osaka (7)	156,496 +4,532
Bee Hive (5)	262,000	Berkshire	260,079 +6,400	Buckingham (5)	89,284 +1,076	Tokyo (8)	138,696 +884
W. Heaton (6)	260,000	Merrimack	259,056 +7,096	Bengal	85,048 +1,050	Amagasaki (9)	132,392 +1,785
Horrockses & Crewdson	252,000 +9,530	Riverside (3)	246,800 +8,276	Curimbhoy (6)	83,396 +1,014	Fukushima (10)	103,616

*　Fine Cotton Spinners' and Doublers' Association Ltd. (registered in 1898).

**　Amoskeag and Pacific had a number of spindles and looms for worsted.

U.K.

(1) Registered as a public company in 1892.
(2) Registered as a public company in 1874.
(3) Registered as a public company in 1898.
(4) Registered as a public company in 1904.
(5) Registered as a public company in 1894.
(6) Reorganized as a private company in 1914 and absorbed by Crosses & Winkworth in 1921.

U.S.A.

(1) Leased all mills of New England Cotton Yarn in January 1913.
(2) Holding company organized in 1911.
(3) Incorporated in 1882; operated in Danville, Va.

India

(1) Founded in Madura in 1889.
(2) Founded in Cawnpore; two-unit firm.
(3) Founded in Nagpur in 1874.
(4) Founded in Bombay in 1898.
(5) Founded in Perambur, Madras.
(6) Founded in Bombay in 1888.

Japan

(1) Fifteen-unit firm at this time.
(2) Eleven-unit firm.
(3) Three-unit firm; founded in 1896.
(4) Two-unit firm.
(5) Five-unit firm. Incorporated by amalgamation in 1900.
(6) Six-unit firm.
(7) Three-unit firm.
(8) Two-unit firm, absorbed by Amagasaki in 1914.
(9) Two-unit firm.
(10) Six-unit firm.

TABLE 4   Mule Equivalents in 1913.

U.K.		U.S.A.		India		Japan	
Firm	Spindles	Firm	Spindles	Firm	Spindles	Firm	Spindles
F.C.S.D.A.	3,243,674	Amoskeag	2,283,000	Maneckjipetit	449,517	Kanegafuchi	862,073
Crosses & Winkworth	432,500	Union	675,000	Madura	159,804	Mie	650,701
Iwell Bank	326,160	Fall River	1,347,447	Victoria	190,000	Fujigasu	345,007
Howe Bridge	316,000	Pacific	1,078,600	J. Sassoon	233,655	Nippon	200,278
Bolton Union	290,478	B. B. R. & Knight	743,363	Campore	144,412	Osakagodo	239,776
Times	264,144	Parker	722,748	Central India	234,948	Settsu	235,086
Broadstone	262,504	Massachusetts	780,342	Century	261,539	Osaka	430,932
Bee Hive	262,000	Berkshire	321,199	Buckingham	182,346	Tokyo	219,516
W. Heaton	260,000	Merrimack	707,860	Bengal	158,982	Amagasaki	247,513
Horrockses & Crewdson	680,850	Riverside	742,620	Curimbhoy	148,172	Fukushima	155,424

recent work.[1] However, as suggested later in this paper, the way to survival in the industry seems to be through vertical integration and, to some extent, through diversification.[2] In this respect the strategies for existence of Japanese textile firms are most interesting to business historians.

First, the characteristics of the growth of firms in four countries will be discussed, after which tentative reasons for existing differences will be offered. Those aspects of the business climate associated with the growth of firms will be reviewed in the latter part of the paper.[3]

II.

The countries selected for discussion are the U.K., U.S.A., India and Japan: the countries that primarily competed with one another in the Asian market.[4] The years selected for comparison are 1884, 1897, 1913, 1928 and 1938. The largest share-floating boom of the firms occurred in the U.K., U.S.A. and India at almost the same time—that is, 1870 to 1875, and the firms established at that time were mostly public limited companies.[5] In Japan, on the other hand, an equivalent boom took place from 1887 to 1889, and the firms built then were in operation by 1892.

The best criterion for measuring the size of a firm will be determined according to the specific viewpoint of each scholar. The number of spindles has usually been the criterion used to determine the size of a cotton spinning firm. The author will also adopt this criterion,[6] but will also take their integration into consideration. To show the process integration, one ring would be equivalent to 1.5 mules in terms of capital cost; similarly, one loom would be equal to 45 mules, and one doubling spindle to half a mule.[7] It is impossible, however, to express functional integration in such a measurable way. On the basis of the Tables 1–6 and other facts yet to be cited, the characteristics of growth of each country's firms can be summarized as follows.

(1)   U.K.   Spindles in the Lancashire cotton industry increased remarkably through the two largest share-floating booms of 1873–75 and 1904–07, amounting to the unimaginable figure of 59 million at the beginning of World War I. The mills, which were about

TABLE 5   The Ten Largest Spinning Companies in 1928.

	U.K.			U.S.A.	
Firm	Number of spindles & looms	Type of integra- tion	Firm	Number of spindles & looms	Type of integra- tion
F.C.S.D.A.	3,295,460	C. S.	Amoskeag (1)	790,000 +29,600	C. Wo. S.W.F.Se.
Amalgamated Cotton Mills (1)	1,064,802	C. S.W.F. Se.	Lockwood Green (2)	570,966 +8,523	C. L. S.W.F.
Howe Bridge	714,800	C. S.	Pepperell (3)	512,016 +14,704	C. Wo. S.W.F.Se.
Crosses & Winkworth	500,016	C. S.	Riverside	472,220 +13,500	C. S.D.W.F.
Swan Lane (2)	400,000	C. S.	Pacific	468,648 +11,076	C. Wo. S.W.F.Se.
Laburham (3)	345,000	C. S.	Fall River	358,952 +8,396	C. S.W.F.Se.
Iwell Bank	333,924	C. S.	Lonsdale	294,756 +8,230	C. S.W.F.
Atlas (4)	323,732	C. S.	Nashawena (4)	275,000 +6,100	C. S.F.
Horrockses & Crewdson	320,000 +8,300	C. S. W.	Berkshire	265,724 +6,000	C. Wo. S..W.
Lees & Wrigley (5)	300,000	C. S.	B.B.R. & Knight	237,440 +6,394	C. S.W.F.Se.

U.K.
   (1)   A loose combination born in 1918.
   (2)   Registered in 1901.
   (3)   Registered as a public company in 1905.
   (4)   Registered as a public company in 1898 and absorbed Texas, a public company; later amalgamated with Egyptian Cotton Mills.
   (5)   Most energetic family business, converted to a private company in 1905.
U.S.A.
   (1)   The figures include a large number of spindles used for worsted.
   (2)   Temporary holding company.
   (3)   Began to operate in Biddeford, Me. in 1850; absorbed Massachusetts Cotton Mills.
   (4)   Incorporated in New Bedford in 1909.

India			Japan*		
Firm	Number of spindles & looms	Type of integra- tion	Firm	Number of spindles & looms	Type of integra- tion
Madura (1)	335,606	C. S.	Dainippon	896,676	C. Si.(R)
				+9,550	S.W.F.
United	245,232	C. S.	Toyo	859,940	C. Si.R.
Sassoon (2)	+4,750			+12,257	S.W.
Bombay	181,544	C. S.W.F.	Kanegafuchi	680,852	C. Si.
D. & M. (3)	+4,848			+8,007	S.W.F.
Maneckji	153,363	C. S.W.	Fuji	595,952	C. Si.
Petit	+4,622			+2,713	S. W.
Sholapur (4)	111,360	C. S.W.	Nissin (1)	480,518	C.
	+2,209			+2,965	S.W.
Victoria	104,336	C. S.W.	Osakagodo	476,800	C.
	+1,500			+3,638	S.W.
Swadeshi	102,592	C. S.W.	Kurashiki (2)	296,840	C. (R).
	+2,722			+1,812	K.S.W.F.
Central	100,352	C. S.W.	Fukushima	255,308	C.
India	+2,220			+1,996	S.W.
Century	100,156	C. S.W.	Kishiwada (3)	203,392	C.
	+3,130			+1,150	S.W.
Shapurgi	97,284	C. S.W.	Wakayama (4)	138,822	C.
Broacha (5)	+723			+1,463	S.W.

India
  (1) Registered in 1889; absorbed Coral in 1924 and Tinnevelly in 1927.
  (2) Five-unit firm registered in 1920.
  (3) Originated in dye works in 1879; established integrated firm.
  (4) Founded in Sholapur in 1874.
  (5) Founded in Bombay in 1916 through purchase of three closed mills.
Japan
  (1) A latecomer founded in 1907.
  (2) A local but established firm founded in 1887.
  (3) Registered in 1892.
  (4) Registered in 1893.
  * Tables 5 and 6 do not contain the spindleage of Japanese firms' silk mills and their subsidiaries in China.

TABLE 6 The Ten Largest Spinning Firms in 1938.

U.K.			U.S.A.		
Firm	Spindles & looms	Type of integration & diversification	Firm	Spindles & looms	Type of integration & diversification
F.C.S.D.A.	3,938,875 +1,045	C. S.	Cannon (1)	734,846 +13,097	C. S.W.F.Se.
L.C.C. (1)	3,331,443	C. S.	Berkshire (2)	721,104 +11,491	C. S.W.
Combined Egyptian (2)	2,270,995	C. S.	Pacific	574,164 +13,778	C. Wo. S.W.F.Se.
Crosses & Winkworth (3)	1,116,105	C. S.	Riverside	466,132 +11,627	C. S.W.F.
Amalgamated Cotton	701,020 +1,275	C. S.W.	Lonsdale	363,232 +7,998	C. S.W.F.
J. Hoyle (4)	431,001 +8,783	C. S.W.F.	Pepperel	317,684 +9,764	C. Wo. S.W.F.Se.
Swan Lane	400,000	C. S.	Textiles (3)	313,000	C. S.Se.
Iwell Bank	333,924	C. S.			
Horrockses & Crewdson	320,000 +10,737	C. S.W.F.	Kendal (4)	244,504 +5,025	C. S.W.F.Se.
Lees & Wrigley	300,000	C. S.	Merrimack	202,540 +6,553	C. S.W.F.Se.
Bolton Textile (5)	292,636	C. S.	Erwin (5)	192,848 +5,427	C. S.W.F.

India			Japan*		
Firm	Spindles & looms	Type of integration & diversification	Firm	Spindles & looms	Type of integration & diversification
Madura	476,180	C. S.	Toyo	1,861,560 +18,937	C.Si.R.Wo. S.W.F. Carpet, Thread
Bombay Dyeing	183,886 +4,850	C. S.W.F.			Lace, Hosiery Tire cord (Rubber)
Central India	115,136 +2,166	C. S.W.			(Pulp)
			Kanegafuchi	1,225,164 +12,275	C.Si.R.Wo. S.W.F.
Sholapur	111,360 +2,234	C. S.W.			Soda, Soap, Carpet, (Pulp)
Century	104,548 +3,096	C. S.W.			(Natural resources Development)
J. Sassoon	101,112 +2,223	C. S.W.	Dainippon	1,183,278 +12,060	C.Si.Wo.(R) S.W.F.
W. Victoria (1)	95,069 +1,615	C. S.W.	Fuji	753,674 +4,208	C.Si.R. S.W.
Muir (2)	88,852 +1,624	C. S.W.	Nissin	702,060 +6,608	C.R. S.W.F.
S. Broacha	88,848 +1,060	C. S.W.	Kurashiki	576,480 +4,148	C.(R) S.W.F.
Swadeshi	80,000 +1,740	C. S.W.	Kureha (1)	543,800 +5,210	C.R.(Wo) S.W.F.
			Kinka (2)	477,808 +905	C.Wo. S.W.
			Fukushima	390,428 +2,112	C.Wo. S.W.
			Tennma W. & S. (3)	316,240 +644	C.Wo. S.W.

* The figures for Japanese firms do not include spindleage of spinning subsidiaries in China.

U.K.

(1) Registered in 1929 through amalgamation of forty-five firms at this time.

(2) Amalgamation of firms in 1929, engaged in spinning yarn of fine counts made from Egyptian cotton.

(3) Crosses & Windworth Consolidated Mills controlled several other firms.

(4) Established integrated firm grown from merger of firms connected with the Hoyles.

(5) Competitive process-integrated private firm, originating in Bacup.

U.S.A.

(1) Organized in Concord, North Carolina, in 1887.

(2) Berkshire Fine Spinning Associates, Inc.; rapid growth in 1930s.

(3) Founded in Gastonia, N.C.; twelve-unit firm.

(4) Fully integrated Southern firm; head office in Boston.

(5) Organized in Durham, N.C., in 1892.

India

(1) Founded in 1920; successor of Victoria Mills.

(2) Founded in Cawnpore in 1874.

Japan

(1) Registered in 1929; most successful entry after World War I.

(2) Registered in 1926.

(3) Founded in the boom year of 1887; a rare case of a comparatively small surviving firm.

NOTES ON TABLES 1~6

Mule, ring and doubling spindles are undifferentiated in these tables, and so are wide and narrow looms. Figures do not include spindles and looms for woolen and silk cloth, except for some American firms mentioned in the footnotes.

Abbreviation

C: Cotton; L: Linen; Wo: Wool; Si: Silk; R: Rayon; S: Spinning (and sometimes doubling); W: Weaving; F: Finishing (including bleaching, dyeing, printing, etc.); K: Knitting; Se: Selling; ( ): subsidiary.

Sources

Company Files & Directories

U. K.

Company files in Public Record offices and Company Registration Office.

Warrall's *Cotton Spinners' and Manufacturers' Director*, Annual Editions.

Warrall's *Textile Directory of the Manufacturing Districts in Ireland, Scotland, Wales and Counties of Chester, Derby, Gloucester, Nottingham*, Annual Editions.

U. S. A.

Dockham's *American Report and Directory of the Textile Manufacture and Dry Goods Trade*, Annual Editions.

Textile World (ed.), *Textile Establishments in the United States, Canada and Mexico*, Annual Editions.

Business Records, Archive and Corporate Departments at Baker Library, Harvard Graduate School of Business Administration.

India

Bombay Millowners Association, Annual Reports, Appendixes.

Company Files in Company Registration Office of Bombay.

The Investor's India Year-Book.

India Textile Diary and Reference Book.

Times of India: Calendar and Bombay Directory.

S. M. Ratnagur, *Bombay Industries: Cotton Mills*, 1927.

M. P. Ghandi, *Indian Cotton Industry, 1938 Annual.*

Japan

Rengo Boseki Geppo (Japan Cotton Spinners' Association), Monthly Reports.

Mensi Boseki Jijyo Sanko (Statistics for Cotton Spinning), Half-Year Reports.

equal in number to the firms, showed a small decrease from 1,085
to 936. The driving force of this rapid raise was basically the public
companies, which had been expanding since the 1870s.[8] Each firm
began by operating roughly 40–60,000 spindles during the former
boom, while this figure increased to 80–90,000 during the latter.
These figures made them worthy to be called large firms in those
days, even if they were not ranked among the ten largest.[9] Private
firms converted from partnerships were included among the ten
largest companies but gradually lost their positions in the course of
time, although this tendency does not appear as obvious in the
tables as in reality.

The various managements were very keen to build mills as large
as possible, equipped with the newest machines. They were competitive, driving small integrated firms out of business.[9] Spinning
firms in Lancashire rarely wanted to have another establishment or
unit[10] apart from their original site, much less an establishment
outside Lancashire. They used to extend old mills or build new
mills on the same land. When a site was filled with mills and other
buildings, it meant the end of their growth. Some of the firms
listed in Table 1 owned two or three establishments. These were,
however, quite few in number[11] and usually were private companies, where the main expansion took place before the share-
floating boom of public companies.

Except for a few cases, including the Fine Spinners of 1898,
amalgamations in the spinning sector were very rare before the
world depression in 1929, when the government intervened in
economic matters. As mentioned above, the fact that most of the
firms remained single units is partly due to a lack of amalgamation,
as well as to the fact that they did not dare to build a new mill
on a second site detached from the original one. The most significant
consequence is that early upper-ranking firms failed to keep their
position in terms of size, as those with newly-built mills entered
the upper ranks, surpassing them. This trend is evident in Tables
1–3.

So far growth was horizontal, as indicated by the figures on
spindleage. As far as vertical integration is concerned, it is well-
known that the tendency was slight before World War II.

However, several integrated firms operating mainly in the domestic market showed good performance for a long time, although they were not listed among the largest ten. Horrockers, J. Hoyle, Tootal, J. Ryland, Barlow & Jones and Ashton Brothers are examples.[12]

(2) U.S.A. Integrated firms with both spinning and weaving processes were established early in the nineteenth century. These used all the yarns produced in their mills, in contrast with Indian and Japanese firms which sold a considerable part of their yarns, even though they were integrated. In 1900, 41% of the spindleages were located in Massachusetts.[13] They were dispersed in a number of towns, so that Fall River, the national center of printed cloth, had only 15% of all the spindles in the country.[14] However, quite a number of large firms were located in Fall River and in Lowell in the nineteenth century.[15] Rapidly growing firms later emerged in other states.

Southern states developed their own spinning industry after the Civil War, but it was not until after the beginning of this century that the industry in New England began to fear competition from the South. Even at that time, the spindle share of southern states only amounted to 25%.[16] Afterwards the transfer of production of coarse cloth to the southern states became decisive, especially after World War I. However, this did not necessarily mean the decay of large New England spinning firms. Some firms were building their mills in the southern states even at the end of the last century,[17] and large mills in the South generally belonged to New England's prominent firms. Firms originating in the South were usually small, although some of them in time amalgamated and grew into larger ones.

The merger movement, which in the industry amounted to a horizontal combination, was not at all successful.[18] Accordingly, horizontal growth in the ten largest firms was almost entirely due to internal expansion.[19] However, it must be recognized that, from a comparative point of view, process-integrated American firms were very desirous of building full vertical integration, especially during the period between the two world wars. They had integrated their finishing processes by the late nineteenth century.[20] It seems that the driving force for full integration often came not from spinning but from selling agents: a process of backward integration. Most of the ten largest firms took an active interest in building their own sales departments.[21]

(3) India. India's first mechanized spinning firm was formed in 1854. After the enactment of the Companies Act in 1857, the largest floating boom of 1870–72 and the following booms of the 1880s came into being mainly in Bombay.[22] The number of spindles amounted to 6.6 million on the eve of World War I, climbing to 10 million by World War II.[23] During this period the position of Bombay gradually declined compared with other regions.[24] Ahmedabad rose to prominence late in the last century and Madras between the two world wars.

A characteristic of Indian spinning firms was that their lives were comparatively short; the machinery of a liquidated firm was often used by creditors to begin a new firm. Just five of the firms registered in Bombay in the last century survived until World War I.[25] Most of these were one-unit firms; even among the largest ten before World War I only a few were multi-units. At that time the average number of spindles per firm was roughly half that of a Japanese company, and the latter was a little smaller than an English firm.[26] However, a few prominent firms did emerge. Prosperous even today, Bombay Dyeing originated from Bombay Dye Works in 1874,[27] and the group of mills controlled by the Sassoon Managing House was consolidated into E.D. Sassoon United Mills Ltd. in 1920.[28]

Some of the firms registered during this early period were called spinning and weaving companies because they were equipped with looms. However, the proportion of yarn used within an Indian firm's own weaving mills to yarn sold outside never equalled Japan's, because a vast number of hand weavers still survived until World War II.

Another managerial characteristic was that the spinning firms, managed by an agency house, constituted a sort of "trust" controlled by a family. The managing agency system, a transformation of a Western institution in the sense that the directorate was just formal, not substantial, could also be found in Asian countries other than India.[29] Except for Sassoon and Bombay Dyeing, a group of firms managed by the same agency house was not usually consolidated into a legal entity.

(4) Japan. The first mechanized cotton spinning firm was Osaka C. S. Co. Ltd., registered in 1882. The years 1887–89 saw the first and largest share-floating boom equivalent to those in the U.K., U.S.A. and India.[30] Although Japan had not yet enacted a unified companies act at that time, these firms were usually public companies whose shareholders originally numbered more than ten[31]; the number increased rapidly since management had no intention of limiting the sale of shares. Beginning with an operation of 10,000–20,000 spindles in a mill, they planned to increase them to 40,000 soon afterward, a project which was comparable to the scale of production in England at that time.

Total spindleage in Japan rose steadily following that first share-floating boom, but even so it amounted to only 2.5 million in all, or less than one-tenth of spindles concentrated in the Oldham district on the eve of World War I. The rapid increase in spindleage was remarkable until the 1920s and 1930s, when the export of cloth rose notably; during the period the spindleage was decreasing in the U.K. and U.S.A. Japanese spindleage caught up with that of India in 1935, numbering more than 10 million, and hitting its peak in 1937. The number of firms peaked in 1900, when it reached 79, and was never over that level until 1937. The market share of the five largest firms rose prominently after a merger movement around the turn of the century; these five maintained more than a 50% share until the beginning of World War II.

In size, the largest Japanese firms did not compare with those in Bombay late in the last century. The reason they had approached the size of Western firms by the time of World War I was because of the influence of the merger movement which spread from the U.S.A. at the end of the last century. Managements of spinning firms in Japan quickly responded to the movement. This was characterized in Japan by large firms absorbing smaller or poorly-performing ones without watering the estimated assets of these absorbed firms.

Before the merger movement, which was active for several years after 1899, almost all the firms were of the one-unit type. After this

merger movement amalgamation proceeded between the two
largest firms after the beginning of World War I.[32] Emphasis also
ought to be put on the fact that large firms often built new mills
independently all over the country in addition to obtaining old
mills by means of absorption. This meant that the large firms
managed a number of comparatively small mills dispersed all over
the country. It seems that the management took no real interest
in expanding the size of a mill or mill group on a particular site.
The reason mills were not concentrated in one district reflected the
policy that new mills should be built in regions where they could
benefit by cheap labor or be located near a weaving district. Thus
the Kanegafuchi C. S. Co., the largest firm in Japan on the eve of
World War I, owned fourteen units outside the Tokyo district where
it had originated. Its largest unit, with 90,768 spindles and 1,480
looms, was located in Kobe, about 400 miles from Tokyo, and
specialized in the production of cloth for export. This was, so
far, the firm's horizontal expansion. The situation as far as integration was concerned was different in Japan than in the U.S.A. and
U.K. Some Japanese firms added weaving to spinning early in the
1890s. However, the demand in Japan was for traditional cloth
woven by narrow looms; cloth woven by wide looms made in
England was not fit for the domestic market and was largely
exported to Asian markets. These exports of cloth increased steadily
until the middle 1930s. Firms with process integration also developed
in accordance with the increase in exports. Another reason for
this export increase and, to some extent, for process integration
was the rapid prevalance of low-cost power looms which had
developed in Japan.[33] The power loom was invented by S. Toyota
in 1897. The Toyota automatic looms prevalent late in the 1920s
raised the productivity of the weaving process to a height comparable to that in Western countries.[34] Besides the integrated firms,
a number of small weaving firms which had until the end of World
War I specialized in production for the domestic market began
to export their products.

Professor A. D. Chandler, Jr. has pointed out that backward
integration played an important part in consumer goods industries.
In fact, merchant firms in the U.S.A. were often anxious to

integrate backwards. In Japan the process only went halfway. Even full process integrations were not well advanced, because spinning firms integrated the finishing processes only to a limited extent. Although exports of printed and dyed cloth were unparalleled with grey cloth in the 1930s, very small firms were prevalent in this field. Despite control through financing, large spinning firms rarely internalized the processes by absorption, so that rationalization of the processes lagged behind. Another characteristic was the fact that spinning firms relied entirely on trading firms in order to sell their products abroad, and on traditional merchants for domestic markets. Having concentrated their attention largely on production, managements took no real interest in functional integration.

Oligopolistic firms gained high profits in the 1920s and 1930s, and they could reinvest huge retained earnings[35]; their first strategy for growth was to build spinning mills in China, and they all entered that country to begin spinning in the 1920s. Around 40% of China's spindles in 1930 were operated by subsidiaries of Japanese firms.[36] The second plan was more worthy of attention: besides the textile industries of silk and wool, they began the production of rayon in the chemical industry field. Their strategy was obviously one of diversification. Kanegafuchi C. S. Co. began to produce pulp and soda, materials for rayon, and finally settled on soap-making.

It would be true to say that Japan was the only country where spinning firms grew to be "big business" before World War II. During its golden age Kanegafuchi C. S. Co. founded a research institute with a staff of more than three hundred.[37] It seems that Kanegafuchi's conspicuous policy of diversification was for the most part a failure, but the experience proved valuable for the company's post-World War II development.

III.

The tables clearly illustrate the growth of firms in terms of horizontal expansion. However, the above statement also shows that the growth of firms in the industry was generally attained by

means of a vertical integration strategy. This was the underlying
long-term policy, especially of successful firms. These two tendencies
of growth could be anticipated to some extent. But it should be
emphasized that particular situations in each country caused this
inherent economic tendency to condition the development of firms,
and thus of the industry as a whole, more strictly than scholars
sometimes recognize. At the same time it must not be implied
that the limiting factors were absolutely impossible to break through,
giving significance to the role of innovative firms as mentioned
above.

The author fears that only a detailed explanation of the unique
conditions would make his argument persuasive.[38] However, the
following is at least a tentative and rough outline of his views.
The case of the U.S.A. is treated first.

(1) In the U.S.A. there was originally no social prestige attached to landownership such as that which still lingered in England,
and the lack of strong traditions made the market mechanism
most workable in this country. The characteristics of American
firms in their formative period lay in the process integration of
spinning and weaving from the very beginning: a situation entirely
different from that in England. This is because spinning firms
could not find the hand-weavers who in nineteenth-century England
were closely connected with small landholdings. Besides integration, by which is meant that all yarn was used in the same firm
for weaving cloth, it should be noted that even before the late
nineteenth century large firms often controlled the finishing processes
through the addition of a finishing mill to their own mills or through
the holding of stock in a local finishing firm. The reason for this
is that Philadelphia, the main center of the finishing process, was
some distance from the large weaving districts. This long experience
with full process integration seems to have made the firms sensitive
to the changeable demands in consumer markets.

The firms in Fall River might be separately treated from other
large firms widely dispersed in New England. It is said that Fall
River was under the strong influence of Lancashire, especially of
Oldham. This is somewhat true since, aside from the fact that
Fall River people came from Lancashire, the firms here were

public companies from the beginning, closely located in a small area, and all making printed cloth.[39] They showed limited growth, as was the pattern of English firms.[40] The difference was that in the course of the depressed 1880s a couple of outsiders came on the scene, making the business climate in the city more dynamic than before; since many firms had depended upon the financing of local banks, some of them were forced to close during the depression; in the course of time[41] new competitive firms, including the Fall River Iron Works, appeared.

Large firms located in other regions were active in extending their spindleage and integrating other processes and functions. Their main goal seemed to have been integration, for after investing in the southern states they became keen on functional integration. Familiar with conditions in the consumer goods market, they knew they would gain most through full integration. The management of these firms was rather local-minded, in spite of the fact that family control had ended and some of the managers were university graduates.[42] Despite their policy of diversification to other natural fibers these firms took no interest at all in the new fiber, rayon, which was actually a product of the chemical industry. They were not financially strong enough to invest in this new field because the industry was not brisk in the U.S. after World War I, at the time when new fibers looked promising. Consequently, they concentrated on a policy of full integration, sometimes including other kinds of natural fibers.

(2) U.K. S. J. Chapman and T. S. Ashton once debated the growth of Lancashire and Yorkshire textile firms during 1884–1911. They concluded that firms' average spindleage had increased steadily during the period, putting their emphasis largely on "typical" or "representative" firms.[43] However, a comparative study here shows us that none of these large firms had conspicuous growth considering the increase in spindleage. This is primarily due to their lack of energetic internal expansion and amalgamation. It has been argued that entry into the industry was so easy that a number of small firms became predominant, and as a consequence competition became severe. This may be partly true. If existing firms had expanded more vigorously, it would not have been so

easy for new firms to enter. It seems most characteristic that the rapid increase in total spindleage, especially at the beginning of this century, was attained by the emergence of new firms.

As is widely known, spinning firms in England could be classified into two types: established private companies making fine yarns, densely located in Bolton and Manchester, and newly founded public companies making coarse and medium yarns, concentrated in Oldham and Rochdale but also dispersed in other districts of Lancashire.[44]

Some firms in the former group still directed so much of their energies to expansion that they ranked among the ten largest in the tables. However, these were only a minority. The object of forming Fine Spinners was obviously defensive, since it did not increase its spindleage very much after the formation.[45] The consequence was that on the eve of this century some vigorous public companies engaged in producing yarn of high quality were born, and large private spinners, including the large shareholders of Fine Spinners, had, generally speaking, passed their prime of life.

An interesting aspect here might be how the profit that had been gained from large and well-established firms was used. It is not certain whether the well-known practice in the early nineteenth century of successful entrepreneurs' withdrawing their profit in order to invest in securities or landed properties can be applied to this later period[46]; it might be presumed applicable to some extent. New companies were also evidently floated by them; in any case, their expansion was not to be continued.

As far as the latter is concerned, managerial ideology of the co-operative society seems to have been of great importance. It should be first said that under the financial structure of England in those days company floating by labor aristocrats was really marvelous. It has sometimes been suggested that these firms were under the substantial influence of cooperative management.[47] According to the author's argument, almost all of the managerial characteristics of firms such as Oldham Limiteds originally stemmed from this influence, although there is no room here for details. A unique "loan" system came from the cooperative society's management which, under the Industrial and Provident Act of 1852, could accept a deposit as its capital within an established limit.[48] Co-operative societies in Lancashire in the 1870s and 1880s often backed some of their capital by lowering each member's maximum deposit when they found it excessive. Likewise, spinning firms often repaid some of their paid-up capital to shareholders at the time of brisk trade on condition that they could call on it again. Thus, among ten firms founded in Royton and Shaw from the largest floating boom of 1873–75 to the end of the last century, four firms reduced their paid-up capital,[49] an unusual management policy for a modern enterprise. The last factor, though not the least important, is that all the directors in the firms were engaged part-time, with very small renumeration, and had other occupations. In addition, the management of these firms modelled on that of cooperative societies was too "democratic" for the board to have its entrepreneurial decision passed at general meetings.[50] Under these circumstances it was almost unrealistic to expect a long-term strategy for growth from the board.

(3) India.   In reference to the business climate, it should be first mentioned that Indian entrepreneurs could not expect government support in the transplantation of the cotton industry, though it was a debatable question to what extent the colonial custom system became a barrier in developing the domestic cotton industry. Presumably such patriots as J. N. Tata could not have had such nationwide support as the Japanese entrepreneurs could expect to have.

As far as management and firms were concerned, the industry was under the substantial influence of the Lancashire cotton industry; this was natural, since Indian firms employed many English managers or engineers even up to the eve of this century.[51] The predominance of mule spindles in the late nineteenth century would support this argument.[52]

The most notable managerial characteristic in India was the managing agency system. Agents, as general merchants, initiated spinning firms primarily to keep the merchant's commission permanently high.[53] In India company promotion required so much entrepreneurship that entrepreneurial profit was assumed to be as permanent as the agent's renumeration.[54] Managing agents were

familiar with market conditions and patterns of consumption. The
Indian merchants were responsible for the exports to China having
risen as conspicuously as they did in the 1870s and 1880s. In those
days many general merchants tried floating spinning firms, but the
difference in performance between firms was so substantial from the
beginning as those in Japan. Mortality was high and life cycle
was short. Consequently firms of good performance had the opportunity of managing previously closed mills, but they rarely did.[55]
Although they sometimes controlled several firms as the largest
shareholders, they took no interest in the growth which could
have been achieved by internalizing them. The reasons why the
growth of firms was comparatively slow might be different from
those in England. The firms usually employed three or four times
more workers than English firms, so that labor management became
a severe limiting factor, considering that even one-unit firms usually
used a sort of sub-contracting system in mill management.[56]

Another aspect of the managing agency system lay in the house
or family control of agency firms, which before World War I was
usually a partnership. Obviously the grouping of the firms bore
similarity to the firm group controlled by the *zaibatsu* in Japan.
In both countries family coercion supplemented modern organization-building, a characteristic distinct from Western countries.[57]

(4) Japan.   There were also a number of barriers in Japan to
the transplantation of mechanized cotton spinning firms. The communication between the U.K. and Japan was more difficult than
that between the U.K. and India in terms of distance and language.
However, Japan was a state of one nation, religion and language.
After two centuries of seclusion the Japanese people, and particularly
the government, came to firmly believe that they had to learn
everything from Western countries.

Looking on Western institutions and modern technology as
models, they were enthusiastic in assimilating them, particularly
modern company management and the machinery system. The
Meiji government was quick to put emphasis on public companies
with modern plants, and thus made every effort to make them
prevalent. In the face of increasing imports of yarn and cloth, the
idea that mechanized spinning mills had to be transplanted rapidly

penetrated the country. This was, above all, a nationalistic cause.

As far as business climate is concerned, the first thing to be considered was the government's assistance to the industry. It has sometimes been argued that the Japanese cotton industry developed free of assistance, but this was true only as compared to other industries in Japan. During the industry's earliest years the government financially assisted private firms to modernize, and later the Bank of Japan took a positive attitude toward additionally discounting spinner's bills which commercial banks had discounted for the first time, thus allowing them to save a good deal of their working capital.[58] The consequence was that after the splendid success of the Osaka Spinning Co. Ltd., which had no direct financial support from the government, the floating boom of 1887–89 produced fifteen firms more or less modelled upon that firm. At that time the All Japan Spinners' Association came into being, originally as a medium of information on textile technology.[59]

However, factors limiting new entries were great, and lack of capital and management resources were most notable. Accordingly, together with the most energetic and continual expansion of forerunners such as those mentioned above, from the formative period of the industry a great difference in terms of performance appeared among the existing firms. This was presumed to depend mostly upon management resources—that is, whether or not they included persons who had mastered Western higher education or who could get new information which was accessible to only a limited number of people.

Another case of modelling upon Western countries was the merger movement which raged in the U.S.A. For fear that they could not compete with industrialized countries if they were slow in responding to the movement, managements were quick to absorb small firms of poor performance. Great waves of amalgamation resulted partly from bankers' intervention during depressed periods, but mainly from the idea that bigness was good in itself. This movement had a nationalistic cause also in that by any means the country's industries had to survive in competition with foreign imports. Leaders of large spinning firms were often professional managers, having graduated from universities since the turn of the last century. Because this was then nationally considered one of the most strategic industries,[60] spinning firms were able to recruit graduates while many of the heavy industries remained infants up to the time of World War I. On the advent of World War I, Kanegafuchi and Toyo had about one hundred university or college graduates respectively as officials. Characteristically, they did not stick to the established way of management, getting ample business information from a number of school friends and making good use of it in their business. Young graduate managers usually were not hesitant to leave for mills located far from the head office. After all consideration, it can be truly said that Japanese spinning firms were skillful in their building of modern organizations. On the other hand, their way of management was paternalistic because the industry's labor force was composed of female workers recruited from agricultural regions where very close family sentiment survived.[61]

Having succeeded in stopping imports, they then became active in expanding exports of yarns and piece goods; "increase of exports" became a national slogan because of Japan's continuing trade imbalances at that time. However, while they were most anxious to consolidate and organize a number of mills throughout the country as effectively as possible, these managers usually did not take the trouble to develop their own marketing system, not having intended full integration in the first place. At the start of this century, having accumulated voluminous reserves, large spinning firms found themselves superior to trading firms in their negotiations and so thought it convenient to avail themselves of trading firms in return for a small commission.[62] At the same time, as far as marketing information was concerned, even large spinning firms could not take the place of trading companies with their many branches throughout the world; such trading companies were also engaged in importing cotton. Spinning firms did not innovate traditional wholesale routes for the domestic market for fear that this would conflict with vested interests; satisfied with high profits, in both cases they left the matter as it was, preferring to retain harmony. As a result, the Japanese cotton industry was unbalanced in terms of full integration up to the time of World War II.

Concluding Remarks

The firm's goal is profit, in the sense that without profit private business cannot survive. However, it ought to be recognized that management's attitudes toward earning these profits differed widely.

In the U.K. the managerial ideology of family business remained influential in private companies, while that of the cooperative society was dominant in public companies. Management's motives in both cases seemed to lie in maintaining their firms as steadily as possible. American firms quite consciously sought full integration for profit maximization. The original integration of spinning and weaving made it easy for them to realize the policy of full integration. Indian merchant-oriented agency houses were inclined to look for short-term profit maximization. The basic problem there lay in labor or mill management. This necessarily set limits to the growth of firms in India. The national consensus to "stop imports" and then "increase exports" was management's motivation to encourage the aggressive growth of firms in Japan. This policy for growth seemed to succeed as a result in creating long-term profit maximization.

Most of the capital needed was raised by subscription of shares in each country mentioned here. As far as government assistance was concerned, Japanese firms received ample support when compared with those of other countries, even if assistance was not direct in its nature. On the other hand, it was a splended achievement that in the face of the capital export-oriented financial system of England (the so-called Macmillan Gap) the Lancashire petit bourgeoisie succeeded in floating the most modern and large-scale firms at that time using the "loan" system. The same admiration is due to the managing agency system in India, where shortages of entrepreneurship and capital were remarkable during the formative period of the industry.

As for managerial organization, it must be admitted that organization-building was one of the factors limiting the growth of firms. British management had no firm belief that scale economy could be achieved by multiplying units, while Japanese management did so believe. It seems that this attitude of the Japanese towards the scale economy was associated with their skillful organization-building. Moreover, according to Prof. A. D. Chandler, Jr.'s paradigm, this building was also in accordance with the recruitment of graduated professional management. If "big business" is defined as separation between ownership and management accompanied by the emergence of professional full-time managers, then large Japanese spinning firms succeeded in their metamorphosis to big business. Despite this, the structural imbalance stemming from the lack of full vertical integration seems, from the present viewpoint, to have been the weak point of the industry in Japan; one result is the industry's recent suffering from developing countries' competition.

In concluding this paper, the author cannot but confess that he has left much ground unexplored. Despite mention of the significance of leading firms and followers' response to them, the argument was not developed in a concrete form. The purpose of this paper was primarily fact-finding and not necessarily an evaluation of the facts.

NOTES

* In the preparation of this paper Mr. D. A. Farnie was so generous as to show the author invaluable records he took great pains to collect. The author is also most indebted to Dr. L. Hannah, director of the Business History Unit at the London School of Economics, where this draft was prepared, and Professor C. Erickson, who always encouraged the author when he was working at LSE in 1974–75.

1. A. D. Chandler, Jr., *The Visible Hand: The Managerial Revolution in American Business*, 1977.
2. See H. S. Davis and others, *Vertical Integration in the Textile Industries*, 1938, pp. 14–6.
3. The author has so far published ten articles with detailed evidence in reference to a comparative study of cotton spinning firms; three of these were written in English, as follows: "The Strategy and Structure of Cotton and Steel Enterprises in Britain, 1900–39," in K. Nakagawa (ed.) Strategy and Structure of Big Business, 1976; "The Growth of Cotton Spinning Firms and Vertical Integration," *Hitotsubashi Journal of Commerce and Management*, Vol.

14, No. 1, 1973; A Century of Cotton Spinning Firms in Japan, The Japan Society of London, Bulletin 93–4, 1981.

The sources he has used are mainly the following: company files stocked in the Company Registration Office (London and Bombay), local newspapers, trade journals and various reports of associations connected with the industry. Business records in manuscript form were used to a limited extent. Large Japanese spinning firms have kept richer business records than those in other countries. All of their large firms except Kanegafuchi are proud of their detailed company histories, which were in some cases supervised by scholars. Kanegafuchi has a history in manuscript form written for private circulation. T. Kinugawa's six volumes entitled *Honpo Menshi Boseki Shi* ("A History of Cotton Spinning in Japan") are invaluable for their rich information on the industry's formative period. The best and most authoritative industrial history covering the period up to World War I was written by N. Takamura. In discussing the characteristics of the growth of firms, the author's emphasis will be largely on the period before World War I.

4. As far as the figures on spindleage are concerned, Germany and Russia followed the U.S.A. before World War I, but it seems that neither country's impact on the international market was influential.

5. Needless to say, the distinction between private and public is not clear-cut. In England an act of 1907 made it legally clear.

6. The only criticism of this criterion I could find does not seem to be persuasive. See S. D. Mehta: *The Indian Cotton Textile Industry: An Economic Analysis*, 1953, pp. 188–200.

7. R. Robson, *The Cotton Industry in Britain*, 1957, p. 138; *Estimate of Long-Term Economic Statistics of Japan since 1868*, Vol. 11: "*Textiles*," S. Fugino and others, eds., 1980, p. 94.

8. After public companies became prevalent, promotion from operative spinner to master spinner was very difficult compared with the previous period.

9. This was especially true in the Oldham district, which accounted for more than 28% of the whole spindleage before World War I.

10. In this paper one "unit" actually means one "site" where one to three mills were built. In the American census of production it appeared as an "establishment."

11. S. J. Chapman and T. S. Ashton, "The Sizes of Business Mainly in the Textile Industries," *Journal of the Royal Statistical Society*,

Vol. LXXXII, 1914, p. 471.

12. A. & A. Crompton, one of the small integrated firms, was an
     interesting case. The management was so entrepreneurial that in
     addition to bleach works built in 1885, the firm established a weav-
     ing mill at Bucharest and took on shipping business. It was said
     that the "Crompton" brand could be found in every townshop
     in southeastern Europe. Public Record Office, BT 31, 19880/2298/
     21; J. E. Hargreaves, *A History of the Families of Crompton and Milne
     and of A. & A. Crompton & Co.*, 1967, pp. 102–6. Also see *The British
     Trade Journal*, 1887, pp. 277–8, 429–30; *Manchester of Today*, 1888,
     pp. 79–81; *Textile Manufacturer*, 1885, p. 328, 1891, p. 121, 1893,
     pp. 188, 425.

13. *Census of the United States.*

14. *Fall River Weekly News*, 6 December 1880.

15. Among the twenty largest firms in 1886, two and five were located
     in Fall River and Lowell, respectively. There were a number of
     other large firms in Fall River.

16. M. Copeland, *The Cotton Manufacturing Industry of the United States*,
     1923, p. 43.

17. In 1897 Dwight had mills of 30,000 ring spindles and 1,000 looms
     in Alabama and Massachussetts and also a mill of 30,624 ring
     spindles and 1,036 looms in Georgia. *Dockham's American Report*,
     16th ed., 1897, pp. 57, 76.

18. A. D. Chandler, Jr., *The Visible Hand*, 1977, pp. 72, 227–8.

19. Several combinations emerged as results of mergers, one of which
     was Parker Mills, ranked 6 in Table 3. See M. Copeland, *op. cit.*,
     p. 161.

20. M. C. D. Borden, a New York prints merchant, controlled Fall
     River Iron Works and American Printing Co. as well. On the
     other hand, Pacific Mills had already internalized its print section
     in 1897. *Fall River Weekly News*, 1 April, 1881; 3 March 1881, etc.;
     Dockham, op. cit., pp. 100, 280.

21. See R. S. Smith, *Mill on the Dan*, 1960, pp. 454–5; E. H. Knowlton,
     Pepperell's Progress, 1948, p. 253ff.

22. S. M. Ratnagur, *Bombay Industries: The Cotton Mills*, 1927, pp. 10–20;
     S. D. Mehta, *The Cotton Mills of India: 1854–1954*, 1954, pp. 40–63.

23. From Bombay Millowners' Association, Annual Reports.

24. The ration of Bombay in the years of 1897, 1913, 1928 and 1938
     decreased to 54%, 44%, 40% and 29%, respectively.

25. S. M. Ratunagur, *op. cit.*, p. 37.

26. The rough average spindleage figures of firms in India and Japan were 29,000 and 58,000, respectively, in 1913.

27. The firm internalized its manufacturing process through the absorption of two spinning firms in 1918. The company history, *Jubilee of Bombay Dyeing & Manufacturing Co. Ltd.*, no date, p. 15.

28. *Indian Textile Journal*, April 1920, p. 130.

29. As an example, Hong Kong Cotton Spinning, Weaving & Dyeing Co. was managed by a commission system. *Indian Textile Journal*, November 1899, pp. 40–41.

30. Fifteen firms were floated during these three years.

31. Existing records show that original subscribers were fairly many, usually more than ten, subscribing 1/4 to 2/3 of all shares.

32. Osaka and Mie were amalgamated in 1914 into Toyo Spinning Co., which absorbed Osakagodo in 1931, Likewise Dainippon Spinning Co. was registered in 1918 through the amalgamation of Amagasaki and Settsu.

33. The Toyota power-loom, originally patented in 1897, became prevalent by the end of World War I.

34. It was said that a male operative could handle 50 Toyota automatic looms. *Nichibo Nanajugonen shi* ("Seventy-five Years of Nichibo Company Ltd."), 1969, p. 168. Platt Brothers bought out the patent of this automatic loom, in order to sell it in Europe, in 1929.

35. They usually paid a 15–35% dividend, paying more than 10% even during the most depressed years of 1929–31.

36. Of around 4 million spindles, more than 1.5 million were managed by Japanese subsidiaries, largely in Shanghai and Tian Tao, whose units were usually larger than Chinese ones. Firstly the Naigaimen Co. operated a spinning mill at Shanghai in 1911.

37. The Kanebo Company Ltd., *Kanebo no Hachiju Nen* ("Eighty Years of Kanegafuchi Spinning Company Ltd.") 196–?, p. 223.

38. The author would like to emphasize the omission of a number of facts which would have enabled this paper to become more persuasive.

39. As in Lancashire, a trade union was very well organized in Fall River. It is also interesting that the news of the share prices and dividends of the firms located in Fall River appeared quite regularly in the *Oldham Chronicle*.

40. However, it should be added that as far as print cloth is concerned, the southern states were not suitable for its manufacture, this being one of the reasons why the firms in Fall River did not invest

in the region.

41. J. S. Brayton, a local banker, controlled several firms, together
     with 20% of the spindles of Fall River, in the course of the depres-
     sion, and these firms, as well as the Fall River Iron Works, did not
     want to be members of the Fall River Manufacturers' Association.
     The latter especially took a leading part in determining the short-
     time operation and standard wage in the district. *Fall River Weekly
     News*, 29 August 1894.

42. For example, N. Durfee and J. S. Brayton, the most noted business-
     men in the city, were both graduated from Brown University.
     F. M. Peck & H. H. Earl, *Fall River and its Industries*, 1877, pp. 53–
     4; R. V. Lamb, *The Development of Entrepreneurship in Fall River*,
     Ph.D. thesis, Harvard University, 1935, p. 47.

43. S. J. Chapman and T. S. Ashton, *op. cit.*, p. 512.

44. The author considers so-called turnover companies basically a sort
     of Oldham Limited, because they usually became public in nature,
     having a number of shareholders.

45. One of a few notable examples is McConnel & Co. Ltd., whose
     number of spindles increased to 350,000 after the amalgamation.

46. M. B. Rose, "Diversification of Investment by the Creg Family
     1800–1914," *Business History*, Vol. XXI, 1979. What matters is
     neither objects of investment nor motives, but that the Cregs were
     metamorphosing from entrepreneurs into investors: they are
     rational from investor's view.

47. T. Allison, *The Cotton Trade of Great Britain*, 1886 pp. 133–4; D. A.
     Farnie, *The English Cotton Industry and the World Market*, 1979, p. 216ff.

48. See G. J. Gray, *Loan Capital: How to Deal with It*, pamphlet, 1892;
     p. 216ff: W. Nuttall, *Co-operative Share Capital: Should It Be Trans-
     ferable or Withdrawable?* Pamphlet, 1872.

49. They were Moorfield, Duke, Smallbrook, Fern and J. Clegg, the
     last of which was a private company when it reduced its paid-up
     capital in 1913. Company Registration Office, Company File, no.
     9131; P.R.O., BT 31, 14517/9184, 14726/17891, 14762/19447.

50. *Oldham Chronicle*, 14 May, 1881, 6ii; 25 February, 1888, 8v-vii; W.
     Marcroft, *Sun Mill Company: Its Commercial and Social History*, 1877,
     p. 67. The managerial ideology of a "cooperative spinning company"
     can be summed up in a word as "democratic" as against the "aris-
     tocratic" management of private firms.

51. *Indian Textile Journal*, October 1901, p. 3; S. M. Rutnagur, *op. cit.*,
     p. 294; *The Gazetteer of Bombay City*, Vol. 1, p. 492ff.

52. The fifteen firms founded during the boom of 1888–90 had 292, 296 mule and 81,000 ring spindles in 1891, while the same number of Japanese firms founded during the boom of 1887–89 were equipped almost exclusively with ring spindles. *Indian Textile Diary and Reference Book*, 1891, pp. 8–9.

53. Dr. Victiany's Ph. D. thesis is useful in understanding the historical background for the emergence of Bombay mills. A. M. Victiany, *The Cotton Trade and Commercial Development of Bombay 1857–1875*, University of London, 1975, p. 212ff.

54. On the other hand it should be remembered that the agitation against this system was quite strong after the early 1870s. *Indian Textile Journal* also took positive part in the campaign in the late 1890s. *Times of India*, 5 March, 1873, 2ii-iii; 10 June, 2v; 12 June 2ii; 14 June 1876, 2v-vi.

55. As an exception, N. Kowasjee, an agency house managing four firms, went bankrupt in 1879. Then E. D. Sassoon Mills, a private company, took over N. Alexsandra Mill, and Oriental S. & W. Co. bought Colaba Mill, while influential M. Petit Manuf. Co. added Fleming Mill as a second unit.

56. *Indian Textile Journal*, December 1894, p. 54: October 1901, p. 4.

57. Cf. K. Nakagawa's suggestive article, "Dainiji Taisenzen no Nippon ni okeru Sangyokozo to Kigyosha Katsudo" ("Industrial Structure and Entrepreneurship in Pre-World War II Japan"), *Mitsui Bunko Ronso*, No. 3, 1968.

58. K. Yamaguchi (ed.), *Nippon Kinyushi Kenkyu* ("Studies in the History of Corporate Finance in Spinning Firms"), 1970, pp. 35–7.

59. The Association later on took a position against poaching skilled laborers and for arranging the ration of operating spindles in depressed times.

60. T. Yamabe was a typical example. Having worked at the London School of Economics, he became a mill engineer in response to a request from E. Shibusawa, the main founder of Osaka Spinning Co. and leading businessman in Japan. He went to live in Blackburn, where he worked at J. & W. W. Briggs, an integrated firm, for about one year. Afterwards he was appointed president of Osaka Spinning Co.

61. Interestingly, S. Muto, president of Kanegafuchi Spinning Co., often spoke in support of paternalistic labor management.

62. It is most difficult to determine how much profit trading firms make from export of piece-goods. However, the following case is some-

what suggestive. The Kureha S. C., an energetic late-comer in the 1920s, was founded by the Itochu Trading Co., then specializing in trade of yarn and cloth. The latter's performance was so bad that it could not make dividends during the decade after World War I. However, it gave ample support to Kureha, which rapidly grew to be an influential spinning firm in the 1930s. It should be also remembered that when Osaka and Mie exported their cloth for the first time to Korea through the Mitsui Trading Co., the latter did it with no commission.

COMMENTS

1

Dwijendra Tripathi
Indian Institute of Management

Professor Yonekawa has done a signal service to the conference by explaining the relevance and justification of its theme. A longitudinal look is perhaps the best instrument to comprehend the business dynamics of a society, and a comparative look provides much more penetrating insights. Comparison, to be meaningful, however, has to be in relation to some experience which the societies in question share in common. It is appropriate for this conference, therefore, to focus its attention on the cotton textile industry, which, besides being the oldest organized industry in each of the countries represented here, has also been the forerunner of industrialization in each of these societies.

Our concern in this conference is the impact of business climate on business decisions. Professor Yonekawa has rightly pointed out that business climate encompasses much more than mere factors of production. Business climate, to my mind, consists of the amalgam of a number of constantly changing and mutually interacting factors which impinge on the decision-making of an entrepreneur at a given point in time. Broadly speaking, these factors include social-cultural values and influences, social-political structure and conditions, economic infrastructure and social overheads such as education, communication and credit facilities, national goals and policies, and the impact of the activities of others with whom the decision-maker may be in direct or indirect contact or whom he looks upon as his reference groups. For convenient reference I would like to call the amalgam of these factors a "constellation of forces." All major business decisions result from inter-

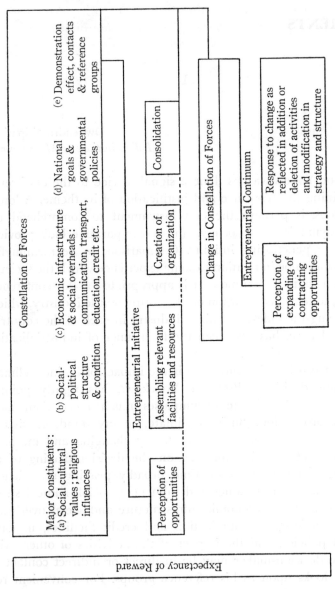

Entrepreneurial Process

Expectancy of Reward

action between the constellation of forces and expectancy of reward.
(See the enclosed schematic presentation.)

Even though certain elements in the environment may be
common, the constellation of forces impinging on the operations of
various organizations differ as the personal values and attitudes
and contacts and reference groups of principal decision-makers
differ. This is why Professor Yonekawa has emphasized the need to
focus on individual firms rather than on the industry as a whole.
I am not quite sure, however, that I would go along with his support
for the Schumpeterian distinction between innovator and follower
firms. I would have no objection if the firms in question belong to
one and the same milieu. But since the risk in innovating a certain
technology or production function is basically the same as that
in adapting it in milieus different from the one in which the original
development might have taken place, the distinction between
innovation and adaptation is neither convenient nor useful.

This minor conceptual problem, however, in no way detracts
from the value of Professor Yonekawa's presentation. With great
care he has collected data about the size of textile firms in four
countries which are as different from one another as any four
countries can be. His tables clearly bring out the differences in the
patterns of growth in these countries. The rationale for selecting the
years 1897, 1913, 1928 and 1938 as points of comparison, however,
is not quite clear to me, and it would be interesting to see whether,
with different reference years, Professor Yonekawa's findings would
undergo any modification.

The possibility of such modifications notwithstanding, there is
no question that the pace and pattern of growth registered by the
textile companies in each of these countries were different. Japan,
for instance, in spite of later entry into the field, overtook and
surpassed India in some respects by 1937. Why did it happen? I
doubt that lack of government support in one country and vigorous
government encouragement in the other explains the whole phenomenon. It seems to me that an important ancillary factor in the
slower growth in India was that fields other than cotton textiles became more attractive areas of investment, and cotton manufacturing reached a sort of plateau by the middle of the 1930s. If the

merger movement never gained momentum in India as it did it in Japan, and if Indian manufacturers concentrated on developing single-unit firms, unlike their counterparts in Japan, it was because it was not necessary for the Indians to resort to these devices to achieve the economy of scale. Under the managing agency system, it was possible for a single family to control and manage several separate firms as if they were part and parcel of one another.

Professor Yonekawa has offered some hypotheses to explain the differences in the patterns of growth in the countries he has covered. But since he is primarily interested in "fact-finding and not an evaluation of facts," the task of explanation devolves on his audience. Perhaps the conference should take up where Professor Yonekawa has stopped.

2

Keiichiro Nakagawa
University of Tokyo

Although it is not always clear which of the two subjects, business strategy or business climate, Professor Yonekawa had tried primarily to deal with, I find many interesting statements in his paper on both of these subjects along the lines of comparative business history.

For example, he emphasizes that only in Japan did cotton spinning firms grow into multi-unit big businesses through horizontal mergers and construction of new mills. As stated in his conclusion, he himself has not elaborated on the leader-follower relations among the Japanese cotton mills. However his paper seems to suggest that the several leading firms, which grew into nationwide big businesses through merger and new mill construction, stimulated the development of the Japanese cotton industry in the twentieth century. In the U.K., on the other hand, most of the spinning firms remained one-unit enterprises, avoiding both merger and new mill construction; thus they could not activate the competitive development of the Lancashire cotton industry after the late nineteenth century.

I think this is one of the most interesting points to be discussed at this meeting, and I would like to know why the British firms avoided mergers and did not build new mills at new sites. Was it due to economic reasons or to human factors?

Professor Yonekawa seems to maintain also that only in Japan could the cotton mills recruit educated and able professional managers. If true, I would like to ask what the reason was for such a unique development. Was this due to the great backwardness of Japan at the start of its industrialization, or the concept of the cotton spinning enterprise as a kind of "national affair"; or was it the formation of cotton spinning firms as public joint stock enterprises from their very beginning? It seems to me that all of these three factors may have contributed to the early development of managerial enterprises in the Japanese cotton industry. In this context, I would be interested to know more about the nature of similar social settings of the cotton mills in the other three countries. By discussing this we can successfully explore the relations between the cotton industry and the business climate.

Another subject to be considered when we study the structure and strategy of cotton mills is, of course, the nature of the market. Professor Yonekawa has not covered this matter, probably to avoid too much complexity in his paper. However, it is very difficult to discuss business climate and business strategy without considering the nature of markets in detail. What were the differences among the four countries, the U.K., U.S.A., India and Japan, in the nature of their markets and ways of marketing? Is it possible to assess quantitatively the quality of the yarns produced by representative cotton mills in each country and the diversity of piece goods manufactured in each nation? Can we follow the process of the changes in main products in the course of each country's industrialization?

I stress the importance of the nature of markets and products because it directly affects the character of technology and the labor force in the cotton industry. Professor Yonekawa has touched on these problems briefly at various points in his paper, and I should be quite happy if he and other experts in this industry could favor us with a little more detailed explanation.

Professor Yonekawa emphasizes that the Japanese cotton mills received substantial support from the government, compared with other countries. However, it seems to me that the mutual cooperation between the firms themselves rather than the Japanese government's support greatly contributed to the development of the industry. The case in point is, of course, the Japan Cotton Spinners Association, which was organized first for the mutual exchange of technological information, then acted to stabilize the labor market, and finally played quite an important role as the agent for extensive, repetitive and successful curtailment of operations. What the government did seems to have been only to support such mutual cooperation among the mills.

In comparison with Japan, the British cotton mills seem to have been much more individualistic in their behavior. I recall that Professor Farnie maintained that in Lancashire an unrestrained and hyperintelligent individualism excluded any kind of communalism or collectivism. What then was the business climate in India? If Japanese business nationalism orginated in the country's desperate economic backwardness, there should have developed in India also some nationalistic support for cotton mills as well as mutual cooperation among the mills. Professor Yonekawa stated that J. N. Tata could not have such nationwide support as Japanese entrepreneurs could expect to have. However, it is not clear to me what kind of nationwide support was favored for the Japanese mills. On the other hand, we know that when Tata failed to raise capital at the London money market for his projected iron and steel mill, the Tata offices in Bombay were besieged by an eager crowd of native investors.

At any rate, I should be very happy if all participants could continue to discuss and expand on matters concerned with the business climate during this meeting.

The Structure of the British Cotton Industry, 1846–1914

Douglas A. Farnie
University of Manchester

I. The Revolution in Textile Consumption

Between 1780 and 1900 the average per capita consumption of textile fibers quintupled, as may be seen in Table 1. The increase in cotton consumption accounted for 69% of that dramatic increment in total consumption as the per capita consumption of cotton increased thrice as fast as that of non-cotton fibers in response to a demand of unprecedented elasticity. As the cheap new fiber established its economic preeminence it transformed the pattern and the extent of textile consumption. Until the 1820s the most important fiber in the world had been flax which had provided the basis for the dominant textile industry of Continental Europe, especially in France, Germany and Russia. The total consumption of cotton first surpassed that of flax in the 1820s and then, in the 1850s, surpassed that of all other textile fibers put together. By 1860 cotton accounted for an estimated 53% of total fiber consumption while flax ranked third in order of importance after cotton and wool, having become the main casualty of the rise of the new fiber to supremacy in the economic world. The expansion of the cotton industry enabled Britain to establish its commercial hegemony at the expense of the Continent as British consumption of cotton accounted for 48% of the increase in its total consumption between 1780 and 1860.

The new monarch of the world of textiles, "King Cotton," was however dethroned during the Cotton Famine of the 1860s and regained its prewar eminence only during the early 1890s. The

TABLE 1 The World's Consumption of Textile Fibers, 1780–1900.

	Cotton	Wool	Flax (in millions of pounds)	Jute	Silk	Total of all Fibers	Share of Cotton (%)	Consumption per capita Cotton All Fibers (in pounds)	
1780	220	440	500		30	1,190	18.49	0.27	1.44
1800	303	460	600		30	1,393	21.75	0.34	1.55
1820	402	520	700		33	1,655	24.29	0.39	1.62
1830	806	607	750		34	2,197	36.69	0.75	2.03
1840	1,210	694	800		35	2,739	44.18	1.06	2.40
1850	1,335	886	900	60	37	3,218	41.49	1.11	2.68
1860	2,451	1,074	925	130	40	4,620	53.05	1.91	3.60
1870	1,675	1,579	1,200	410	42	4,906	34.14	1.22	3.58
1880	3,501	1,915	900	900	45	7,261	48.22	2.41	4.99
1890	4,817	2,250	800	1,310	50	9,227	52.21	3.13	5.99
1900	6,767	2,500	750	1,500	52	11,569	58.49	4.16	7.12

Source: *Textile Recorder*, vol. 20, 15 Dec. 1902, 251, S. N. D. North, "The World's Supply and Consumption of Cotton," reprinted from the *Proceedings of the New England Cotton Manufacturers' Association* and supplemented by estimates of population derived from C. McEvedy and R. Jones, *Atlas of World Population History* (Harmondsworth, Penguin, 1978), 342.

Cotton Famine clearly revealed the role of cotton as the main driving force of the textile revolution: it reduced the per capita consumption of all fibers for the first time in eighty years, relegated cotton to its relative position of 1830 and benefited all other fibers, but stimulated none so much as jute. Thereafter the cotton industry revealed true resilience in recovering from a depression without precedent in its history. Between 1870 and 1900 the consumption of cotton increased more than thrice as fast as that of all other fibers. The consumption of jute grew only slightly less fast than that of cotton, whose position as the cheapest of all fibers was lost to its new rival. The competition of Calcutta with Dundee in the manufacture of jute introduced in 1880 the first manufactured commodity into the northbound traffic of the Suez Canal and presaged the future migration of the cotton industry eastwards and homewards.

II. The Uniqueness of the British Cotton Industry and Its Reflection in the Mirror of Scholarship

The increase in cotton consumption benefited most of all Great Britain, whose cotton industry expanded to a size unsurpassed in spindleage by any other state until 1958. Britain dominated the textile industry of the world to an unparalleled degree, employing in its cotton industry in 1850, 60% of the world's spindles and 53% of its power looms. In 1910–13 its cotton industry consumed only 20% of the world's mill consumption of cotton but employed 39% of the world's spindles and 30% of its power looms, produced 25% of the world's cotton textiles and exported 70% of the volume of cotton piece-goods entering into world trade, shipping abroad at its peak in the boom year of 1913 734,768 tons of yarn, thread and piece-goods.[1] That preeminent position was one never achieved by any other producer and was the creation of a unique industry.

The British cotton industry differed profoundly from other cotton industries in so far as it pioneered the application of mechanical power to both spinning and weaving and therefore became a medium for the employment of capital rather than of labor. It developed its own distinct technology, spinning medium counts from middling Orleans cotton on the mule (whose spindles outnumbered those on the ring frame until 1959), running its spinning machines at very high speeds and replacing its machinery to a degree as yet unrecognized[2] but using the lowest amount of cotton per spindle in the world after Switzerland. Within Great Britain the cotton industry dethroned the woolen industry from its historic pre-eminence and continued its career of expansion for over forty years after the spindles spinning flax reached their maximum number in 1880 and those spinning wool reached their maximum in 1885. Its longevity proved remarkable in view of the low profit-margins apparently endemic to the industry. The British cotton industry was however much more export-oriented than that of other states and generated a near-universal commerce which revolutionized the textile trade of the world and provoked widespread and deep-ranging defensive reactions abroad. The cotton industry of Lancashire served as both a stimulus and a model to other states. Not only did its raw cotton market serve the cotton industries of Europe, but also its ancillary machine-making industry equipped most of the spinning industries of the world. Its most famous cotton broker, Thomas Ellison, became from 1875 the leading cotton statistician of the world,[3] and its technical press supplied the trade from 1875 with its premier journal in *The Textile Manufacturer*.

Has Britain's greatest industry produced a harvest of business history in the twentieth century appropriate to its world-historical significance during the nineteenth century? A brief perusal of scholarly media suggests that editors of learned journals have shunned the business history of the cotton industry and that publishers have concluded that public interest in the business history of a moribund industry was too limited to bring them either profit or prestige. Thus the *Economic History Review* published between 1927 and 1978, 1165 articles, none of which dealt with the business history of the cotton industry, and established a self-denying pattern imitated by other periodicals. The Cambridge journal, *Economic History*, published 139 articles between 1926 and 1940 but included only one on the business history of the cotton industry, a study in the social history of a rural factory community. *Textile History* proved to be most interested in the history of the woolen industry in harmony with the undoubted importance of wool in British history: only two of the 107 articles published therein between 1968 and 1979 concerned cotton firms and neither of those related to Lancashire. The *Bulletin of the John Rylands Library* became almost a house organ of the University of Manchester and published sixty volumes between 1903 and 1978 but printed only two articles on cotton firms. The most distinguished record in this field was achieved by the Liverpool periodical *Business History*, which devoted five articles of the 190 published between 1958 and 1978 to the business history of the cotton industry. In respect to monographs, only four academic histories of firms have appeared.[4] None was sponsored by a business concern and three were published by Manchester University Press, which was forced to remainder its most recent venture into this sphere.

Can any explanation be offered for the absence of any extensive study of the business history of the Lancashire cotton industry? Firstly, no industry-wide associations existed before 1940 to generate the necessary statistics. Secondly, most firms were small and short-lived, leaving no records behind for the benefit of later historians. Surviving archives were few in number, and those few were intensely exploited.[5] A recent attempt by the University of Liverpool to build up a cotton industry archive failed to elicit any significant response from the trade. Moreover, the hypnotic fascination of the archives of the central government in London for visiting scholars forced upon them a metropolitan perspective and entailed a neglect of individual firms because of the virtual separation of the industry and the State during the era of its expansion. The tremendous vitality of the industry during its greatest age was based in part upon the preservation of rigorous business secrecy, in accordance with the strength of family traditions and the patterns of an oral culture. Such secrecy was enforced by the severity of inter-firm competition which doomed one attempt in 1898 to compile a daily market report of the sales of cloth made upon the Manchester Royal Exchange. That tradition influenced the University of Manchester through its close links with the staple trade of the region and was maintained by J. & P. Coats, which declined to permit the publication of a completed academic history of its business activity.

Until the publication of the works of G. W. Daniels in 1920 and of A. P. Wadsworth & J. de L. Mann in 1931, the main concern of early histories of the industry was with the inventor rather than with the businessman, and that bias was faithfully maintained in a long succession of boringly derivative works. Then the triumph of the neo-Keynesian macro economic approach inevitably diverted attention from the micro economic history of the firm. Nor did Marxist historians reveal any disposition to study the history of individual concerns before reaching positive and all-embracing conclusions. Thus the inertia of accumulated intellectual capital, reinforced by a natural distrust of originality on the part of scholars, has favored the macro economic approach at the expense of other avenues of investigation. That tradition has not yet been modified either by the new social history or by the new econometric history with their preference for the aggregative method. The use of aggregate data in such invaluable works as Worrall's *Cotton Spinners' and Manufacturers' Directory*, published annually from 1882–84, has nevertheless remained surprisingly limited. The greatest single gap in the historical literature of the cotton industry must surely be found in the absence of any reliable long-term series of annual statistics of production.[6] The sobering conclusion must follow that little is known with certainty about the detailed history of the industry and that an immense abyss of ignorance lies beneath the confident platitudes periodically emitted by self-appointed pundits on the history of the industry: it may be added that no other industry has generated so much punditry upon the basis of so little real evidence. Thus the projected *Dictionary of Business Biography* faces a major challenge in its bid to resurrect the history of the leading businessmen of the past. The following generalizations on the subject must of necessity be tentative and provisional.

III.   The Growth of the Industry's Markets

During the nineteenth century the cotton industry paradoxically developed fastest in states without any source of supply of raw material, and those states became the main suppliers of the great markets of the world for cotton goods, so raising the volume of international trade to new heights. Europe and Britain had no domestic source of supply of cotton but together controlled 89% of the world's spindles in 1850, 78% in 1890 and 69% in 1913. The lack of raw cotton was made good by its import from the U.S.A., which stimulated the growth of transatlantic trade. The expansion of American supply provided Lancashire with its greatest single advantage in the production and export of cotton manufactures. The U.S.A. supplied the right staple of cotton in the right quantity at the right price so that the resulting expansion of Anglo-American trade laid the basis for the rise of cotton as a world power. The long-term decline in the price of raw cotton from the maximum level of 1799–1801 lasted until 1898 and may have contributed to the Kondratieff long waves of economic life in 1814–50 and in 1873–96 insofar as the re-entry of the U.S.A. into the world market after the Anglo-American war of 1812–14 and again after the

Civil War of 1861–65 ushered in the main periods of declining prices. The Cotton Famine seems to have been less a simple shortage of raw cotton than "the famine of a good staple."[7] Thereafter the U.S.A. regained in full its prewar position in the world cotton market in 1879–81, enabling the British cotton industry to increase its dependence upon the markets of Asia.

The industry's pronounced export bias endowed it with its own peculiar importance in the economic history of Great Britain and of the outside world: the increase in the value of its exports accounted for 25% of the increase in the value of the United Kingdom's export trade between 1784–86 and 1912–14. That distinctive orientation seems to have been molded by two factors in particular, by the influx of foreign merchants to Manchester from the 1820s and by the immense demand generated within the vast empire built up by the East India Company. Foreign merchants acquired control by the 1860s of some 75% of the overseas trade of Lancashire,[8] and provided the main exogenous contribution to the industry's expansion. Within the spectrum of foreign markets, a secular and fundamental shift away from Western Europe and North America towards Asia and Latin America began in the 1830s and was completed between 1860 and 1887, as may be seen in Table 2. Increasingly the industry found its main outlets in Asia, in the two largest markets of the world for cotton goods: India ranked as the main market from 1843 until 1939, while China ranked second only to India from 1869 until 1926. Indian demand alone raised Lancashire to the summit of its relative importance and increased the industry's export bias to an all-time peak in 1881 when 74.5% of the value and 90% of the volume of its product was exported, leaving only 11% of the total spindleage to furnish the needs of the home trade. Chinese demand was relatively less important than Indian but nevertheless detonated the greatest single boom in the whole history of the industry, in 1920, when the export of cotton manufactures reached their all-time maximum value.[9] Together those two markets reached the peak of their relative importance to the cotton industry in 1888, taking 38.73% of the total value of its exports, and the zenith of their absolute importance in the boom year of 1913, taking 38% of the value of

TABLE 2   Relative Shares of the Main Markets of the World in the Exports of the British Cotton Industry, 1820–1913.

	Volume of exports of piece-goods (in millions of yards)					Proportion (%)				
	1820	1850	1873	1896	1913	1820	1850	1873	1896	1913
Europe	141.875	261.208	533.374	372.086	442.043	57.12	19.23	15.31	7.13	6.25
America	79.831	464.878	753.429	921.217	916.939	32.14	34.23	21.62	17.65	12.96
U.S.A.	23.802	104.230	109.531	55.300	44.415	9.58	7.67	3.14	1.06	0.63
West Indies	26.928	100.824	104.813	96.610	95.524	10.84	7.42	3.01	1.85	1.35
Latin America	26.024	224.332	498.998	741.660	666.501	10.48	16.52	14.32	14.21	9.42
Levant	7.888	155.692	516.128	497.134	677.633	3.18	11.46	14.81	9.53	9.58
Asia	14.191	426.366	1520.329	2990.447	4363.380	5.71	31.39	43.63	57.31	61.67
India	14.191	314.453	989.790	2038.025	2919.408	5.71	23.15	28.40	39.06	41.26
China		73.209	349.744	542.816	716.533		5.39	10.04	10.40	10.13
Africa	4.409	34.359	94.067	265.330	436.900	1.78	2.53	2.70	5.08	6.18
Total	248.360	1358.183	3484.943	5218.249	7075.252	99.93	98.85	98.06	96.70	96.63

	Value of exports of cotton manufactures (£m.)					Proportion (%)				
	1820	1850	1873	1896	1913	1820	1850	1873	1896	1913
Europe	10.666	9.599	22.230	13.033	21.641	64.57	33.97	28.74	18.79	17.23
America	4.316	8.226	16.946	13.584	20.262	26.13	29.11	21.91	19.59	16.13
U.S.A.	1.195	2.504	4.392	2.455	3.721	7.23	8.86	5.68	3.54	2.96

West Indies	1.525	1.451	2.074	1.149	1.458	9.23	5.13	2.68	1.66	1.16
Latin America	1.419	3.623	9.448	9.184	11.805	8.59	12.82	12.21	13.24	9.40
Levant	0.414	2.601	9.493	5.738	9.196	2.51	9.20	12.27	8.27	7.32
Asia	0.851	6.887	24.465	30.017	59.178	5.15	24.37	31.63	43.28	47.12
India	0.851	5.221	15.006	18.434	35.651	5.15	18.48	19.40	26.58	28.38
China		1.021	5.913	5.882	12.095		3.61	7.64	8.48	9.63
Africa	0.257	0.571	1.843	3.536	7.747	1.56	2.02	2.38	5.10	6.17
Total	16.517	28.257	77.354	69.355	125.601	99.92	98.68	96.93	95.03	93.97

Note: In order to maintain comparability between the various markets, their component states have been maintained so far as possible unchanged from one bench-mark year to the next. Thus Europe includes Wallachia and Moldavia in 1850 and 1873 (Roumania in 1896 and 1913), Gibraltar, Malta and the Channel Islands but not the Azores, Madeira or the Canaries. The Levant comprises Turkey (including European Turkey in 1913), Syria, Egypt, Aden (in 1896 and 1913) and Persia in 1873–1913 on Arnold Talbot Wilson's principle of 1909 that Asia began at the River Indus. Asia includes Mauritius but excludes the islands of the Pacific. India excludes Burma, Ceylon and the Straits Settlements but China includes Hong Kong. Africa excludes Egypt but includes the neighboring islands except for Mauritius and especially the Azores, Madeira, the Canaries and Madagascar.

Source: *Tables of the Revenue, Population, Commerce &c. of the United Kingdom and its Dependencies, Part I. From 1820 to 1831* (Parliamentary Papers, 1833, vol. 41), 65; *Tables of the Revenue, Population, Commerce &c. of the United Kingdom, Part XX. 1850* (Parliamentary Paper, 1466 of 1852), 127; *Annual Statements of the Trade of the United Kingdom for 1873, 1896 and 1913*. The statistics shown above differ in the details of their distribution from those presented in D. A. Farnie, *The English Cotton Industry and the World Market, 1815–1896* (Oxford, Clarendon Press, 1979), p. 91.

its exports. The result of that shift towards Asian markets was to
encourage the manufacture of cheaper goods, to create a contrast
between the high-valued goods produced for Europe and the
cheaper unfinished cloth destined for Asia, to reduce the relative
importance of the finishing industries and to increase the average
amount of cotton consumed per spindle from 1810 until 1888.
Moreover, India and China became the ultimate heirs to British
primacy when India acquired the largest spindleage in the world
in 1974 and when China acquired the second largest spindleage to
India in 1976. Thus the wheel of fortune came full circle as Lancashire's former largest markets emerged as the successors to its
manufacturing primacy.

IV. The Extension in Supply of the Factors of Production

Both capital and labor apparently remained cheap in comparison
to other countries and were rarely in short supply, except at the
peak of a cyclical boom. The supply of labor had expanded under
the influence of the process of "proto-industrialization" during the
eighteenth century and came largely from the native population of
Lancashire, which increased throughout the eighteenth and nineteenth centuries faster than that of the rest of the country, reaching
its peak proportion of 13.4% of the total population of England
and Wales in 1901. Female labor supplied the bulk of the labor
force, and the female population of Lancashire increased more
rapidly than the male population between 1831 and 1901, despite
the imposition of protective factory legislation. As the cotton
operatives severed their links with the land and with agriculture,
they became a distinct group with an industrial tradition and ethos.
Steeped in the pervasive atmosphere of modern industry, they developed a high degree of productivity, acquired the pride as well
as the mentality of the artisan grades of labor and transmitted
a sense of vocation to the younger generation. Their unions remained non-political in organization, having been organized long
before the establishment of the Independent Labour Party in 1893.
Controlled by men, those unions gradually imposed from the 1850s
district wage-lists upon the employers and secured for the operatives

an increasing share of the product of industry. Thus the diffusion of prosperity in association with the continued expansion of the industry fostered what despondent neo-Marxists have called "class collaboration" within the society of industrial Lancashire. Perhaps the greatest example of that cooperative spirit was the creation of the Manchester Ship Canal (1887–94), or "the People's Canal," which was financed by the capital of 39,000 shareholders, large and small, and was excavated to the same depth as the Suez Canal in order to link Manchester to its markets in Asia.[10]

Capital was never in short supply to finance the expansion of local industry but overflowed into other sectors of the nation's economy as industrial East Lancashire replaced commercial Merseyside from the late 1830s as the main center of wealth-creation within the county. Thus investments were made outside the cotton industry in joint-stock banks in the 1830s,[11] in railways in the 1840s, in iron, steel and coal companies in the 1860s, in insurance and building societies in the 1870s, in urban real estate and municipal loans in the 1890s[12] and in art throughout the century.[13] There is however little or no evidence of the diversion of investment to agricultural land, especially in the later nineteenth century, and it remains debatable whether or not the "entrepreneurial ideal" of the cotton employers then succumbed to the seductive embrace of the landed tradition.

A new source of finance was opened up to the industry in 1856 through the statutory authorization of joint stock companies with limited liability. Such companies drew upon the savings of small investors and included the "working class limiteds" of Oldham which, as specialized spinning companies, gave a marked impetus in the 1870s to the functional separation of spinning from weaving. The new limiteds served as savings banks to the local manufacturing population and made full use of loan capital which private masters could never have used in the same way lest they ruin their credit in the market and increase their fixed charges to an uncomfortable level. In response to the invasion of their own domain by the massed power of small investors, organized into joint stock companies, private employers created their own private limited companies, which became from 1885 the dominant force in the joint-stock movement within the cotton industry. In the twentieth century such employers remained in possession of the commanding heights of the industry, especially by means of the trust and the trade association.

V. The Expansion of the Ancillary Trades

As both seller and buyer the cotton industry exerted from the 1830s a growing influence upon the economy. Its backward linkages, however, stimulated the expansion of agricultural production in the "Cotton Kingdom" of the American South rather than in Britain, while its forward linkages remained those of a producer of consumer goods rather than those of a manufacturer of capital goods so that its influence was correspondingly limited. The industry's main products were two, yarn and cloth, and its sole "intermediate" product was yarn, which furnished a basic input to a range of other textile trades. In those industries the stimulus to the complementary investment of capital seems to have been relatively limited and late. Only in the manufacture of sewing thread was a new industry so developed, especially from the 1830s, upon a factory basis at the expense of the manufacturers of linen thread, as to become from the 1860s more capital-intensive than any other branch of the cotton industry. The export of yarn, which reached its peak volume in 1884, further restricted the domestic influence of such forward linkages.

The expanded production of cotton cloth did not transform the basis of the clothing industry which remained a dependent fief of the woolen industry and was revitalized by the advent of shoddy (manufactured from "reborn" wool) and of ready-made clothing. That new trade developed outside Lancashire, which clung with habitual conservatism to its traditional fustian, the parent of the cotton industry. One particular branch of the clothing industry however settled in Manchester from the 1830s as the manufacture of rainwear developed production on a factory basis and became the greatest single consumer of rubber in the kingdom. In close association with the growth of exports, the packing industry expanded into one of Manchester's most specialized and profitable activities, aided by the manicipality from 1894 through the supply of hydraulic power. That trade became the object of a great merger in 1896 by Lloyd's Packing Warehouses, which in turn financed the construction of a range of modern warehouses in the city and so secured a clientele of tenant-customers. Yarn, thread and cloth together embraced the full range of the industry's products: its by-products were few in number, unlike those of the coal industry. Almost the sole by-product was the cotton waste made in growing quantities as production mounted. That waste supplied the raw material used by the cotton waste industry and also by the paper-making industry, which settled in Lancashire close to an expanding source of supply of its basic input.

The cotton industry grew to such an immense size that it created a correspondingly vast range of auxiliary industries to supply its needs as well as to handle its products. Those subsidiary industries had no parallel elsewhere in the world in their number, extent or function. Thus mill-building became a specialized activity, generating employment for the whole range of building trades and calling into existence specialized mill architects, especially in Oldham. The perfected type of Lancashire mill was even exported *en bloc* to countries where its structure had to be fundamentally modified to suit different conditions of climate. The demand for mill-stores created, especially from the 1830s, satellite trades which supplied the industry with minor inputs including lubricating oil, sizing material, chemicals, bobbins, shuttles, belting and ropes. Those trades generated profits which might be ploughed back into the industry through investment in limited companies. The demand for power and light created an extensive coal mining industry which was scattered among numerous small pits but produced in the aggregate the largest volume of coal destined for local consumption, supplying the industry with the cheapest power in the world. The coalfields of Lancashire and Cheshire rose in status from the fourth largest producer in the 1800s to the largest after the northeastern field by 1830, retaining that position until 1883 when they were surpassed in output by South Wales. The demand for light was met by the use of coal-gas, in the production of which Lancashire ranked second only to London throughout the century.

The demand for chemicals created from the 1790s the heavy chemical industry of the lower Mersey region, making Lancashire the center of a vast new industry in addition to the oil, paper, rubber and engineering trades.

The immense demand for machinery generated the most important of all backward linkages and created from the 1840s the textile machine-making industry, which developed to an extent without parallel elsewhere in the world. Home demand alone remained huge because Britain operated until 1893 a majority of the world's spindles. As Lancashire became the workshop of the realm, engineering expanded to embrace the manufacture of locomotives, wood-working machinery, paper-making machinery, rubber-processing machinery and machine tools. Textile machine-making was however given a great stimulus by the abrogation in 1843 of the laws prohibiting the export of machines, by the Great Exhibition of 1851 and by the Cotton Famine of 1861–65. More concentrated in size and in location than the cotton industry, textile engineering became similarly divided between a few large firms and a host of small firms. From the 1840s the large firms, led by Hibbert & Platt (or Platt Brothers, as it became in 1854), employed machine-tools while the small firms preserved older labor-intensive techniques of production. Spinning machinery remained the industry's primary product, manufactured first for the home market and then for the export trade. Those spinning machines gave rise to a vast export trade in yarn and to the spread of the handloom abroad, which in turn created the export demand for spinning machinery. So vast was the demand for the new machines that it fostered extreme specialization, supporting by 1880 82 spindle and flyer manufacturers, 51 bobbin manufacturers, 50 manufacturers of card clothing and by 1928 65 shuttle makers and 111 reed, heald and slay manufacturers in addition to the main body of textile engineers.

Competition seems to have remained unchecked within the machine-making trade, since Platt Brothers never acquired the monopolistic position of J. & P. Coats, did not establish any cartel with other engineers until 1931 and manufactured only 15% of the total value of the textile machinery exported between 1893 and

1913. In the supply of the world market that industry enjoyed one great advantage in its close association with heavy engineering, which supplied the necessary steam engines to foreign clients. Thus it equipped the cotton industries of Europe, Latin America and Asia and supplied with mechanical sinews a range of new Manchesters which were destined to become the heirs and successors of Lancashire. Textile machines supplied the most valuable portion of Britain's export trade in machinery and millwork for a century from 1843 to 1942 and surpassed in weight from 1906 the volume of the exports of cotton manufactures. Those exports were predominantly shipments of spinning machines because of the high survival-capacity of the handlooms of the world, which increased in number throughout the century and reached their peak number of an estimated 7,000,000 in 1900. The largest tonnage of those exports was recorded however in 1908, five years before the peak tonnage of exports of cotton manufactures, a paradox which requires explanation. Only in 1961 did the value of textile machinery exports surpass the total value of cotton yarn and cloth exports.

The auxiliary industries were a product of the peculiar size and density of the cotton industry of Lancashire: they enhanced the intensity of economic activity within the whole region and made available a range of capital-saving goods and services unparalleled elsewhere in number or quality. The unique pattern of the Lancashire economy apparently gave rise to Marshall's idea, first expressed in 1891, of the difference between the "external economies" and the "internal economies" available to a business firm, a distinction based upon the special relationship between the Lancashire cotton industry and the world market. The external economies generated by the ancillary industries permitted the division of labor and the specialization of function to be carried to a degree unknown elsewhere. Such economies even became to some extent a substitute for the internal economies of large-scale production and enabled the industry to survive and flourish upon a basis of small-scale enterprise. As the industry expanded in size and its 2,000 constituent firms became more specialized in function, a vast haulage industry grew up which linked together the different towns and trades of "Cottonia," adopted the internal combustion engine in the 1890s and stimulated the local manufacture of trucks, buses and cars from the 1900s. The service sector established a degree of functional autonomy and directly encouraged the expansion of industry through the foundation of room and power firms, through the flotation of limited companies financed by contractors and through the extension of credit to clients investing in new machinery. The decline of the ancillary trades seems to have occurred from 1927 after the cotton industry of Lancashire reached its maximum spindleage. Both the chemical and the engineering industries continued to flourish, however, because they had attained a large measure of functional independence of their parent trade.

V. The Transformation of Oldham into the Hub of the Spinning Industry

In 1850 Oldham was one center of the cotton industry among others; by 1870 it had established within a single quinquennium a preeminence in cotton spinning which was to endure as long as the industry itself. It doubled its spindleage from 3,000,000 in 1866 to 6,000,000 in 1871[14] and surpassed first Manchester and then Bolton in spinning capacity; it became the leading mill-town in the world, the largest center of consumption of raw cotton and the greatest producer of cotton yarn. By 1871 Oldham alone had more spindles than any single country in the world outside the U.S.A. and had in particular exceeded in spindleage France, deprived of Alsace by the Franco-Prussian War. During the next forty years the town maintained its primacy as the cotton industry continued to expand. Between 1866 and 1884 Oldham added 6.6 million spindles or 81% of the total increment made by the whole of the British cotton industry; between 1884 and 1914 it added a further 7.4 million spindles or 39% of the total increment within the industry. By 1880 Oldham had almost as many spindles as France and Germany combined.[15] Its spindleage first exceeded ten million in 1886 and rose to seventeen million in 1914, or as many as had Russia, India and Japan together; in 1914 its spindles still surpassed those of any single country in the world apart from

TABLE 3   Average Size of the Spinning Firm in the Lancashire Cotton Industry, 1850–1914.

Spinning spindles	
1850	11,818
1870	16,872
1890	36,504
1884	40,732
1896	51,008
1914	75,358

Source: Returns of the Factory Inspectors, 1850, 1870, 1890. J. Worrall, *The Cotton Spinners' and Manufacturers' Directory*, 1884, 1896, 1914, excluding doublers and doubling spindles.

the U.S.A. Its share of the total spinning capacity of the British cotton industry rose from 19% in 1870 to 24% in 1884 and to 29% in 1914. When it attained its absolute peak capacity in 1927 it held 30.4% of the total number of spinning spindles in the industry while the second center of spinning, Bolton, had only 13.5%.

During that process of unprecedented expansion Oldham remained a center of specialized spinning firms and then became the home of joint stock companies, with large mills and highly productive machinery capable of spinning all domestic rivals out of existence. Thus the degree of the town's specialization in spinning was surpassed in 1884 in only three small cotton towns and by 1914 only in two, Dukinfield and Middleton. The rise of Oldham as a specialist center of spinning transformed the whole pattern of industrial organization in Lancashire. It precipitated the decline of spinning in northeast Lancashire and further encouraged in that district the complementary growth of specialized weaving firms. Together the massive expansion of specialized spinning and specialized weaving firms contributed to the relative decline in importance of the combined or integrated firm. Thus a horizontal reorganization of the structure of industry took place while yarn and cloth agents developed an interstitial function of key importance, so discouraging any potential reversion towards vertical integration.

The fundamental distinction between spinning and weaving firms reflects the divergent technological development of the two processes of production.[16] Spinning had been mechanized first and had found markets outside as well as inside Lancashire so that specialized firms might embark upon a long and profitable career. Such concerns expanded notably in size from the 1870s under the influence of the joint-stock movement and became more rather than less specialized.

Because the expansion of spinning capacity was largely concentrated within a single town it may be unprofitable to speculate upon the origins of specialization as a general trend within the Lancashire cotton industry unless prior consideration is given to the dynamic consequences of the rise of Oldham. If the impact of that town upon the economy of Lancashire was so revolutionary then it may be unnecessary to invoke the influence of other more general factors. Regrettably the economic history of Oldham has never been written. Nor has the impact of the emergence of so vast a complex of productive power been studied. Thus a question of the utmost importance to an understanding of the greatest of British industries has never been posed, still less answered. At this rudimentary stage of investigation it may be useful to suggest a plausible explanation of this unprecedented phenomenon. The hypothesis is that the explosive speed of Oldham's expansion was based upon an unbreakable local alliance forged between the cotton spinning and the machine-making industries, which enabled the town to benefit by all the advantages accruing to a late starter and to establish a virtually impregnable position as the hub of the spinning universe. Such an explanation may well account for all of the recorded phenomena and will certainly avoid the primary error of antedating the era of the town's rapid expansion.

The textile industry had been established in Oldham during the seventeenth century and had been transformed from the 1790s by the rise of the cotton industry into a staple manufacture of coarse yarn and cotton velvets. By 1850 the town was ranked as an old cotton town in sharp contrast to such new towns as Ashton-under-Lyne. "Oldham is the pariah of the cotton-trade. The refuse from all the other Lancashire towns is brought here, and worked up into the coarsest and trashiest of fabrics."[17] That judgment was penned just before the rapid mutual expansion of machine-making and cotton spinning began in the town, ushering in four decades of unparalleled prosperity. That process of expansion was all the more remarkable in view of the great disadvantages under which Oldham labored. As a frontier town within a frontier community, it was sited upon the easternmost edge of Lancashire, far distant from the raw cotton market in Liverpool as well as from both of the two main routes crossing the Pennines. The high altitude of 700 feet above sea level was not offset by any countervailing advantages since the town lacked any water supply, a river, a canal or any visible natural resources. The comparative isolation of Oldham from the progress of civilization was reflected in the limited and late establishment of even minimal municipal amenities.

There was a growing home demand for yarn which enterprising spinners might supply. Exports of yarn had been expanding more slowly than exports of cloth since 1843 and suffered much more than cloth exports during the Cotton Famine; they did not surpass their level of 1860 until 1872, when they attained their all-time peak value. The demand for yarn in the Blackburn district origi-nated from the demand for cloth in the Asian market and had always been more important to Oldham than the export demand. The expansion of power-loom weaving in Blackburn and that of mule spinning in Oldham became powerful complementary trends, mutually reinforcing each other as Oldham extended its spinning power even faster than the specialized weaving capacity of northeast Lancashire. To respond to that derived demand more effectively than any other center was the achievement of Oldham, turning to the fullest advantage such resources as it could muster. Located only 6.5 miles from Manchester, the town lay close to the greatest yarn market in the world in the Royal Exchange and well within the magic radius of ten miles necessary for effective carting within the duration of a single day.

For the manufacture of yarn Oldham had an incalculable advantage over other towns in the presence of the firm of Platt Bros., which undertook the systematic improvement of the tech-nology of cotton spinning and perfected first the technique of carding and then that of roving, both indispensable preliminaries to the most effective spinning. During the thirty years after 1845,

Platt Bros. transformed itself from an assembler of parts supplied
by other makers into a fully integrated engineering enterprise,
turning out a range of machines unequalled by any other manufacturer. During the 1860s it became the largest machine-making
firm in the world as well as "the largest manufacturing establishment in Great Britain."[18] During the crisis of the Cotton Famine
Oldham became the first town in Lancashire to use Indian cotton
in place of the American staple, and Platt's perfected the self-
acting mule for the spinning of coarse counts, producing three
successive models in 1868, 1886 and 1900 and becoming the largest
manufacturer of mules in the world. The skill and resources of
Platt's enabled Oldham to survive the Cotton Famine much more
easily than any other cotton town and supplied the town with its
greatest single advantage. The enterprise of John Platt (1817–72)
laid the foundation not only of a global commerce in machinery
but also of the productive power of Oldham as the metropolis of
cotton spinning. Platt's mules were the true basis of the supremacy
of Oldham. They were unrivalled in length, in speed and in productivity, which was raised by as much as 5% by the cold moist climate
of the locality and was undoubtedly far superior to that of spindles
laid down outside Oldham. The constant replacement of plant was
encouraged by Platt's, by the establishment of a depreciation rate
of 7.5% on machinery as the norm, by the growing competition between spinners and by the operation of the Oldham speed spinning
list of 1875. Such extensive replacement of spindleage created
a thriving local trade in second-hand machinery, which further
enhanced the superiority of the town over its rivals. Platt's effectively compensated Oldham for its lack of other advantages and
especially for the limited local development of steam-engine manufacture. In return Platt's reaped greater profits than its host industry
and never passed a year without a dividend until the decade of
1927–36; during the 110 years between 1869 and 1978 the firm
paid an average annual ordinary dividend of 12%.

  Oldham had not become a center of the cotton industry during
the age of the waterwheel; it was a product of the age of the steam-
engine, the self-acting mule and the railway. The deeply entrenched
local tradition of small capitals was based primarily upon the

cheapness of land in comparison to its price in neighboring towns. Land was not locked up in large estates but was split up by the hilly nature of the locality into many separate properties and was thus easily purchasable. That distinct advantage was reinforced by another local custom which was not found in any other spinning town. The system of renting "space and turning" to several tenants within a mill remained peculiar to Oldham. That practice reduced the amount of capital necessary to begin business and made possible the exceptionally rapid expansion of specialized spinning firms especially in the coarse trade, which was most suited to the small firm as well as to the high level of local humidity. It prevented the establishment of effective barriers to entry upon the industrial scene and enlarged the opportunities for social mobility but also accentuated the degree of competition, especially for labor, among employers. Thus the typical unit of production remained relatively small and capacity was widely dispersed among 203 separate firms in 1914.

The history of the crucial decade of the 1860s remains a wholly blank chapter in the unwritten economic history of Oldham. Apparently the town derived substantial comparative advantages from its response to the challenge of the Cotton Famine. That crisis not only gave an immense stimulus to innovation in the textile engineering industry of Oldham but also established the cotton waste trade upon a broad and unshakeable foundation, adding another valuable external economy to the resources available to local employers. The expansion of world demand and supply during the postwar boom of 1871–73 precipitated the great mule mill-building boom of 1873–75, when joint stock companies began to replace family firms as the basis of local enterprise, especially as the flotation of "turnover" companies accompanied that of "working class limiteds." The availability of loan capital for secure investment at 5% notably extended the supply of capital, facilitated the payment of higher ordinary dividends than would otherwise have been possible and encouraged the flotation of companies even beyond the due needs of trade, attracting capital from neighboring towns to "Diviborough"[19] and making it the leading center of the joint stock company in England. The mania for company-promotion was fostered by the ancillary trades which were the direct beneficiaries of mill construction, including architects, contractors, builders, engineers and suppliers of mill stores. Platt's workmen became leading shareholders in the new limiteds[20] while mill officials in nearby Shaw became leading promoters in the 1880s of new vehicles for their managerial talents. Vested interests were thus created in the continuation of company flotation, and four fresh waves of promotion followed between 1880 and 1909[21] whenever dividends rose to an attractive level. The new mills were built in brick from the ample supplies of local clay and proved highly efficient units of production. The average spindleage of the town's spinning mills (excluding doublers) rose from 41,500 in 1884 to 56,900 in 1896 and to 77,330 in 1914. The average size of spinning firm in Oldham surpassed that of Manchester during the early 1890s, but only in 1926 did an Oldham firm secure a place among the ten largest spinning firms in Lancashire.[22] The competitive capacity of the new mills was strengthened by their hard-driving managers and by their sharp-minded salesmen, so intensifying the pressure upon established firms, stimulating them to increase their productivity and transforming the local spinning trade into "a huge machine for paying wages."[23] The burden of change was borne by the private employers who suffered a disastrous loss of their family fortunes[24]; the benefits were reaped by the ancillary trades and by the consumers of the world as well as by the operatives. The boom of the 1870s raised Platt's to the summit of prosperity and enabled it to pay in 1876–77 its all-time highest dividend of 37%.

The industrial micro-climate of Oldham, based upon a superbly balanced economy, proved highly favorable to the development of the spinning industry and fostered among both employers and employees the dominant values of individualism, self-reliance, self-help and thrift. A well-established pattern of commercial freedom was reinforced by the entrenchment of Liberal power in the local Town Council during the forty years following 1854. Oldham became "peculiarly a working man's town," largely created by people who had risen from the ranks.[25] Its cotton operatives carried the fierce insularity of Lancashire to a pitch unattained elsewhere; they became notable for their independence, their industry and their productivity, which had earned for them since 1841 the highest gross pay in Lancashire.[26] Their town became the first and only cotton town to enjoy a full week's holiday all at once.[27] From the 1850s on those operatives founded a wide range of provident clubs and societies. They made Oldham into a center of consumers' cooperation second in importance only to Rochdale; their cooperative societies developed a distinctly individualistic approach to their mission,[28] undertaking the functions of building societies and aiding the joint stock movement both directly and indirectly, especially through their support of the pioneer Oldham limited, the Sun Mill established in 1858. Local educational facilities had been based originally and solidly upon the Sunday school but were notably extended into the technical field under the influence of Platt Bros. through the successive agencies of the Mechanics' Institute (1837), the Lyceum (1839), the School of Science and Art (1864) and the Municipal Technical School (1891). Thus the mechanical ability of the population was developed to the full and the influence of industrial progress became diffused throughout the whole of the workfolk, creating an abundant local supply of mill managers for service abroad as well as at home. The industrial atmosphere of the town became even more aggressive after it had surpassed both Manchester and Bolton in spinning capacity and fostered the bold ambition to capture the textile engineering trade of Manchester.[29]

The rapid rise of Oldham provides a sharp contrast to the economic history of Bolton, which grew relatively slowly and like a tree rather than like a mushroom but which remained preeminent in the value if not in the quantity of its production. Oldham established an unassailable superiority in the spinning of coarse counts at the expense of other towns which found it impossible to preserve their traditional status. The Osaka of Great Britain never suffered any effective challenge to its hegemony and only began to decline from 1928 when the British cotton spinning industry as a whole began to decline. The influence of its expansion extended throughout much of industrial Lancashire. The rise of Oldham first checked any further expansion of spinning in northeast Lancashire after 1875 and then contributed to its absolute decline from 1877, especially in Burnley, Blackburn and Rossendale. The emergence of a specialist spinning sector secured a necessary complement in the birth of specialized weaving firms, which required commercial skills superior to those necessary in spinning. As Burnley expanded its weaving capacity in the 1880s, Oldham became the main source of supply of yarn for manufacture into its staple product of cheap narrow printing cloth. Weaving remained much less concentrated in location than did spinning, and no single center achieved the dominance established by Oldham within the spinning trade. Burnley indeed surpassed Blackburn in loomage in 1894 but never mustered more than 14% of the total number of looms in the industry. The core of the new pattern of horizontal organization remained the divorce of spinning from weaving, an achievement for which the rise of Oldham was primarily responsible.

The horizontal reorganization of the structure of industry was apparently an almost inevitable product of the rapidity of the expansion of market-demand and of the delay in the mechanization of weaving. That trend created a division of labor based upon the separation of firms in terms of both function and location; it was accomplished largely through the spread of specialized spinning firms from the 1850s, through the diffusion of small private power-weaving firms especially in the 1880s and through the increase in the number of both yarn and cloth agents serving as the necessary mercantile intermediaries, rather than through the passive and relative decline of the firm which combined spinning with weaving. Spinning remained the preserve of specialized firms more than did weaving. In 1884, 58% of the firms of Lancashire which spun at all spun only and controlled 61% of the total number of spindles. By 1914, 71% of the firms which spun at all spun only and controlled 78% of the spindles. In contrast, 55% of the firms which wove at all in 1884 wove only and operated only 43% of the looms. By 1914, however, 78% of the firms which wove at all wove only and operated 70% of the looms.

The concomitant decline of the combined firm during the ninety years after 1850 created a divorce between the large integrated enterprises and their specialized rivals. By 1914, combined firms represented 14% of the total number of firms and controlled 22%

of the spindles and 30% of the looms. Such concerns remained the preserve of the leading industrial clans of the county, such as that of the Lees who created Tootal, Broadhurst, Lee & Co. and supplied chairmen not only to Tootal's (1863–1906, 1922–52) but also to the Calico Printers' Association (1908–64), to the Fine Cotton Spinners' and Doublers' Association (1922–40) and to the Lancashire Cotton Corporation (1955–64).

VII. The Influence of Competition upon the Structure of Industry

The singularity of the British cotton industry became increasingly reflected in the structure of the individual firm, which differed markedly from that of other industries at a comparable stage of maturity. The typical firm specialized in one main process of production and tended to remain limited in size in comparison to firms in other industries. The spread of such specialized firms took place through the creation of new businesses rather than through the dissolution of existing combined firms. That trend has been interpreted as a response to the growth of the market, so justifying Adam Smith's dictum that "the division of labor is limited by the extent of the market." The sheer extent of the market available to the industry in the 1850s, coupled with the rapidity of its expansion, made an overpowering impression upon all contemporary observers.[30] The gross value of production quadrupled between 1850 and 1914, enhancing the power of the influences fostering specialization in the service of the world market and distinguishing the British cotton industry from others oriented primarily to the supply of domestic needs. Production expanded by means of the multiplication of individual units of production rather than by means of an increase in the capacity of established firms. The total number of manufacturing firms increased to a maximum in 1913, the year of the peak volume of production. Thereafter the number of firms declined in harmony with the reduction in the volume of production and the shrinkage of overseas markets. Thus throughout the era of the industry's maturity firm and mill remained largely identical, the typical unit of enterprise was relatively small and the representative employer was a yeoman of industry rather than a captain of industry.

The industry remained readily accessible to small capitalists not only because of the expansion of its markets and of the range of its products but also because of its geographical concentration within the Lancashire area, the absence of any restrictions upon entry, the divorce of textile engineering from the cotton industry proper, the continual improvement in the technology of manufacture and in its productive capacity, and the comparative insignificance after 1845 of patent-based monopolies.[31] Entrance to the industry was further encouraged by the relatively small scale of economic operation, by the renting of room and power, by the increasing separation of the spinning and weaving processes and the development of a thriving market in yarn, and by the high functional efficiency of the great markets of Liverpool and Manchester. Small businessmen were undoubtedly the primary beneficiaries of the ready extension of credit by ancillary interests such as brokers, engineers and banks, the increasing use of loan capital, especially after the advent of limited liability, the phenomenal expansion in the regional facilities of transport and communication, and the growth of a wide range of external economies offered by the auxiliary industries of the region. Small employers found an outlet for their capital and enterprise first in spinning and then in weaving, where the average size of firm grew much more slowly than in spinning.

A high rate of entry to the industry was partly balanced by a high rate of exit since the recurrence of cyclical depression tended regularly to decimate the ranks of employers. The high mortality rate among businesses and the rapid turnover of concerns made the average life expectancy of the firm relatively brief and created a shortage of old-established family dynasties. Industrial expansion seems to have been greatest where conditions of entry were the easiest as in Oldham and Burnley, but least where opportunities of access were more restricted, as in Manchester and Bolton. On the whole the economic structure of the region remained open rather than closed during the era of the industry's drive to maturity. Such an open structure fulfilled a democratic function in maintaining freedom of access to the industry and in helping to moderate antagonisms which might otherwise have threatened the foundation of social peace upon which rested so vast a superstructure. The business climate of the region undoubtedly encouraged the entry of new men but imposed strict limits upon the expansion of their operations.

The manufacturing firms of Lancashire were the creation of a myriad of independent businessmen with an intense regional, and even a local, consciousness. Those employers were denied the psychic security stemming from landed estates. They lacked any model for social emulation in the absence of a dominant gentry and in the weakness of the aristocratic ideal. Even when fortified by a strong religious sense they remained almost wholly dependent upon their own personal capacity, and inevitably they elaborated a proud ethic of individualism. As hard-headed and self-made men, they depreciated the value of formal education in favor of practical experience. Their range of experience tended however to limit their aims.[32] Their main goal in life seems to have been the achievement of status in local society, and their great fear seems to have been that of failure to accomplish the ascent from the ranks. Once the goal of social ascent had been achieved, its very achievement tended to inhibit further output of effort, especially on the part of the successor generations, who no longer made the continued expansion of the firm one of their primary goals.

Most firms had been established as family concerns, and they proved slow to free themselves from the restraining influence of the household. The pattern of relationships within enterprises was based more upon personal and even upon family ties than upon impersonal criteria. Such firms were governed by strong forces emphasizing the particularistic traditions of kinship and locality rather than by universalistic forces making for limitless growth at the cost of shedding their local roots, character and function. They did not pass under the influence of demonic entrepreneurs or of dynamic amalgamators. They derived no impetus to growth from the introduction of radically new products capable of creating a whole new market or of transforming an old one. Nor did they diversify into fields outside the cotton industry, least of all into the new sectors of the world economy expanding from the 1890s.

In general they remained dedicated to the manufacture of a single product. Within their chosen sphere of activity they became diligent servants of the greatest market economy ever developed.

The pervasive influence of competition within Lancashire molded the basic structure of industry and limited the range of opportunities open to individual firms. Those concerns remained more divided by the struggle to survive than united by any common overriding interest. Inter-firm competition was never effectively inhibited by any permanent or effective trade association. Masters' associations tended to be weak, unrepresentative and rarely capable of united action save on matters of hours and wages, so that the precious individual authority of the many employers remained unimpaired. General employers' associations were formed only in 1889–90 after the establishment of operatives' amalgamations in spinning in 1870 and in weaving in 1884; they were founded as separate associations for the spinning and weaving trades. Temporary associations were indeed established in favor of the extension of cotton supply (1857–72) and in opposition to factory legislation (1853, 1855) as well as to the Indian cotton duties (1874, 1894). No structure of affiliated organizations was however built up to cater for the long-term needs of the industry. Thus there was no association for parliamentary purposes before 1899 and no association for either cotton supply or cotton growing until an American corner of the cotton market in 1903 created a general crisis. Nor was there any organization for the compilation of statistics, for market research, for the analysis of the costs of production, transport or merchandising or for the calculation of stocks and sales. The Textile Institute was founded only in 1910, the Shirley Institute for scientific research only in 1919, the Cotton Board only in 1940 and the British Textile Employers' Association only in 1969. The Manchester Cotton Association was indeed founded in 1894 and Manchester Liners in 1898 as corollaries to the Manchester Ship Canal, but those organizations found the task of moderating Liverpool's hold upon the trade of Lancashire a Herculean one. Thus the cotton industry remained largely unorganized in an economic world increasingly regimented into rings, trusts, conferences and unions[33]; its employers were condemned to undergo what Marshall in 1907 termed "the ordeal of economic freedom."

The firms constituting the industry undoubtedly benefited from the evolving pattern of horizontal organization, which created a plurality of markets and made manufacturers as consumers hostile to any monopolistic aspirations to control prices in the sole interest of sellers. They never, however, secured the freedom to reshape their economic environment or even to modify their own structure. Their freedom of action was reduced in proportion as the central institution of the Manchester market in the Royal Exchange perfected its function through the completion of a world-wide network of cables in 1870–72 under the influence of the Manchester merchant John Pender (1816–96).[34] Barriers to the diffusion of knowledge were reduced by the improvement of internal communications and by the influence of the trade press as well as of the ancillary industries. Thus firms could acquire no means of increasing their market power or of carving out a secure niche free from the bracing blasts of competition. They lacked any experience as oligopolists or as monopolists and could not even have contemplated acquiring such a position. Hence they never felt the need to fight in order to preserve their own minute share of the aggregate market.

In consequence the strategy enforced upon firms by a state of perfect competition became primarily the quest for survival amidst a host of rivals. Managerial functions were restricted to the bare minimum necessary simply for survival. The perspective of firms was inevitably limited to the short term, and frustration of all but minimal expectations became inevitable. Such firms dared not make the quest for dividends or for profits their primary aim if the means to achieve such an end threatened their very existence. Employers secured from business the necessary subsistence for themselves and their workfolk, especially when levels of activity were raised during periods of cyclical boom. By continuing to exist, however, such small employers accentuated the degree of competition because the pressure of fixed costs encouraged the expansion of production and discouraged any uneconomic resort to short-time working. Thus they contributed to, and accepted, the long-term decline in the general rate of profit accruing to the trade. By reinforcing the competitive structure of industry they maintained its character, its ethos and its vitality, but they inevitably made

impossible any fundamental remolding of its structure. The ferocity
of the struggle for survival tended to stunt the growth of individual
firms and precluded most from embracing policies oriented towards
expansion.

Those firms which grew in size beyond the limits of the individual
mill remained atypical.[35] From the 1850s large firms tended to
develop in the cotton industry outside rather than within Great
Britain. Thus the role of world leader played in succession by the
firms of Arkwright, Peel and Horrocks passed from England to
Russia in the 1860s, to the U.S.A. in the 1900s and to Japan by
the 1920s.[36] The average size of English firms in the 1890s nevertheless remained more typical of the cotton industries of the world
as a whole. The external economies available to those firms in
Lancashire became more important than the internal economies,
masking the relatively high costs inseparable from their small size.

The joint stock movement strengthened the dominant individualistic pattern of industrial organization. Economies of
scale were undoubtedly reaped from the 1870s by the limited
spinning companies of Oldham, which underwent the most dramatic
increases in size within the trade. The new companies nevertheless
remained separate enterprises, each standing firmly upon its own
individual legal foundation and mustering such a relatively limited
capital that cotton spinning companies were quoted only rarely
upon the London Stock Exchange, remaining essentially local
emanations. The managers of the new companies aspired to pursue
their career within the established structure of industry rather
than to transform that structure. They increased the degree of
competition within the spinning industry while narrowing the
range of functions fulfilled by the former employers. That restricted
managerial role was reflected in the physical layout of the mill
and in the allotment to the chief executive of a firm of office space
appropriate to his limited function: in a distinct innovation in
1884, a Bolton firm built mills with spacious offices and elegant
directors' rooms.[37] The pattern of small-scale enterprise was preserved during the great company reflotation boom of 1919–20
and presented strong resistance to the ensuing rationalization
movement, which was regarded in Lancashire as inspired by

managerial megalomania fostered by a clique of metropolitan intellectuals.

The size of firm was governed by factors quite distinct from those regulating the size of mill and especially by the lack of the managerial capacity necessary to control ten million or even one million spindles. Firm and mill experienced a long-term increase in size until the 1920s but tended to remain broadly identical. Only after the industry had ceased to expand and had begun to suffer in the 1930s from a secular depression did the average firm begin to expand, under pressure from the banks, more rapidly in size than the average mill.[38] Until then firms had been largely freed from any external pressure unduly forcing their growth. They had however been cut off from direct contact with the ultimate consumer by the intermediary of the Manchester merchant and thereby from any chance of interpreting early warning signals from their markets. Hence they did not expand their operations overseas into the markets being lost to local competition, and they never acquired the global vision of the Coats family.

The cotton firms of Lancashire were the product of the age of the Industrial Revolution and of a society which had become "industrial but not modern."[39] They may best be understood in terms of their own time and their own world; they may be understood much less effectively in terms appropriate to the later age of the multinational corporation. In their service of the world market during the period of the industry's maturity their achievements were substantial. However, they did not develop the world-conquering ethos of the "haute bourgeoisie" of "corporate capitalism," and they did not become powerhouses of unending growth, either from their own resources or through amalgamation. Thus they did not and could not become pioneers along the path to be followed in Japan by Dainippon, Toyobo and Kanebo. Nor did they become the parents of the modern business corporations of the United Kingdom. Hence they failed to retain a central position in the economy of the nation and suffered both attrition and relegation to the periphery. Thus the pioneer sector of the Industrial Revolution did not become a seedbed of monopolistic tendencies, and its firms did not become vehicles of "monopoly capitalism."

VIII. The Amalgamation Movement of 1898–1900

Competition varied in its incidence and was usually more intense
in the weaving trade than in the spinning industry, in the export
trade than in the home trade, and in the manufacture of prints and
fancies than in that of domestics intended for the home market.
It remained the severest where firms were most numerous and
where the product was simple, undifferentiated, easily gradable,
sold in bulk and therefore substitutable. Thus it proved the keenest
in the standard plain goods trade where prices were fixed in the
"slaughterhouse" of the Manchester Exchange. Inevitably competition became less acute during phases of expansion than during
periods of depression and overproduction, when the pressure of
fixed costs discouraged employers from resorting to short-time
working so long as they could cover their variable costs.

The extent and the intensity of such competition should not,
however, be exaggerated and was in fact limited in a few favored
sectors. A wide and extending range of products dissolved the
superficial unity of the industry into a congeries of dissimilar and
unconnected complexes of firms, producing different materials for
different markets. Certain highly specialized firms acquired niches
protected from the worst ravages of competition. Thus in fine
spinning a limited number of firms in Manchester spun a limited
supply of Sea Island cotton for a restricted market. In the home
trade the increasing frequency of fashion changes in dress goods
extended the range of differentiated products and effectively
partitioned the market among a limited number of suppliers. Large
manufacturers used patents in order to preserve a monopoly of
the most advanced technology and trademarks in order to distinguish their products in perpetuity under the legal recognition
granted in 1887. In the fine trade of Preston an old established
market connection remained essential to success, and a few firms
reaped the pecuniary harvest accruing to the reputation of their
name and mark. In the thread trade, as in fine spinning, price
leadership by a single firm proved an acceptable means of market
control to a happy few oligopolists.

In such favored niches of the industry the formal restriction of competition was accomplished through the reorganization of business structures in the amalgamation movement of 1898–1900. The creation of large-scale organizations was pioneered by Horrockses of Preston through an amalgamation devised in 1887 to resolve a bitter conflict between the senior and junior partners,[40] and by J. & P. Coats through the cartel in 1889 and the trust in 1896. The Coats combine proved so successful that it stimulated a wave of emulatory foundations in quest of comparable profits. Did that trust movement usher in a new era in the history of the British cotton industry? The resulting flotation boom of 1898–1900 in Manchester proved most successful in the case of the finishing trades, where competition from outside was already precluded either by the immense capital necessary for entry, as in calico-printing, or by the control of a limited supply of the vital water by the established firms, as in bleaching. The boom proved intense enough to encourage many abortive proposals for combinations in a wide range of associated trades, to attract London financial interests into Manchester and to stimulate the foundation of the city's first financial weekly.[41] The extensive horizontal integration of separate firms into seven separate combines undoubtedly rein-forced the trend towards the vertical segregation of the processes of production. Within the central sector of spinning, however, only one solitary horizontal combine was formed, in order to exploit the privileged access enjoyed by its member firms both to a limited supply of specialized raw material and to a highly specialized market. The creation of that trust was inspired by wholly tradi-tional motives: "The Fine Cotton Spinners' Association has reverted to something like the system which prevailed in the eighteenth century, when apprentices of good family were placed in the Manchester trade."[42]

The other amalgamations were inspired more by a wish to avoid the losses inseparable from cutthroat competition than by a desire to secure access to economies of scale. They were carried out by men who were business politicians rather than by industrial statesmen.[43] In operation they tended to inhibit rather than to favor innovation: "The combine is safe and dull, dismal and respectable, a bureaucracy facing live industries outside and

TABLE 4   Average Annual Ordinary Dividends Paid by Nine Textile Combines, 1898–1917.

Title of combine	Date of registration	Average dividend %	Period of time
J. & P Coats Ltd.	6.8.1890	31.5	20 years from 1897–98 to 1917–18
Winterbottom Book Cloth Co. Ltd.	26.11.1891	17.45	10 years, 1908–17
English Sewing Cotton Co. Ltd.	16.7.1897	8.9	19 years from 1899–1900 to 1917–18
Fine Cotton Spinners' & Doublers' Association Ltd.	31.3.1898	8.0	20 years from 1898–99 to 1917–18
Bradford Dyers' Association	3.12.1898	7.8	19 years, 1899–1917
English Velvet & Cord Dyers' Association Ltd.	7.4.1899	6.37	19 years, 1899–1917
Bleachers' Association Ltd.	7.6.1900	3.83	18 years from 1900–1 to 1917–18
British Cotton & Wool Dyers' Association Ltd.	12.2.1900	3.5	18 years from 1900–1 to 1917–18
Calico Printers' Association Ltd.	8.11.1899	2.44	18 years from 1900–1 to 1917–18
Rylands & Sons Ltd.	25.10.1873	11.3	20 years, 1898–1917
94 Limited Spinning Companies of Oldham		7.05	20 years, 1898–1917

Source: *Stock Exchange Official Yearbook*, 1899–1919. F. W. Tattersall, *Cotton Trade Review* (1969), 15. The United Turkey Red Co. Ltd., registered on 30 December, 1897, published no record of any ordinary dividend until the year 1914.

abroad, a place where old men in charge enlarge on their long and mostly useless experience, and expect their cheap young men to make no mistakes—in fact, to make nothing. They hire out their services and machines—at rack-rent monopoly prices—to small middlemen of greater inspiration."[44] In general they did not become successful enough in financial terms to encourage imitation, least of all by old-established firms with no strong wish to sink their individuality within impersonal combines.

Not one of the combines in the finishing trades could reproduce the success of J. & P. Coats, despite the increased demand beginning in the 1890s for dyed, bleached and printed goods. Thus no model was established for effective imitation by others, so precluding the exertion of any widespread demonstration effect. The amalgamation movement of 1898–99 succeeded in Japan but proved a comparative failure in Britain, limiting the drive towards combination before the great depression of 1929–32. True success in forming amalgamations was achieved not by the cotton employers but by their operatives.

IX. The Unique Achievement of J. & P. Coats of Paisley

The most aristocratic branch of a prosaic industry proved in the long run to possess the greatest power of survival. The firm of Coats, established in 1824, acquired an unparalleled eminence in the world market and fulfilled a unique function. Its highly specialized product of sewing thread was originally manufactured for the markets of Europe and the U.S.A. Coats pioneered the establishment of foreign subsidiaries by the thread industry after the U.S.A. introduced a protective tariff in 1842, increasing its investment in American plant after the tariffs of 1861 and 1875. The explosive expansion of the firm's operations was detonated by the world-wide diffusion of the sewing machine, invented in 1846. Coats adapted its production to the new device and developed a machine cotton unrivalled in strength and in fineness. For the large-scale manufacture of the new six-cord thread high-speed doubling was essential, and Coats pioneered the adoption of the ring frame for doubling from 1867. The firm doubled the number of its hands from 3,000 in 1858 to 6,000 in 1890,[45] replaced G. A. Clark & Co. as the largest manufacturer of thread and established a duopoly with Clark's from 1876.

Archibald Coats (1840–1912), "the Napoleon of the thread trade,"[46] incorporated the firm as a limited company in 1890 with a capital of £3,750,000. In 1895–96 he amalgamated the family business with four of the largest and strongest firms in the trade, increasing the spindleage of the combine to 500,000 and its capital to £7,750,000 and securing control of 80% of the industry's capacity. For thirty years thereafter J. & P. Coats maintained its position among the top three manufacturing firms of Great Britain and remained until 1928 under the chairmanship of a member of the family. The strength of the combine derived not from the technology of manufacture[47] but from its huge capital, its efficient management and its discreet practice of preserving the nominal independence of the member firms, so as not to force the existence of its monopoly upon the notice of the public. Above all, the cosmopolitan dominion of Coats was based upon the extensive marketing connections of the firm, upon its foreign subsidiaries, upon its world-famous trademarks and upon its immense turnover, stemming from the peculiar nature of the demand for thread. That commodity was an instrumental article which was absolutely essential to the clothing industry but which embodied only a minute part of its total costs.

The position of supremacy established by J. & P. Coats in 1896 was reinforced by the establishment in 1898 of a perfect duopoly with the English Sewing Cotton Company, enabling Coats to pay during each of the next two years the all-time record ordinary dividend of 45%. Thread exports reached their peak volume in 1900, sixteen years after the peak volume of yarn exports in 1884. Thereafter the subsidiary plants abroad catered for local demand and generated the vast bulk of the firm's profits. Coats remained unique in its possession of foreign subsidiaries, in its pronounced export bias and in its high degree of profitability. It became the most financially successful combine in the world; it never passed a year without a dividend and returned to its ordinary shareholders an average dividend of 17.2% during the ninety years 1890–1979 as well as an "almost unprecedented rate of twenty per cent" to its preference shareholders. Its returns made millionaires of at least eleven members of the Coats family who died between 1883 and 1930, leaving on average an estate of £2.27 million. The great thread combine successfully survived criticism from Alfred Marshall in 1919 and from M.P.s in 1919–20[48]; thereafter it maintained with Scots discretion the specialized supremacy of the British cotton industry into the later twentieth century.

X.   The Cotton Industry, Society and the State

The cotton industry differed from the woolen industry in its exotic nature and in its dependence upon foreign sources of supply; it could not be absorbed into the traditional agro-industrial structure of the British economy. Its rapid rise generated widespread emotional opposition to the emergence of a new estate of "cotton lords," although down to 1910 only a single peerage was in fact bestowed, in 1856, upon a cotton manufacturer. The economic consequences of the industry's expansion were however more momentous than either the political or the social consequences. The new industry grew from infancy to maturity under a protectionist regime but helped to transform the commercial policy of the State, in the unique conjuncture of the 1840s, through the campaign for the repeal of the Corn Laws and for the establishment of free trade. In its infancy the cotton trade had supplied the State with revenue from both an excise duty on prints (1712–1831) and an import duty on raw cotton (1798–1845). In maturity the industry secured the abolition of the import duties on cotton in 1845 and on cotton cloth in 1846, freeing itself from "the shackles of protection" and creating a phenomenon without precedent in history, an unprotected industrial market economy. Thereafter the industry maintained no fiscal links with the State and enjoyed in its own northern realm a unique degree of freedom in an age when Manchester seemed to be the very center of the universe. The Manchester Chamber of Commerce served when necessary as an effective intermediary between the trade and the government.[49] Manchester lacked however the traditional ties with the State maintained by Liverpool and rarely seems to have been able to manipulate foreign policy in its own interests.

The cotton industry remained loyal to the cherished policy of free trade and turned a deaf ear to the successive siren calls of fair trade in the 1880s, of bimetalism in the 1890s and of tariff reform in the 1900s. As a counterpart to the restriction of government activity, the balance between public and private expenditure tilted heavily in favor of the creative private sector of the economy. The gross product of the cotton industry surpassed in value the

public revenue itself from 1852 to 1893. Government expenditure
began to rise from 1835 but declined as a proportion of G.N.P. to
a low point in 1873 and only began to rise significantly faster than
G.N.P. from 1895 when naval expenditure first exceeded military
expenditure. The cotton employers had been largely converted
from political Liberalism to Conservatism during the Home Rule
crisis of 1886. Then the imperial renaissance of the 1890s under-
mined the moral basis of economic liberalism in so far as it catered
to material interests rather than to ideals. The change in national
temper from the sturdy individualism of "Manchesterdom" to the
collectivist ethic of the modern age was reflected but not pioneered
in Lancashire.[50] As political and social values came increasingly to
be exalted above the economic calculus, the cotton industry became a political casualty of the new climate of opinion, its decline
being in British history as unprecedented a phenomenon as had
been its rise. The industry's employers had always been dominated
by the short-term perspectives of the market economy. They
remained faithful to their inherited ethos and disdained until
1958 to seek tariff protection. Their virtual independence of the
aid of the State and of its associated records may well be the fundamental reason why the business history of their trade remains
as yet unwritten.

NOTES

1. R. Robson, *The Cotton Industry in Britain* (London, Macmillan,
   1957), 4, 357–9.
2. *Business History*, March 1981, 84–86, "Platt Bros. & Co. Ltd. of
   Oldham, Machine-Makers to Lancashire and to the World: an
   Index of Production of Cotton Spinning Spindles, 1880–1914."
3. *Textile History*, 1978, 76, "Three Historians of the Cotton Industry:
   Thomas Ellison, Gerhart von Schulze-Gaevernitz, and Sydney
   Chapman."
4. G. Unwin, *Samuel Oldknow and the Arkwrights. The Industrial Revolution at Stockport and Marple* (Manchester University Press, 1924,
   1968).
   R. S. Fitton and A. P. Wadsworth, *The Strutts and the Arkwrights,*

1758–1830 (Manchester University Press, 1958).

R. Boyson, *The Ashworth Cotton Enterprise: The Rise and Fall of a Family Firm, 1818–1880* (Oxford, Clarendon Press, 1970).

C. H. Lee, *A Cotton Enterprise*, 1795–1840: *A History of McConnel and Kennedy, Fine Cotton Spinners* (Manchester University Press, 1972).

I have excluded from this list Frances Collier, *The Family Economy of the Working Classes in the Cotton Industry 1784–1833* (1964) and B. W. Clapp, *John Owens, Manchester Merchant* (1965) on the grounds that they deal respectively with the social and the mercantile aspects of the industry rather than with the central process of manufacture.

5. This remark does not apply to the records of the English Sewing Cotton Co. Ltd. (1909–47), listed at M128 in the Archives Department of the Manchester Central Library or to the records of Horrockses Crewdson & Co. Ltd., deposited in the Lancashire Record Office, Preston, in 1969–79 and listed at DDHs and DDX 103.

6. The estimates presented by Mark Blaug in 1962 diverge too widely and too often from those of the meticulous Ellison to remain acceptable for much longer.

7. *Manchester City News*, 15 April 1865 3iii, "Plant Bros. & Co., of Oldham." B. M. Ratcliffe (ed.), *Great Britain and her World 1750–1914. Essays in Honour of W. O. Henderson* (Manchester University Press, 1975), 153–78, "The Cotton Famine in Great Britain."

8. *Third Report of the Royal Commission on the Depression of Trade*, 1886, Q. 8320, J. C. Lee (1832–95), chairman of Tootal's from 1888 to 1895, 10 March 1886.

9. *Business History*, January 1979, 105, "An Index of Commercial Activity: the Membership of the Manchester Royal Exchange, 1809–1948."

10. D. A. Farnie, *The Manchester Ship Canal and the Rise of the Port of Manchester 1894–1975* (Manchester University Press, 1980), 7.

11. F. Stuart Jones, "Instant Banking in the 1830s: The Founding of the Northern and Central Bank of England," *The Bankers' Magazine* (London), March 1971, 130–35; idem, "First Joint Stock Banks in Manchester, 1828–1836," *South African Journal of Economics*, 1973, 16–36; idem, "The Cotton Industry and Joint-Stock Banking in Manchester 1835–50," *Business History*, July 1978, 165–85; idem, "The Manchester Cotton Magnates' Move into Banking, 1826–

50," *Textile History*, 1978, 90–111.

12. *Northern Finance and Trade*, 28 July 1897, 52.

13. C. P. Darcy, *The Encouragement of the Fine Arts in Lancashire 1760–1860* (Manchester, Chetham Society, 1976, Vol. XXIV—Third Series).

14. *Co-operative News*, 9 September 1871, 11, "Co-operation in Oldham." *Co-operative Wholesale Society Annual*, 1884, 186, 188, "Growth of the Cotton Business in Oldham. Statistics of the Cotton Trade and Population."

15. *C. W. S. Annual*, 1884, 187–8, 212.

16. D. A. Farnie, "The Textile Industry: Woven Fabrics," in C. Singer (ed.), *A History of Technology*, Vol. V. *The Late Nineteenth Century (1850–1900)* (Oxford, Clarendon Press, 1958), 569–94.

17. *Chamber's Repository of Instructive and Amusing Tracts* (Edinburgh, Chambers, 1852; Manchester, Shipperbottom, 1972), i, 28, "The Cotton Metropolis."

    A. B. Reach, *Manchester and the Textile in 1849*, ed. by C. Aspin (Helmshore Local History Society, 1972), 79–87, "Oldham."

18. Platt Bros. & Co. Ltd., *General Meetings Minute Book, 1868–1902*, 28, S. R. Platt at the shareholders' meeting of 23 July 1874, DDPSL 1/90/1 in the Lancashire Record Office, Preston.

19. *Oldham Chronicle*, 8 September 1877, 5i; 15 September, 2vi; 10 November, 2vi.

20. Platt Bros. & Co. Ltd., *General Meetings Minute Book, 1868–1902*, 19, S. R. Platt at the shareholders' meeting of 8 January 1873.

21. In 1880–84, 1889–92, 1899–1901 and 1905–9.

22. S. Yonekawa, "The Growth of Cotton Spinning Firms and Vertical Integration. A Comparative Study of U.K., U.S.A., India and Japan," *Hitotsubashi Journal of Commerce and Management*, Oct. 1979, 4. Lees & Wrigley had been the largest firm in Oldham since 1914 and increased its spindleage from 180,000 to 300,000 during 1925.

23. *Oldham Chronicle*, 19 January 1889, 6iii; 26 January, 6v, J. Taylor, chairman of the Sun Mill.

24. *Oldham Chronicle*, 22 December 1900, 8vi, S. Andrew, "The Oldham Cotton Trade. A Quarter of a Century's Experience."

25. *Oldham Chronicle*, 21 December 1867, 7iii, John Platt, chairman of Platt Bros.

26. G. H. Wood, *The History of Wages in the Cotton Trade* (Manchester, Sherratt, 1910), 116.

27. Allen Clarke, *The Effects of the Factory System* (London, Richards,

1899), 31.

28. *Co-operative News*, 9 September 1871, 41; 18 May 1872, 266.

29. *Oldham Chronicle*, 3 January 1884, 2vi.

30. T. Bazley, "Cotton Manufacture and Trade," in *The National Encyclopaedia: a Dictionary of Universal Knowledge* (London, Mackenzie, 1875), vol. V, 10.

31. In 1846 the patent secured in 1832 by Richard Roberts (1789–1864) for his self-acting mule expired.

32. P. G. Hamerton, *The Intellectual Life* (London, Macmillan, 1873), 416–23, "To an Energetic and Successful Cotton Manufacturer"; *ibid.*, 424–29, "To a Young Etonian who Thought of Becoming a Cotton Spinner."

33. *Manchester Guardian*, 9 October 1895, 8iv, J. B. Tattersall (1845–1925), president of the Oldham Master Cotton Spinners' Association from 1891 until 1917.

34. D. A. Farnie, *East and West of Suez. The Suez Canal in History, 1854–1956* (Oxford, Clarendon Press, 1969), 158–61, "The Trade of the Indian Ocean, 1870–1874;" *ibid.*, 185–87, "The Trade of the China Seas, 1870–1874."

35. D. A. Farnie, "John Rylands of Manchester," *Bulletin of the John Rylands University Library of Manchester*, Autumn 1973, 93–129.

36. S. Yonekawa, *op. cit.*, 6, 11.

37. *Lancashire, the Premier County of the Kingdom* (London, Historical Publishing Company, 1888), 76, John Bayley & Sons Ltd.

38. John and Sylvia Jewkes, "A Hundred Years of Change in the Structure of the Cotton Industry," *Journal of Law and Economics*, October 1966, 116–117.

39. E. A. Wrigley, "The Industrial Revolution and Modernization," *Journal of Inter-Disciplinary History*, Autumn 1972, 258.

40. Horrockses Crewdson Papers in the Lancashire Record Office, DDHs 84, Correspondence regarding Shares, 1885–87, deposited by T. V. Hermon in 1977.

41. *Northern Finance and Trade*, 7 July 1897–21, April 1899 (1168 pp.).

42. *Manchester Guardian*, 24 October, 1904, 5i, in a critical review of S. J. Chapman, *The Lancashire Cotton Industry* (1904).

43. S. J. Chapman, *The Lancashire Cotton Industry* (1904), 174.

44. *Textile Manufacturer*, July 1929, 232, in a review of *Some Thoughts on the C. P. A.* (Manchester, Falkner, 1929).

45. *Textile Manufacturer*, March 1890, 118.

46. *Northern Finance and Trace*, 17 November 1897, 407, 409. *The Times*,

13 May 1912, 11iii-iv.

47. J. Watson, *The Art of Spinning and Thread Making* (Glasgow, Watson, 1878), 108–13, 259–307.

    J. Nasmith, *Modern Cotton Spinning Machinery, Its Principles and Construction* (Manchester, Heywood, 1890), 274–81.

48. A. Marshall, *Industry and Trade* (London, Macmillan, 1919), 595–7.

    J. M. Rees, *Trusts in British Industry 1914–1921* (London, King, 1922), 103–113.

49. A. Redford, *Manchester Merchants and Foreign Trade 1794–1858* (Manchester University Press, 1934); idem, *Manchester Merchants and Foreign Trade Vol. II;, 1850–1939* (Manchester University Press, 1956).

50. *Manchester Guardian*, 25 October 1951, 3iii-iv, A. P. Wadsworth, "Political Lancashire. Swing since the Reform Bill."

COMMENTS

1

Heidi Vernon Wortzel
Northeastern University

Great Britain, as a textile-exporting country, had a unique set of strengths that it was able to exploit. D. A. Farnie posits that Britain's application of mechanical power for spinning and weaving was responsible for the employment of capital rather than labor. Developing a distinct technology based on mule spinning at very high speeds, by 1850 Britain had 60% of the world's spindles. Allowing for an interlude for the American Civil War, Britain's output grew until it reached a peak of more than seven hundred thousand tons of yardage, thread and piece goods in 1913.

Not only was Great Britain unique in its capability as far as textile production was concerned; it was also the source and inspiration of subsidiary industries that had no parallel elsewhere in the world. Mill building, mill stores, coal production and the textile machinery business all grew out of the spinning and weaving business.

According to Farnie, Britain dominated the textile industry of the world until 1958. By the mid-1970s, India and China, two countries that had been purchasers of British goods, became "heirs to British primacy," and finally surpassed it.

To what does Farnie attribute the decline of the textile business in Great Britain? Part of the answer, he says, lies in the cotton industry's policy of free trade. Textile manufacturers in Manchester were unable to manipulate foreign policy for their own interests. Farnie declares, "As political and social values came increasingly to be exalted above the economic calculus the cotton industry became a political casualty of the new climate of opinion." There seem to be factors in addition to those to which Farnie has alluded. No one would quarrel with the contention that Britain's textile industry was the world's first modern industry. Likewise, it is clear that the textile business was one of the first to successfully employ machinery and mechanical power. Yet there are some unexplored issues that might deserve further attention.

What about technological factors that might have contributed to Britain's decline? It might be useful to point out that there was an alternative to mule spinning. Ring spinning was invented and perfected in the United States and by 1870 had become America's most important form of spinning. Indeed, by the beginning of World War II, mule spinning was no longer used in the United States. Great Britain was the world's last important cotton textile industry to introduce ring spindles. This is not to suggest that the failure to switch from mules to ring spinning was responsible for Britain's decline. It is merely an issue that might be mentioned as a subject of debate in this context. The large body of literature on mule versus ring spinning might shed additional light on the subject of British competitiveness.

What of Britain's export business? While Farnie correctly notes the shift toward Asian markets, and India and China in particular, he does not mention the importance of Japan as the really serious threat to Britain in the third markets. Much of the decline of British influence in that area can be attributed to Japan's entry into the international economy and not only to the rise of local industry.

Japan had been a good customer of Great Britain as early as the late 1860s. Britain, in fact, supplied more than 100 million yards of cotton cloth to Japan between 1905 and 1910.[1] Japanese output increased rapidly, and by 1913 its exports were about five times as great as its imports. Like Britain, Japan's cotton textile industry grew without the support of tariffs and other government assistance. After 1914, British exports of cotton goods went into a steep decline while Japanese competition experienced a record rise.

---

[1] Lars G. Sandberg, *Lancashire in Decline* (Columbus: Ohio State University, 1974), p. 110.

The rise of Japanese exports had serious implications for Britain's markets in India and China. In the post-World War I era, Indian imports of British goods dropped sharply. By 1938–39, imports of piece goods were down by 73% from their prewar level.[2] The rise of the domestic Indian market was certainly the immediate and overwhelming reason for the drop in British exports. Nevertheless, it should not be overlooked that in the 1930s, Japan overtook Great Britain as a supplier of the Indian market.

The second disaster area for the British cotton textile industry was China. In the post-World War I period, the domestic Chinese textile industry expanded rapidly. The Chinese government, like that of India, was determined to protect its domestic markets and imposed tariffs. Japan, not Britain, was the primary target of the protection, but British trade, which was already sadly depleted, was virtually destroyed.

There seems to be an abundant crop of issues for historians and economists to reap in the field of British textile history. Farnie raises some tantalizing and provocative questions that will, I suspect, continue to intrigue us for some time to come.

2

Naosuke Takamura
University of Tokyo

I would like to raise some questions about the British cotton industry in view of the contrasts with the history of the spinning industry in Japan.

My first question concerns horizontal reorganization. Professor Farnie mentioned that the trend towards specialization in spinning and weaving in the English cotton industry increased in the late nineteenth and early twentieth century. The industry in Japan during this period was developing in quite a contrasting way. Spinning

[2] *Ibid.*, p. 182.

firms installed power looms, and the consumption of cotton yarn used by such firms to weave cotton cloth increased from 3% in 1899 to 19% in 1914. By 1914, five of the six largest firms combined spinning with weaving. In this way they could stabilize management by handling both yarn and cloth and better cope with fluctuating market prices. Professor Farnie indicated that one reason for horizontal reorganization in England was "the rapidity of the expansion of market demand and the delay in mechanization of weaving." However, the rapid expansion of market demand was seen in cotton cloth rather than in cotton yarn, especially in the overseas market, the use of automatic looms also increased during this period. I would be interested in knowing why, despite these factors, the trend toward specialization increased in English firms at that time.

My next question concerns the supply of capital. Professor Farnie mentioned that "capital was never in short supply to finance the expansion of local industry but overflowed into other sectors of the nation's economy." In Japan, which was behind in industrialization, there was little available capital, and spinning firms therefore began as stock companies. They attempted to pay enough dividends to satisfy stockholders and to increase their capital by assingning new shares, as well as by increasing available equipment. Why did capital overflow into other sectors in England? Is it possible that the English spinning industry was not attractive enough for investors who expected a generous profit? What other reason could there be?

Finally, I would like to ask about the enlargement of the various enterprises. Professor Farnie mentioned that it was rare in England for spinning firms to enlarge the scale of their operation by amalgamation. However, Professor Yonekawa stated that the big spinning firms in Japan enlarged quickly through amalgamation and an increase in equipment; this occurred in the early twentieth century, during the same time that Oldham firms were evincing little interest in enlarging. Large-scale Japanese firms were benefiting because they could trade cotton yarn and cloth with trading companies; they could also raise funds through banks and were therefore able to enjoy better business conditions than medium and small-size firms.

Why could not a larger business in England have realized the same advantages? Could you explain the reason why some of the firms were less eager to enlarge the scale of their enterprise?

The Business Climate of the German Cotton Industry, 1850–1914

Gerhard Adelmann
University of Bonn

"Business climate" seems to be a rather vague expression, and it is still so if "business climate" means "business environments" "under which the firms of the German cotton textile industry are managed." In fact all economic, social and political conditions form the setting in which the firms and the German cotton industry have been developing. Yet, starting with the method of the business history, i.e. from the firm, or from the entrepreneur, there is a decisive concretization of the term "business climate" because of the sources and reports on the business history and the industrial history of the German cotton industry.

Besides the customs policy as the political reaction on foreign competition, which was looked at primarily, there are other fields of the business climate standing out in literature: the economic, mostly short-term cyclical developments on the market, the development of textile technology (capital as a production factor) and of the labour market (labour as a production factor). In the sources and in research the situation on the capital market, also the sectional aspect of the raising of capital have been standing aside with a few exceptions. Investments, however, with which the entrepreneurs are also reacting on the specific situation on the various markets, have been treated generally.

In today's lecture I'd like to follow up the question of how important the different aspects of the business climate which were looked at as important at the time have been for the development of the German cotton industry and its firms. I'd also like to try to give an answer for some aspects of the business climate, an answer I am going to prove by outstanding examples.

Taking the title of my report I must not only make some pre-liminary remarks on the term "business climate" but also on the second and third components of it, i.e., "the German cotton in-dustry" and "from 1850 to 1914."

It need not be stressed that the "cotton industry" has never been a uniform industrial branch in Germany, just as it has never been in England or in other countries. The cotton industry is divided into the main production steps, spinning, weaving, and finishing, as well as into enterprises combining several of these steps.

In comparison to England it is even more important that in Germany or in the German Reich no German cotton industry in the sense of a regionally concentrated industry existed in the second half of the 19th century. Because of historical, political reasons the German cotton industry emerged as an industry of the various German states since the 18th century[1] promoted by public measures (economic policy=business climate). Even in the 20th century it has been divided into at least three frontier-crossing main districts: the north-western one (in the Rhineland and Westphalia), the south-western one (in Alsace, Baden, Württemberg and Bayerisch-Schwaben) and the central German one (in upper and Lower Franken, Saxony, and lower Silisea.[2] Their business environments/climates had a different setting to a certain extent. They have come closer only in the course of the common development of customs policy after 1834 and of the political development after 1871, i.e., while a German economy developed. As an unreachable aim for the agglomeration, to be strived for, the German con-temporaries looked at Lancashire and the neighbouring counties which held 93.5% of the total British cotton production in 1903.[3] The regional splitting of the German cotton industry caused by political and traffic reasons was a decisive structural element which was influenced very much by the business climate.

The period 1850–1914 doesn't cover the entire period of in-dustrialization in the German cotton industry. The industrializa-tion/mechanization of the cotton industry had rather started at the end of the 18th century in spinning and lasted till the end of the

19th century in cotton weaving. The development of the German cotton industry was a continuous, long-lasting process of mechanization which has to be explained as "industrialization" and not as an "industrial revolution."[4] In cotton spinning the development of mechanized factory production had started in Germany before the period we'll look at. At different times in the various regions a first development stage started at the end of the 18th century (Rhineland, Saxony) and at the beginning of the 19th century, running out in the first half of the 19th century, not later than 1834/36.[5]

Waterframes and handmules, both in centralized plants, existed or barely existed together until 1850. At the end of the 1840s but even more at the beginning of the 1850s the second main foundation stage started. In that stage modern mechanized spinning made its way, in progressive areas by the end of the 1850s, in backward areas not later than the 1860s.

The development of power-loom weaving occurred in Germany in the second half of the 19th century, i.e., in the period we'll look at. The transition from decentralized hand weaving to the usage of power-looms in factories took place at a slow pace until the end of the 19th century and with significant regional differences. Handweaving and power-loom weaving did not only exist side by side in the different regions, but for several decades they were combined by cotton merchants who had factories, in order to satisfy the cyclically varying demand.

Despite of the different development of the German cotton industry in regions and in time, it seems appropriate for this lecture to look at the long time growth of the whole German cotton industry[6] despite the reservations just mentioned. The statistics had to be looked at to find out whether periods emerge which point to changes in the structure of the industry and its enterprises; these periods with different growth rates may have been connected with changes in the business environment/business climate.

In the main part of my lecture I'd like to analyze the most important aspects of the business climate of the German cotton industry for some outstanding time periods.

Table 1 shows the number of spindles in the German cotton

TABLE 1   The Number of Spinning Spindles and the Production of German Cotton Spinning.

Year	Spindles	Growth rate % p.a.	Index of the number of spindles (1913=100)	Yarn production (t)	Growth rate % p.a.	Index of yarn production (1913=100)	Production per spindle (kg)	Self-sufficiency in yarn for weaving (%)
1800	22,000		0.2	93		0.02	4.2	
1815	360,000		3	1,963		0.4	5.1	54
1846	897,300		8	12,294		3	13.7	31
1852	1,045,000		9	17,490		4	17.5	47
1861	2,235,195	8.8	19	58,877	14.4	13	26.3	79
1870	2,600,000	1.7	22	65,518	1.2	15	25.2	85
1875	4,237,609		36	93,613		21	22.0	88
1887	5,037,825	1.4	42	165,122	4.8	37	29.8	97
1898	7,883,714	4.2	66	295,286	5.4	66	37.5	100
1905	8,832,016	1.6	74	350,939	2.5	78	39.7	103
1909	10,162,872	3.6	85	407,280	3.8	91	40.1	102
1913	11,951,583	4.1	100	447,264	2.6	100	37.4	105

Source: Kirchhain 29f., 41f., 61f.; author's calculations.

industry for selected years between 1800 and 1913. Of the figures in Table 1, column 2 with the average annual growth rates is important for the context right now. Column 2 shows the growth rate for the overall period 1852–1913 that is dealt with in the conference and contains the growth rates for some significant shorter periods of time. Taking the average annual growth rates, I got the most important stages of high and low growth of German cotton spinning. The overall growth rate in the number of spindles from 1852 to 1913 is 4.2% p.a., but it is interesting to note that this was not a level rise; the growth rates during selected periods are of varying intensity.

1852–1861: growth rate 8.8% p.a.
(The number of spindles grew by 113.9% in 9 years);
1861–1870: growth rate 1.7%
(The number of spindles grew by 16.3% in 9 years);
1875–1887: growth rate 1.4%
(The number of spindles grew by 18.9% in 12 years);
1887–1913: growth rate 3.4%
(The number of spindles grew by 137.2% in 25 years).

Within that last quarter of a century the following periods had growth rates above the average:

The period 1887 to 1898 with an average growth rate of 4.2% p.a. and the period 1905 to 1913 with an average growth rate of 3.9% p.a., while the years 1898–1905 dropped back quite substantially with an average growth rate of 1.6% p.a.

Stages with growth rates above average were especially the years 1852–1861 (8.8%), 1887–1898 (4.6%), and 1905–1913 (3.9%). The 1850s, the late 1880s, and the 1890s were outspoken foundation periods within the German cotton spinning industry. The last period seems rather to have been a period of extension, a period which, by the way, had alternating high and low growth rates.

Stages with an extremely low growth rate p.a. were the years 1861 to 1875, though not surprising because of the Cotton Famine (average annual growth rate 1.7%) and the period 1875 to 1887 with an average annual growth rate of only 1.4%. This low growth rate would have to astonish a protectionist, as just in 1879 the

TABLE 2 The Number of Weaving Looms and the Production of the German Cotton Weaving Industry.

Year	Looms		Power-looms		Production of cotton textiles in tons	Production per loom in kg
	Total	Growth rate % p.a.	Total	Growth rate % p.a.		
1800	35,000				1,800	51
1815	40,000				3,600	90
1846	150,000				39,470	263
1861	194,250		23,448		75,051	386
1875	226,000		84,721		101,415	449
1898	272,600	0.8	194,726	4.9	294,715	1,081
1905	300,560	1.4	228,700	2.3	340,559	1,133
1909	312,400	1.0	260,323	3.3	398,049	1,274
1913	343,200	2.4	286,003	2.4	426,837	1,244

Source: Kirchhain 29f., 68; Rieger, Verzeichnis der Spindeln und Webstühle, volumes 1893, 1898, 1905, 1909, 1913; Jacobs 55, 86; author's calculations.

German tariffs on cotton yarn and cotton fabric had been raised quite substantially. Apparently the slowed down growth of that period was influenced by the general growth recession and the stagnation of the so-called "Great Depression."

The period 1898 to 1905 also had a low average annual growth rate with 1.6%. On first sight you might explain that development by the increase in price of the American raw cotton and often mentioned "cotton crisis" before World War I;[7] a scarcity of raw cotton production and a world wide growth of spindle capacity that was out of proportion.

Checking the annual changes in the number of spindles according to Kirchhain[8] leads to similar spans of time, in which the changes in the number of spindles were higher than average (1835–1838, 1853–1861, 1891–1898, 1906/07, 1912/13) or lower than average (1841–1844, 1863, 1872–1878, 1881–1887, 1899–1905, 1908–1911).

The number of looms and their substantially lower growth rates shown in columns 2–4 of Table 2 don't indicate such significant changes as in cotton spinning. They do not reveal the different growth periods in the cotton industry in such a distinct way.

Trying to take a close view of the business climate in the German cotton industry, the growth periods of the years 1852–1887 seem to be appropriate to me, as all important aspects of the business climate can be grasped at least in their beginnings. I am going to concentrate on that period, but nevertheless I'd like to point out the most important future trends until 1913 when discussing the various aspects.

1852–1861

The mushroom growth of the 1850s seems to have been influenced by the following factors:

1. The favourable overall national and international market conditions as well as the specific conditions of the cotton market. Mentioning the favourable overall market, I am thinking of the industrialization in Germany having its take-off period at least after 1850.[9] The growing population and the growing job opportunities tended to create more buying power. The demand of the rising number of industrial workers concentrated on the relatively cheap cotton products. Entrepreneurs in the Mönchengladbach area adjusted to that demand by changing their production programme. The terms of trade developing favourably and leading to a relative cheapening of the raw cotton as well as the early industrialization and mechanization of the cotton industry with their cost and price-reducing effects contributed to the relative cheapening of cotton products in comparison to other textiles. A growing demand stimulated by a rising supply with declining prices made cotton a wanted product within the reach of a growing industrial population. The favourable overall market conditions of the 1850s mentioned before need not be explained in this report as they didn't affect just the cotton industry but promoted the overall economic development in Germany, which is called industrialization from the 1850s onwards.

2. Besides the market conditions, the economic measures of the state are to be named in second place of the general frame structures. Taking the economic policies we have to point out once more that they not only affected the German cotton industry but the overall economic development in Germany.[10] Almost all the

German states belonged to the Zollverein after 1853, i.e., around the middle of the century there was already a domestic market in the size of the later German Reich. Of the various political-economic-measures of the German states, of the Zollverein, and of the later German Reich, I am only going to mention the standardization of the mercantile law. I'd also like to remind you of the various laws and rescripts regarding company law which made the foundation of stock companies easier around 1850. I dealt with this question in an earlier paper on the 'Foundation of the Gladbach Stock Company for Spinning and Weaving.'[11] A unification of the industrial legislation also started before the foundation of the Reich in 1871. Economic freedom was introduced quite late in southern Germany in comparison to Prussia, and the emerging freedom of coalition gained quite an importance for the associations of entrepreneurs and the trade unions. The railway policy[12] of the German states dates back to the 1840s, leading mostly to private railway systems but also to state-run railways. All these political-economic measures were not aiming at the cotton industry but rather at the whole economy and especially the whole industrial sector.

Besides the political-economical measures I also have to mention the political-social laws of the state. In the 1850s there were only the laws regulating child labour. But once again, these political-social measures were not aiming at the cotton industry alone but at all industries, even though they were more important for cotton spinning because of its early industrial development than for the other trades which were not that far in industrializing or which employed fewer adolescents and children.

All these political-economic and social measures which had more of an overall effect were outrun by the tariff policy which was aiming at single branches of the economy, especially the cotton industry, the iron industry and later on after 1879 at the agricultural sector. Therefore, as far as government policies are concerned, we only have to deal with the tariff policy and some of the social legislation when examining the business climate of the German cotton industry.

3. Between 1852 and 1861, i.e., the period we're looking at right now, there was no outstanding tariff measure, no outstanding

date in tariff policy. Yet, in those years the raising of the tariff on cotton yarn that had taken place in 1846 really began to be effective according to many contemporaries and some researchers. Seen from the tariff aspect, that period 1846–1865 is also called the period of the three-taler-tariff, as the specific duty on cotton yarn had been raised from 2 to 3 talers.[13]

Estimating the effects of the tariff on the growth in the 1850s, one has to distinguish between the real protective effects of the tariff increase and the stimulating psychological effects of that policy, which had been influenced by the entrepreneurs, on the readiness of investors and entrepreneurs to invest in an industrial branch which seemed to be protected. Yet, to ask for such a differentiation is easier said than done.[14] After this review of the overall frame structures applying to the whole industry I'd like to take a look at the local and individual production facilities in the 1850s. Here we are dealing with those aspects of the business environment which have influenced the layout of the German cotton industry and its enterprises within the frame of the overall business environment.

4. Of the special manufacturing conditions we have to deal with the status of technology, especially of textile technology which was decisive for the possible standard of the technical plant organization of fixed capital. In the 1850s the not novel finding of the technological backwardness in comparison to the further developed cotton industries of neighbouring countries England, Switzerland, Alsace, the Netherlands, and Belgium led to a greater willingness to innovate and to invest of a growing number of entrepreneurs in the German cotton industry. The diffusion of technical progress which had already made its way in industrially progressive countries took place in comparatively backward Germany at such a speed that Jacobs[15] was not wrong when he spoke of a "technical revolution" in cotton spinning. What Jacobs was thinking of was the replacement of older machines and working methods by completely new ones. This technical revolution was the founding of many new modern cotton spinning plants with self-actors powered by steam engines. The transition to bigger plants is shown best in Bavaria. In 1846 the average number of spindles was 4,594; in

1861 already 16,267 spindles. There were 14 employees on every
1,000 spindles. Sometimes, though by no means in general, a joint
stock company[16] was chosen as the type of enterprise for a large
scale firm because of the reduction in risk and the easier way of
raising capital. The foundation of stock companies occurred in the
different regions at different times; at first and mainly in southern
Germany, where 20 stock companies were founded until 1861,
while only 3 stock companies were founded in the Prussian part
of the Rhineland after 1853. In 1861 there were 25 stock companies in the German cotton industry, 6 of them pure spinning
firms, 4 of them pure weaving firms but 15 combined firms with
spinning the main part of the business. Yet I dare to doubt that
those combined mills are a specific structural element of the German
cotton industry which makes it distinct from those of other
countries, especially of England. The importance of the banks and
especially of the stock exchanges in the placement of the stocks was
low not only in the Rhineland[17] but also in Bavaria[18] because the
group of stockholders was regionally limited most of the time.
Personal ties continued to dominate in the foundation and running
of stock companies in the cotton industries for a long time. The
development of the number of self-actors and the amount of horse-
power used in German cotton spinning industry are good indicators
of the accelerating diffusion of technical progress after 1850.
Especially in the 1850s the growth rate of technical progress accelerated substantially. The development of textile technology and
its diffusion was of course not finished with the year 1861, but went
on, partly with a lower pace and under different economic conditions, in the following stages. The highly productive ring spindles,
which could be constructed as early as the 1860s, were only introduced to a significant extent in Germany as late as 1890.[19] I'd
also like to remind you of the slow spreading of the power-looms,
introduced around 1850, in the factory system. The first weaving
automats, the Northrop looms, were only tested by some modern
plants in Germany in the last decade before World War I.[20]

According to the lists of the Bremer Baumwollbörse (Cotton
Exchange), the number of spinning firms and their average size,
measured by spindles operated, developed as follows:

	Germany		Rhineland-Westphalia	
	Spinning firms	Spindles per firm	Spinning firms	Spindles per firm
1893	379	20,790	80	10,332
1905	368	25,500	101	27,050
1914	348	35,600	111	37,200

Source: Rohling 52.

The number of firms slightly decreased between 1893 and 1914 while the spindles per unit increased by more than two thirds.

If you take Rhineland-Westphalia as a regional case study you will find remarkable deviations from the average size of the German spinning firms. In 1914 the average firm of the whole Rhineland-Westphalia region operated 37,200 spindles, an amount slightly above the German average (35,600). However, in the older spinning and weaving Rhineland district, my Japanese listeners are thoroughly informed of by the publications of my colleague Professor Watanabe, there were only 25,814 spindles per unit, especially due to the large number of old small firms in the Gladbach area. In the younger district of Westphalia the average size of a firm amounted to 54,306 spindles. Here several new large-scale spinning mills had been founded since the 1870s partly owing to the cheaper wages in the rural districts near the German-Dutch frontier, e.g. the biggest German spinning firm, Gerrit van Delden & Co., in Gronau operating 319,810 spindles, yet including 138,046 twining spindles, in 5 mills. In number of spinning spindles the Leipziger Baumwollspinnerei AG was ahead by 240,000 spindles.

The average size of a German power-loom firm was much smaller than that of the spinning firm. According to Rieger's lists (quoted by Rohling 53 f.) there existed 493 weaving firms with an average number of 241 looms in 1893, and 851 firms with an average of 336 looms in 1913. There were 325 resp. 698 specialized firms among these weaving firms, their number of looms running below average, while the other firms were combined with spinning mills. The weaving branches of those integrated firms had at least a middling size, as the figures of the following tentative table roughly indicate:

	1893	1913
Integrated firms	114 (30.1%)	153 (44.0% of spinning firms)
Spindles (in thousands)	1,780 (22.6%)	4,921 (41.2% of German spindleage)
Looms	38,209 (36%)	116,503 (40.7% of German power-looms)
Per integrated firm:		
Spindles	15,620	32,183
Looms	335	761

Source: Rohling 54; Rieger 1893, 1913; author's calculations.

Reviewing the structure of the cotton firms, the above table indicates that the process of integration which had begun about 1850 continued after 1890. In 1913, 44% of the spinning firms were integrated firms commanding about 41% of the German spindleage and of the German power-looms as well. As to the importance of the different types of enterprise, I'd like to direct your attention to the fact that in 1913 out of 348 spinning firms only 26% were run by joint stock companies. But these 91 companies, consisting of 44 specialized spinning firms and 47 integrated firms, held 47.4% of the German spindleage. In weaving, the influence of joint stock companies (47 integrated plus 18 specialized weaving companies) was limited to 25.2% of the power-looms (cf. Kirchhain 180; Rohling 61), but 7.6% of the firms.

5. As a further factor in the development of the cotton industry and as an essential aspect of the special business climate the labour market situation emerged in the 1850s. Generally it can be said that the modern factories of the German cotton industry were built in those areas where the textile industry relied heavily upon working people used to textile work. Sometimes these people had worked in the textile business as a side-line to agriculture, sometimes as full-time workers in the older mechanical spinning or in cotton weaving. The situation on the labour market can't be described for the whole of Germany in the upswing period of the 1850s. The situation rather differed quite a lot in the different regions,[21] especially depending on the rate of industrialization. But it also differed depending on the foundation of a plant near a town or in the country. It would not be justified to say that there was

TABLE 3   Number of Occupied Persons in Cotton Spinning and Weaving.

Year	Number of persons in the Spinning Industry	Persons working per 1,000 spindles	Number of persons in the Weaving Industry	Persons working per 100 looms	Total number of persons in spinning and weaving
1800	1,700	77	58,000	165	59,700
1820	12,300	32	(1823) 82,500		94,800
1844/48	18,500	21	208,000	139	226,500
1850/54	20,500	19			
1859/60	31,900	16	218,400	115	250,300
1865/69	31,900	14			
1873/77	51,100	12	227,000	100	278,100
1885/89	53,700	11			
1897/99	73,500	9	246,000	90	319,500
1904/06	78,200	9	261,500	87	339,700
1908/10	84,900	8	265,000	85	349,900
1913	96,800	8	284,000	83	380,800

Source: Kirchhain 73.

a general surplus of workers in the 1850s. There was only a surplus of unskilled workers everywhere in Germany at the beginning of industrialization.

In some regions of the German cotton industry there was already a certain lack of skilled and semi-skilled workers so that workers from already further developed industrial areas had to be recruited. In southern Germany skilled workers from Switzerland or from Alsace were recruited when new cotton spinning mills were built. In Westphalia experts from the nearby Netherlands were enlisted. After 1850 there was hardly any enlisting of English workers. Such a recruitment had only been necessary in the first foundation period of the German mechanical cotton spinning industry at the end of the 18th and in the early 19th century. English technicians were still sometimes needed to install new textile machines. Yet, in general, the qualified workers training the local workers and also the managing technical personnel came from the developed German and continental European cotton regions.

The number of employees in the cotton industry can be seen in Tables 3 and 5. In the spinning industry the number of operatives grew by more than 50%, from 20,500 to 31,900, in the 1850s, while the number of spindles doubled. In the weaving industry, which employed ten times more workers than the spinning industry around 1850, the number of operatives didn't grow substantially, i.e. it grew by 8,000 to 218,400, 23,500 of them working with power-looms. In 1913, 96,800 people were working in the spinning industry compared to 284,000 in the weaving industry. With regard to the manpower per firm I calculated an average of 278 operatives per spinning firm and estimated about 266 operatives per weaving firm.

The sex distribution of the operatives in the German cotton industry was just about even in the 1850s. The proportional share of female workers rose only slightly to about 53: 47 until World War I.[22] Taking the further development into consideration, it has to be mentioned that the labour market situation changed in the cotton areas in the long run depending on the extent to which other enterprises of the cotton and textile industry, or other branches of industry, for instance the iron and steel industry, gained importance. During the period of industrialization the labour market situation changed for the cotton entrepreneurs from a favourable surplus of cheap labour to a definite shortage of workers. The industry tried to react to these consequences by raising wages, measures of industrial welfare policy, but also by rationalization. The competitive situation on the labour market can already be seen in more developed cotton areas in the 1850s.

In location theory the textile industry is counted to the labour orientated industries. Yet you have to restrain from over-estimating the importance of the working force potential for the location of the German cotton industry. After the 1850s the orientation as the available power sources seems to have become more important in modern cotton spinning. As various older and newer locational and regional investigations in textile history have proven for southern Germany,[23] the modern cotton spinning industry moved to places with favourable water power while the existence of a manpower potential was of minor importance for the location of the plants. You can see a certain comparable development of locating plants in Rhineland-Westphalia, Saxony, and Franken, where the nearby coal depots became more important.

6.   As a sixth aspect of the business environment, one which was especially important in the 1850s, the improvement of the lines of communication, especially the building and extension of the railway system in Germany, has to be mentioned, even if the improvement of the traffic system—which is only part of the whole infrastructure—didn't only have an effect on the cotton industry but on the overall economic development. The vicinity or remoteness of transport facilities certainly had some sort of importance in the establishment of enterprises in the cotton industry. It can be proven many a time that single cotton manufacturers tried to influence the building of railways and succeeded indeed. This is even more true for the combined efforts of textile entrepreneurs of a region, making use of the regional chambers of commerce to get a certain route of the railway or later on to achieve reduced freight rates for raw cotton. As early as the 1850s examples can be found for the textile region in the lower Rhineland near Mönchengladbach, Rheydt, or in

TABLE 4   The Number of Spinning Spindles in the German States.

Year	Bavaria		Württemberg		Baden		Alsace-Lorraine	
		(%)		(%)		(%)		(%)
1800	2,000	9.1						
1815			7,000	1.9	10,600	2.9		
1846	56,533	6.3	27,000	3.0	140,000	15.6		
1852	80,000	7.7	37,193	3.5	138,036	13.2		
1861	536,825	24.0	171,566	7.7	296,301	13.3	[1,410,000]	
1870							[1,559,751]	
1875	833,496	19.7	270,042	6.4	368,580	8.7	1,387,382	32.7
1887	924,312	18.4	354,548	7.0	398,172	7.9	1,375,000	27.3
1898	1,390,558	17.6	545,278	6.9	429,768	5.5	1,597,848	20.3
1905	1,578,084	17.9	706,585	8.0	468,784	5.3	1,511,586	17.1
1909	1,897,840	18.7	852,762	8.4	510,586	5.0	1,568,232	15.4
1913	2,309,236	19.3	882,998	7.4	550,436	4.6	1,891,450	15.8

Source: Kirchhain 39ff.; author's calculations.

southern Germany near Augsburg and Hof. Even in the last decades of the 19th century the railway lines and the channels in the backward areas, for instance in the Westphalian cotton industry near the Dutch border, were an important aspect of the business climate, not only an aspect the entrepreneurs reacted to but also an aspect they shaped actively.[24]

1862 to 1870/75

In sharp contrast to the first period I just described, with its mushroom growth, the second and the third period 1862 to 1875 and 1875 to 1887 had only a slight growth. Both periods have this slow growth in common, but the reasons for the slowing down of growth and temporary stagnation differ. In the period 1862–1870/75, mainly political aspects of the business environment negatively affected growth. In the period 1875–1887 mainly economic reasons (the so-called depression) were responsible for the slow growth, even though political aspects, too, for instance the protective tariff policy in 1879, fell into this third period, measures which were supposed to stimulate growth. The period 1862–1875 is generally left out when looking at the economic growth as the statistical unit of the region has changed: i.e., Germany had been

Saxony		Prussia		Other North German states		Germany
	(%)		(%)		(%)	
3,000	13.6	15,000	68.2			22,000
284,000	78.9	55,000	15.3			360,000
500,000	55.7	170,433	19.0	3,334	0.4	897,300
551,820	52.1	227,951	21.8	(10,000)	1.0	1,045,000
707,387	31.7	398,071	17.8	125,045	5.6	2,235,195
						2,600,000
650,000	15.3	695,825	16.4	32,284	0.8	4,237,609
1,001,599	19.9	894,194	17.8			5,037,825
1,869,867	23.7	2,030,377	25.8			7,883,714
1,949,313	22.1	2,617,664	29.6			8,832,016
2,211,953	21.8	3,121,499	30.7			10,162,872
2,405,931	20.1	3,911,532	32.7			11,951,583

enlarged by Alsace-Lorraine in 1871. Looking at the figures without taking Alsace into account, there was only a slight growth of cotton spinning in the area of the Zollverein after 1862, as shown in Table 4. The same is true for the development of the number of weaving looms. On the other hand, growth in the number of power looms was high in times of crisis: the Cotton Famine because of the American Civil War and the competition of the cotton weaving industry of Alsace which was already mechanized to a large extent, thus forcing the transition from hand weaving to power-looms, wherever hand weaving still existed in the German Reich.

After these preliminary statistical remarks I'm going to emphasize the most important aspects of the business climate in this second period 1862–1875. The slow growth of that period was mainly caused by political events and the consequences thereof. Indeed there were three wars: 1) the American Civil War causing the Cotton Famine, the shortage of American raw cotton in 1862–1865; 2) the Prussian-Austrian War of 1866 between Northern and Southern Germany; and 3) the German-French War of 1870/71 with the affiliation of Alsace, the most important French cotton area, to the newly founded German Reich in 1871.

As a further, but also political aspect of the business climate

TABLE 5   Regional Distribution of the Number of Persons Working in Cotton Spinning and Weaving.

	Persons working in spinning						Persons working in weaving					
	1882		1895		1907		1882		1895		1907	
	Absolute number	%	Absolute number	%	Absolute number	%	Absolute number	%	Absolute number	%	Absolute number	%
Schwaben	5,932	10.1	7,445	10.1	8,704	9.0	5,157	2.8	9,846	4.6	10,656	5.1
Lower and Central Franken	3,616	6.2	5,388	7.3	8,654	8.9	13,312	7.1	12,212	5.7	16,864	8.0
Württemberg	3,289	5.6	5,517	7.5	8,646	8.9	7,285	3.9	9,316	4.3	12,603	6.0
Baden	3,753	6.4	4,698	6.4	5,006	5.2	5,387	2.8	9,088	4.2	10,201	4.8
Alsace	15,090	25.8	13,737	18.7	13,761	14.2	25,775	13.7	26,579	12.4	24,065	11.4
Saxony	8,979	15.4	10,630	14.4	17,800	18.3	56,252	30.0	60,411	28.1	63,828	30.3
Silesia	4,362	7.5	2,072	2.8	1,846	1.9	28,695	15.3	27,634	12.9	17,324	8.2
Rhineland	8,144	13.9	13,368	18.2	16,759	17.3	22,574	12.0	28,897	13.4	23,224	11.0
Westphalia	1,796	3.1	4,603	6.3	10,996	11.3	6,898	3.7	12,736	5.9	16,826	8.0
Rest	3,548	6.1	5,999	8.2	4,899	5.1	16,362	8.7	18,236	8.5	15,113	7.2
Germany	58,509		73,457		97,071		187,697		214,955		210,704	

Source: Hamburger 40.

I have to mention the tariff reform, the tariff reduction in 1862, starting off the period of relatively free trade 1865–1879. Protectionists have made that return to the two-taler-tariff responsible for nearly all growth difficulties in the period 1865–1879. Yet the scientific research[25] of the years before the World Wars proved this argument not to be tenable. If we researched the period 1862–1875 for decisive aspects of the business climate for the overall economic development, we'd certainly have to mention the "Years of Foundation" 1871–1873 starting off a second new period of industrialization in the German economy. Yet there were no "Years of Foundation" in the German cotton industry.[26] This should be noted as a distinctive feature of that period. The fact that there were no "Years of Foundation" in the German cotton industry is linked to the political development, i.e., the shock caused by the affiliation of the advanced cotton industry in Alsace while the market of the cotton industry of the German Reich did not expand.

The special aspects of power-politics of the business climate, i.e. the effects of the wars, shall be dealt with right here as they were only existing in this period.

The effects of the Cotton Famine caused by the American Civil War can be seen in the development of the spindleage. The changes in the number of spindles as calculated by Kirchhain show definitely that the number of spindles remained constant 1862–1865 as can be seen from Table 1. Yet, that stagnation doesn't mean that there were no changes in the spindles used. At the time of the Cotton Famine, when about one third of the German spindles were out of work,[27] the composition of the spindleage was changed substantially. Old spindles were replaced by new ones, which could be bought at cheap prices in those years as the English factories producing textile machinery suffered from a shortage of orders.[28]

This unique favourable[29] occasion was taken advantage of by various cotton firms, especially the bigger ones, which were financially well-based and which had also bought big raw cotton supplies at the beginning of the Cotton Famine at favourable terms; these companies were thought to have profits running to millions of

marks.[30] The Cotton Famine also contributed to the decline in the
number of the primitive mules and the half-selfactors in Saxony, a
decline which can hardly be seen from Table 4 on the basis of regional location. According to other sources the decline of the number
of spindles in Saxony was more substantial in the 1860s, and was four
times higher than Kirchhain said. In any case that meant the end
of the era of the small firm in cotton spinning.[31]

In Germany the scarcity and price-rise of American raw cotton
led to a certain reorientation to the coarser East Indian raw cotton
and to the finer Egyptian raw cotton.[32] Yet, both areas couldn't
replace the missing American supplies, so that cotton spindles
were temporarily out of order in Germany. In the German cotton
weaving industry some firms tried to solve the problem by returning
to the weaving of other yarns. In the Mönchengladbach and
Rheydt area, besides the temporary transition to silk weaving, half-
cotton weaving came up in those years of the cotton crisis, that is
weaving with a cotton warp and a woolen weft. For that reason
the later-on quite important wool industry of the Mönchengladbach
area developed.[33] The cotton crisis, which was not just the shortage
of the high-quality American raw cotton but also the general big
increase in prices for all raw cotton, promoted also the transition
from handweaving to mechanical weaving with power looms
because of the deterioration of the material. The coarse yarns
from East Indian raw cotton were well suited for processing with
power looms, as people could only manage the processing of coarse
yarns when mechanical weaving started. Taking a closer look
at the number of power looms in Germany than was possible in
Table 2, you can derive a bigger increase already in the 1860s
when you sum up the regional figures. The number of power
looms increased from 23,500 in 1861 to just about 57,500 in 1875,
not taking the additional power looms in Alsace into account. Already in the 1850s the transition to power-loom weaving and the
decline of hand-weaving had started especially in those areas
where cotton spinning was relatively far developed: in Bavaria,
Baden, and in the Rhineland, while this transition started in
Saxony and Silesia in the 1860s.[34]

The German war between Prussia and Austria and their allied

forces, i.e. the states in northern and southern Germany, in 1866 had no long-term effects on the development of the cotton industry. Only Saxony, lying close to the battlefield, was affected. Here the tendency to reorganize the backward spinning industry in Saxony, starting because of the Cotton Famine, was still enforced. There were also some complaints about consequences in Bavaria, but they are not proven, nor can they be conclusively attributed to the war of 1866. Yet the worsened economic situation and especially the Cotton Famine did affect the Bavarian cotton industry. That way you have to understand the report that "since 1863 out of 15 spinning mills with 375,000 spindles 2 had broken down, 7 were sold under constraint, while 3 had temporarily become insolvent, 1 had reduced its stock capital to a half, and 2 had not yielded for eight years."[35]

Turning now to the third war of that period, the German-French War of 1870/71. Its effects on the overall economic development of Germany have been valued positively, though sometimes overrated and explained by one reason. Yet the German cotton industry almost did not take part in the following overall economic growth of the "years of foundation" 1871–1873. The German yarn production had just regained the level it had attained before the Cotton Famine in 1869/70,[36] when the normal economic growth of the German cotton industry was slowed down by the effects of another political event, the German-French War. The affiliation of Alsace-Lorraine had accommodated to "the patriotic feelings of the German nation," [37] but brought the German cotton industry with the big modern cotton industry of the Alsace, a competitor which might ruin the German firms as the entrepreneurs feared. By affiliating Alsace the increase in spindles (1,490,584) ran up to 56% of the amount of spindles in the old areas, the increase in the number of power-looms ran up to 88%, the increase in the number of calico machines ran up to 100%.[38] Until 1870 the production capacity of the cotton industry in Alsace was directed to the big French market protected by ad-valorem duties. The production capacity was far higher than the market in Alsace-Lorraine. Therefore that production capacity had to press on the German market after the affiliation. When the German authorities asked the cotton entre-

preneurs for their opinion on the affiliation still during the war,
the answers of the chambers of commerce, of the associations and
of the cotton industry spokesmen differed quite a lot. The chambers
of commerce in Saxony, which were in favour of free trade representing the interests of the local cotton weaving industry, had spoken
"for an affiliation right away without any transitional tariff arrangements." A commission of the cotton entrepreneurs in southern
Germany, mostly representatives of cotton spinning, had addressed
the king and had argued against the affiliation. The chambers of
commerce in the Rhineland and in southern Germany had displayed
great reservations and had made several suggestions ranging
from a special customs area to transitional tariff arrangements in
the peace treaty with France.

The political decision fell the latter way: In 1871 the French
market was still open to the cotton industry of the Alsace. There
were reduced tariffs in 1872, and until the spring of 1873 the processing exchange between French weaving mills and dyeing and
printing plants in Alsace were exempt from the tariff.[39] After this
transitional period, the industrialists in Alsace and in the German
Reich looked upon it as too short, the separation from the French
market was perfect while the economic integration of the Alsatian
cotton industry into the market of the German Reich took a longer
time. This integration led to trouble for the Alsatian as well as
for the German cotton firms, especially in southern Germany, even
though not always in the same way and to the same extent, as
interested parties said in reports of the chambers of commerce,
petitions and in the expert hearing during the Enquiry on the
State of the Cotton and Linen Industry of 1878.[40] Yet some
consequences of the political change on the frame structure can't
even be denied after a critical analysis of other reasons. In this
context I can only point out some effects of the integration of the
Alsatian cotton industry. The extremely low growth in the number
of spindles in the years 1870–1875 by only 78,000 (average annual
growth rate 0.6%) and the decline in the number of spindles in
Alsace by 172,369 (11.1%)[41] at the same time were certainly
influenced by that affiliation. The transition of the Alsatian fine
spinning mills to the production of coarser yarns was at least to a sub-

stantial part caused by the—in comparison to the French productive tariff—lower German specific duty which only shut out foreign competition in coarser products. This change in the Alsatian yarn production contributed to the surplus of coarser yarn on the German market, i.e. to a surplus production industrialists complained about, and which was felt especially in the cyclical downtrend following the mid-1870s. The Alsatian weaving industry, already well mechanized, was certainly a competitor for the weaving firms in southern Germany on the domestic and foreign markets, but a competitor they could compete with. Yet, the integration enforced the necessity for the German handweaving plants to change over to power looms also in fine weaving, and this is quite important in regard to the structural change caused by the business environment. I'd also like to mention the consequences on the neighbouring cotton industry in Baden. Of course, you need not look for contemporary complaints about the competition, complaints which have been occurring at all times. Of greater importance for the regional structure is the observation that "the trading area in the southern part of Baden adapted itself to the further developed Alsatian one" after the border had been done away with. A substantial division of labour developed especially after the tariff increase in 1879. In this division of labour the Alsatian industrialists of the different production steps farmed out orders to plants in the southern part of Baden.[42]

1873–1887

Just as the previous period 1862–1873, the years 1873–1887 yet to be researched in regard to the business climate saw a slow growth in cotton spinning. Before 1873 political, non-economic events had hampered growth, after 1873 unfavourable cyclical trends set the conditions of the period. Because of these cyclical trends some contemporaries and several historians later on spoke of the "Great Depression" which is said to have lasted from 1873–1896. I don't want to reopen the discussion on "The Myth of the Great Depression"[43] for the German cotton industry. But I can't figure out any criteria which would justify speaking of a great depression in the German cotton industry even if there were cyclical trends.

In various reports the investment decision to replace outdated equipment was expressly explained by saying "that in these hard times only a plant that is technically up-to-date can stay competitive."[44] The fact that behind these entrepreneurial decisions there were human beings who hesitated to stick to the project despite a worsening economic situation can be seen from the example of the Baumwoll-Spinnerei and Weberei Augsburg. In such a situation in 1877 the board of directors and the business manager of that company "felt obliged to point out to the control board the extraordinary deterioration of the economic situation which had occurred in the meantime before going on with preliminary works for construction." The control board approved of that cautiousness but also stated "that there were no sensible reasons to lose courage and to give up the well prepared project. The business manager should be of good cheer and start with the project. By the time construction was finished the bad times would be over and would have been replaced by a favourable economic situation."[45]

Whatever physical growth rate we are going to check, no matter whether the amount of spindles or power-looms, the yarn production, or the cotton products, all these criteria have a positive growth rate. Only the average annual growth rate in the number of spindles between 1875 and 1887 was extremely low with 1.4% but the average annual growth rate of the yarn production was above average with 4.8%, indicating an increase in productivity by modernization even in this time of the so-called Great Depression.

Even if we take the monetary sphere of the economic development of the period 1871–1896 into account in order to fix the cyclical trends and examine the gross production values of cotton spinning according to Kirchhain,[46] there is no completely other picture. The gross production values of cotton spinning had remarkable declines only in the years 1873/74 and 1878/79, partly made up by upswings in other years. The growth of the gross production value of cotton spinning was at a standstill or on a low level in the 1870s and increased in the 1880s. In 1890/91 the gross production value was higher than the too high level of 1871, and grew substantially in the 1890s. If you drew the conclusion from that development of the gross production values, that the declining returns of the yarn production meant a deterioration of the situation, of the earnings capacity of cotton spinning, without considering the declining prices on the input-markets and the declining production costs of the time, your conclusion would not be justified.

In this context Kirchhain, with his further reaching analysis of the components of growth in cotton spinning, has shown that the medium-and long-term decline of the gross value per kg or of the easier to handle spinning margin was hardly caused by a declining profit margin but rather by a progress in productivity reducing labour costs and capital charges.[47] This reduction of production costs together with the falling prices for raw cotton led to the declining yarn prices.

Taking all these considerations on the "Great Depression" into account I'd like to make two points:

1. The expression "Great Depression" should be replaced by "a temporary stagnation with a generally slowed down growth" in the German cotton industry

2. The period defined that way is much shorter than the one of the so-called Great Depression 1873–96. It is restricted to the 1870s in yarn production and in regard to the number of spindles it lasted until 1887.

Additionally, new research work on other industries, for instance on the iron and steel industry by my collegue from the University of Bonn, Wilfried Feldenkirchen,[48] has led to a reinterpretation and doing away with, the phrase of the so-called Great Depression.

Yet, regardless of what we call this period, the relatively unfavourable economic situation in some years of the 1870s and 1880s remains as an important fact of the business climate which has influenced the development of the German cotton industry. The unfavourable economic situation since the middle of the 1870s has also stimulated the efforts of the entrepreneurs, to influence the central political-economic aspect of the business climate, the tariff policy, by common action, with the aim of having tariffs raised.

In their demand for an improved tariff protection, the protectionist interests of the South German cotton spinners met with those of the iron industry in North Germany. Both organizations were prominently taking part in the foundation of the "Central-verband deutscher Industrieller zur Beförderung und Wahrung nationaler Arbeit" in 1876.[49] The agrarians in Northwest Germany, who turned from radical free-traders to protectionists when cereal exports began to be surpassed by cereal imports in the 1870s, combined with the industrialists. The combination of economic interests and the political interests of Bismarck, leading to a turn in German economic policy, has interested contemporaries and scientific research very much until today. I can only briefly sum up the attitude of the cotton entrepreneurs towards the tariff reform of 1879. That attitude was outspoken in the hearings of the "Enquete-commission on the Production and Market Conditions in the Cotton and Linen Industry" and in the reports of the local chambers of commerce. All representatives of the spinning industry were in favour of an increase and a differentiation in the yarn tariff. The experts of the weaving industry agreed for the first and only time with two people speaking against it. They demanded an increase in the tariff for fabrics, too. The new tariff of 1879 even went beyond the petition of the Centralverband deutscher Industrieller, especially in regard to the differentiation of the yarn tariffs. The tariffs continued to be specific tariffs but were also differentiated according to value by a detailed scale, starting with 12 marks per 100 kg single wire yarn until number 17, going on with additional six marks for the higher differentiations, and ending with 36 marks for yarns beyond number 79. Two-wire and coloured yarns had correspondingly higher tariffs. There was also a differentiation tariff for fabric, with rates between 80 and 350 marks.[50] If you want to judge the protective effect of specific duties, you can't just convert that into an ad-valorem tariff on yarns, as contemporaries did, but you must rather calculate the real tariff by putting the tariff in relation to the gross value added per kilogram (or, which is easier, in relation to the spinning margin). According to the calculations of Kirchhain[51] the real tariff rose from 24.5% before 1879 to 47.4% after the tariff reform, when the tariff was raised from 12 to 18 pfennigs per kilogram for cotton yarn number 30. Taking the further development of the relation between duties and gross value added into account, the following simplified conclusion can be drawn: with a declining spinning margin, i.e., with a growing productivity, the real tariff protection was increased and the more the German spinning industry could make up the technical lead of the English spinning industry.

In my opinion the difference between the contemporary and today's understanding of the tariff effects can be expressed in the following formula: It can't be credited to the tariff protection only, as people thought or said at the time, but rather has to be credited to the productivity progress that the low and partly the medium yarn numbers didn't cost more in Germany than in England, at least in normal years before World War I.[52]

The development of the self-sufficiency rate shows that already around 1875, i.e., before the last tariff increase, the German spinning industry could already cover 88% of the German weaving industry's demand for the average number 24 yarn. According to contemporary experts the possibility of the German spinning industry to compete ranged up to number 24 before 1878, after 1879 to number 36–40. German domestic production and imports from England and Switzerland in yarn numbers 45–60 were just about even around 1905. Before World War I the higher yarn numbers were and continued to be the domain of the English and partly of the Swiss spinning industry. The German yarn import, which rose in absolute weight after 1879 but declined in relation to the growing German yarn production, consisted mostly of higher numbers.[53] Without any influence of the new tariff reductions in the following decades, the German cotton spinning industry could strengthen its third rank in the world in regard to the number of cotton spindles (7.9%) behind Great Britain (38.7%) and the U.S.A. (21.8%).[54] The German spinning industry's market was mainly the domestic market. The multidivisional German cotton fabric and hosiery industry could sell 20% of its productive value on the world market in 1913.[55]

Notes

1. See K. H. Wolff, Guildmaster into Millhand: The Industrialization of Linen and Cotton in Germany to 1850. In: *Textile History*, 10 (1979), 7–74; M. Hamburger, Standortsgeschichte der deutschen Baumwoll-Industrie. Diss. Heidelberg 1911, 21 ff.

2. A Oppel, Die Baumwolle nach Geschichte, Anbau, Verarbeitung und Handel. Leipzig 1902, 662 ff.

3. E. Landauer, Handel und Produktion in der Baumwollindustrie. Tübingen 1912, 163.

4. G. Adelmann, Structural Change in the Rhenish Linen and Cotton Trades at the Outset of Industrialization. In: *Essays in European Economic History 1789–1914*, ed. by F. Crouzet, W. H. Chaloner, W. M. Stern, 95 f. Originally in German in: Vierteljahrschrift für Sozial- und Wirtschaftsgeschichte 53 (1966), 162–184.

5. P. Borscheid, Textilarbeiterschaft in der Industrialisierung, Stuttgart 1978, 29, 36.

6. Cf. the fundamental work: G. Kirchhain, Das Wachstum der deutschen Baumwollindustrie im 19. Jahrhundert. Eine historische Modellstudie zur empirischen Wachstumsforschung. Diss. Münster 1973. New York 1977. with a comprehensive bibliography.

7. Cf. for instance: E. Wurster, Die Baumwollkrise vor dem Weltkrieg. Diss. Erlangen 1918. Bayreuth 1919.

8. Kirchhain, *op cit.*, 51, Table 8.

9. W. Fischer, Bergbau, Industrie und Handwerk 1850–1914. In: H. Aubin u. W. Zorn (Ed.), *Handbuch der deutschen Wirtschafts- und Sozialgeschichte*, Bd. 2, Stuttgart 1976, 528, 553 ff.

10. W. Lochmüller, Zur Entwicklung der Baumwollindustrie in Deutschland. Jena 1906, 27 f.

11. G. Adelmann, Die Gründung der Aktiengesellschaft "Gladbacher Spinnerei und Weberei." In: Spiegel der Geschichte. Festgabe für Max Braubach, ed. K. Repgen, St. Skalweit. Münster 1964, 729 ff.

12. R. Fremdling, Eisenbahnen und deutsches Wirtschaftswachstum 1840–1879. Dortmund 1975, 109 ff.

13. G. Jacobs, Die deutschen Textilzölle im 19. Jahrhundert. Diss. Erlangen, Braunschweig 1907, 22.

14. Cf. among others: U. Dedi, Die oberbadische Textilindustrie unter

dem besonderen Einfluß ihrer Grenzlage. Diss. Göttingen, Säckingen 1935, 51 ff; 58 ff; K. Döhrmann, Entstehung und Entwicklung der Gronauer Textilindustrie. Diss. Münster 1924, 32 f.
The tariff border became a locational factor. In the 1850s as well as in the 1880s, Swiss and Dutch cotton entrepreneurs founded plants on the German side of the border.

15. Jacobs, *op. cit.*, 23 f.
16. Kirchhain, *op. cit.*, 179, Tab. 56; Adelmann, Grüdung, 732 ff.
17. L. Davids, Die Finanzierung von Baumwoll-Spinnereien und webereien im Handelskammerbezirk M. Gladbach. Diss. Köln 1923.
18. H. Rothschild, Die süddeutsche Baumwoll-Industrie. Diss. Berlin. Stuttgart 1922, 19 f.; K. Schmid, Die Entwicklung der Hofer Baumwoll-Industrie 1432–1913. Leipzig und Erlangen 1923, 121 ff.; Firmen-Chronik der Baumwoll-Spinn- und Weberei Arlen 1834–1959. Arlen 1959, 28–30.
19. Kirchhain, *op. cit.*, 47; F. J. Gemmert, Die Entwicklung der ältesten kontinentalen Spinnerei. Diss. Köln 1926, Leipzig 1927, 21.
20. Cf. among others: Hundert Jahre Mech. Baumwoll-Spinnerei und -weberei Augsburg. o.O. 1937, 157.
21. Cf. for Württemberg for example: Borscheid, *op. cit.*, 140 ff.
22. Kirchhain, *op. cit.*, 162 ff.; Schmid, *op. cit.*, 61 ff.; cf. to this aspect, and to labour relations in general the dissertation of my student K. E. Emsbach, Die soziale Betriebsverfassung der rheinischen Baumwollindustrie im 19. Jahrhundert, probably Bonn 1982.
23. Rothschild, *op. cit.*, 11 ff.; H. Riede, Die Entwicklung der württembergischen Textilindustrie. Diss. Heidelberg 1937, 116; Borscheid, *op. cit.*, 41; F. Kreutzberg, Die Entwicklung der M. Gladbacher Baumwollindustrie. Diss. Göttingen 1925, 110.
24. Hundert Jahre Gebrüder Laurenz 1854–1954. Ochtrup 1954, 32, 80; Döhrmann, *op. cit.*, 23.
25. See Jacobs, *op. cit.*, 50; G. Benl, Die handelspolitischen Interessen der deutschen Spinnerei und Weberei von Baumwolle und Wolle seit 1862. Diss. München, Berlin 1928, 12.
26. See Lochmüller, *op. cit.*, 28 and others.
27. W. Fränken, Die Entwicklung des Gewerbes in den Städten Mönchengladbach und Rheydt im 19. Jahrhundert. Köln 1969, 67; Döhrmann, *op. cit.*, 19; Denkschrift zum fünfzigjährigen Bestehen der Baumwollspinnerei Kolbermoor 1862–1912. München 1912, 12, 14.

28. Riede, *op. cit.*, 92; Rothschild, *op. cit.*, 7.

29. Purchase was always favourable in times of economic decline (price variations of up to 100% within a few years) "so that ordering firms frequently employed the tactics of increasing their machinery precisely in times of such depression." Schmid, *op. cit.*, 130.

30. Hundert Jahre Mech. Baumwoll-Spinnerei & Weberei Bayreuth 1853–1953. Mainz 1953, 31; G. Meerwein, Die Entwicklung der Chemnitzer bzw. Sächsischen Baumwollspinnerei von 1789–1879. Diss. Heidelberg 1913, Berlin 1914, 83; Laurenz, 25 (yarn purchase), Jacobs, *op. cit.*, 51.

31. Jacobs, *op. cit.*, 53; Meerwein, *op. cit.*, 86; Borscheid, *op. cit.*

32. The scarcity and price-rise of the American cotton didn't affect Germany as much as England, as about 40% of the import of raw cotton for the coarser German spinning industry came from East India, the Levant and other regions before the Cotton Famine. The proportional share of these countries could be increased during and after the crisis to 60% until 1867. Lochmüller, *op. cit.*, 26.

33. Fränken, *op. cit.*, 67 ff.

34. Jacobs, *op. cit.*, 28 f.

35. Jacobs, *op. cit.*, 53.

36. Kirchhain, *op. cit.*, 29, table 2; Jacobs, *op. cit.*, 54.

37. F. Pfeiffer-Rupp, Die Standortsfrage der Baumwoll-Industrie in Deutschland. Frankfurt/M. 1920, 128.

38. H. Herkner, Die oberelsässische Baumwollindustrie und ihre Arbeiter. Straßburg 1887, 274.

39. *ibid.*, 279 ff.

40. Reichs-Enquête für die Baumwollen- und Leinenindustrie. 1) Stenographische Protokolle der Sachverständigen, 2) Statistische Ermittlungen H. 1–5, 3) Bericht der Enquête-Kommission. Berlin 1878, 1879.

41. Jacobs, *op. cit.*, 53 f.

42. Dedi, *op. cit.*, 56 f.

43. Thus the title of the booklet by S. B. Saul, The Myth of the Great Depression 1873–1896. London 1. edition 1969.

44. Kolbermoor 26.

45. Mech. Baumwoll-Spinnerei u. Weberei Augsburg 97.

46. Kirchhain, *op. cit.*, 147 f.; table 42.

47. *ibid.*, 211 f.; E. Ilgen, Die Preisentwicklung der Baumwollfabrikate seit 1890. Verlauf und Ursachen. (Schriften des Vereins für Sozialpolitik 142, 1. Bd. 3. Teil.) München und Leipzig 1914, 92 ff.

(spinning margin), 127 ff. (weaving margin).

48. Wilfried Feldenkirchen, Die Eisen- und Stahlindustrie des Ruhrgebiets 1879–1914. Wachstum, Finanzierung und Unternehmensstruktur ihrer Großunternehmen. Soon as: Beiheft zur Zeitschrift für Unternehmensgeschichte, Wiesbaden 1982.

49. H. A. Bueck, Der Centralverband Deutscher Industrieller 1876–1901. Bd. 1. Berlin 1902, 136 ff.

50. Lochmüller, *op. cit.*, 30 ff.

51. Kirchhain, *op. cit.*, 185, table 59.

52. Jacobs, *op. cit.*, 81 f.

53. A good third of the fine yarn over no. 47 was reexported as fine cotton. Thus the weavers demanded as temperate a duty on fine yarn as possible. F. W. Rohling, Die Rheinisch-Westfälische Baumwollenindustrie, ihre Bedeutung und die verschiedenen Einflüsse auf ihre Entwicklung. Diss. Bonn, Hamburg 1921, 85.

54. Calculated according to the table by: A. Kertesz, Die Textilindustrie Deutschlands im Welthandel. Braunschweig 1915, 19 und Wurster, *op. cit.*, 152.

55. Calculated according to Kertesz 25 and Wurster 154. Table: Home consumption of cotton textiles in industrialized countries (1912/13). According to this table Great Britain and Germany were the only countries whose production was higher by 67.2% resp. 19.4% than home consumption.

COMMENTS

1

Mary J. Oates
Regis College

In this interesting paper, Professor Adelmann assesses the significant features which account for the growth of the German cotton textile industry. He maintains that in explaining the expansion of firms and the adoption of new equipment and production methods, political and social as well as economic forces must be explicitly considered. The structure of the German industry was clearly affected by positive and negative shifts in the business environment after 1850. Paradoxically, fundamental structural changes were more apparent during years of slow growth than in periods of industrial prosperity. A particularly good example is the "Cotton Famine" era of 1862–65. German entrepreneurs in these years took advantage of lower prices which accompanied the slowing of demand for textile machinery by replacing their outdated spindles with newer models. These years also witnessed additions to plant capacity by larger producers with funds and raw cotton reserves. Both of these developments suggest a rather remarkable perspective on the part of German producers during a serious economic crisis. Their sanguine expectations of recovery were evidently not universally shared since, to quote Adelmann, "... the English factories producing textile machinery suffered under a shortage of orders." A more detailed explanation of those features of the German situation which led to plant retooling and expansion in a downswing would be useful.

Another structural change in German textiles during the 1862–65 period was the decline of small spinning mills. Yet such mills persisted in other countries despite overall increases in average plant scale, selling usually in local markets. What factors account for their rapid decline in Germany at this time? Why did they not reappear after the cotton shortage ended?

Adjustments in product line and markets made by mill managers in the famine years were both fundamental and lasting. Coarser yarns were spun, of necessity, from Indian cotton. This in turn stimulated demand for power looms and lessened demand for handloom weaving. In the German case at least, economic recession in an industry did not indicate industrial stagnation. Important rationalization occurred despite critical material shortages.

Adelmann's discussion of the significance of political events, both internal and external to Germany, and the role of the state in textile development is especially enlightening. The Zollverein created a large market for domestic producers, and high tariffs protected this market, to some extent, from outside competition. Does Adelmann consider protective tariffs to have had any long-term adverse effects on the development process such as encouraging the survival of inefficient producers, processes or technology? It is possible that tariff protection contributed to the slow adoption of ring spindles and power looms. Of special interest are the reasons for the relatively long delay of producers in adopting the automatic loom. The loom had been widely installed in the United States a generation before it was introduced in German mills. Adelmann notes but does not discuss this feature of German textiles.

The paper considers the labor supply, suggesting that changes in this key factor of production reflected environmental changes in German society at large. It would be helpful to know just how extensive and significant changes in the age structure, educational levels and experience of the textile work force were in the 1850–1914 period. Recent research suggests that experienced mill workers were more efficient in pre-1880 factories.[*] Experience and education were also decisive influences on productivity in Japanese cotton mills between 1891 and 1935, while managerial and technical advances were relatively less crucial in this regard.[**]

Adelmann's study of the German cotton textile industry is a

---

[*] Gavin Wright, "Cheap Labor and Southern Textiles before 1880," *Journal of Economic History* 39 (September, 1979): 659–660.

[**] Gary Saxonhouse, "Productivity Changes and Labor Absorption in Japanese Spinning, 1891–1935," *Quarterly Journal of Economics* 91 (May, 1977): 215–218.

challenging contribution to the literature in its emphasis on the role of extra-firm forces on producer decisions and firm development. We are indebted to him for expanding our awareness of the interrelated factors which contribute to industrial growth in individual countries. In such research lie some of the answers to the puzzles which so often confront us in intercountry comparisons.

2

Hisashi Watanabe
Kyoto University

Professor Adelmann presented a view of the total process of development of the German cotton industry in the period at issue. Although it always remained in the shadow of its big predecessors, especially of the British cotton industry, Germany did succeed in becoming one of the leading countries in this branch, at the latest by the end of the 19th century. Professor Adelmann traced its growth as a whole so that we can now have a clearer concept of this problematic component of the German industrial structure. I greatly appreciate his effort, especially his critical investigation of the growth of spinning and weaving during the so-called "Great Depression." I cannot deny, however, that I have several questions to raise, in particular about his point of view.

1) First, I am concerned with his definition of "business climate." Professor Adelmann equates "business climate" and "business environment." Certainly I do agree with his opinion that the term "business climate" is still so vague that one could define it in each way. There should, however, be a certain difference between these two concepts. "Business environment" should refer to external conditions which may be temporary, while "business climate" should be concerned rather with structural conditions consisting of not only external but also internal elements. Therefore the latter has to do particularly with behavior patterns of

economic subjects, such as investors, managers and employees. In this sense, then, the term "business climate" is concerned to a certain extent with a so-called typology of entrepreneurs which J. Schumpeter, F. Redlich and W. Zorn once treated, as well as with that of laborers. In his equalization of the two terms, however, Professor Adelmann has almost excluded this indispensable subjective element from his concept of "business climate," despite being occasionally concerned with the attitude of the cotton entrepreneurs towards the 1879 tariff reform. I myself would like to emphasize the significance of intrinsic or cultural factors in defining this concept, i.e., the perpetual interactions of subjective and objective conditions for business activities which themselves are to be realized by the medium of performance of each economic subject, and thus to characterize the economic and business structure of a country or region historically.

2) I think that the next point is related to the first one. I cannot totally agree with Professor Adelmann in his concentration on the spinning and weaving steps for analysis of the characteristics of the German cotton industry. Certainly this would be appropriate for analysis of the Japanese cotton industry. In my opinion, however, the spinning in Germany represented rather passive, or even a negative, aspect of the development of the cotton industry.

3) The second point leads us to the third one. Generally speaking, the cotton industry has been regarded as a strategic branch in the process of industrialization of most countries. In early stages of the industrialization process, however, a serious problem in the balance of trade may develop if the country is not one of the raw cotton producing countries such as the U.S.A. or India. In the period at issue such circumstances still afflicted the Japan economy. This was the case in Germany too. You can see this structural imbalance of trade in Table 1 (attached) (columns 1, 2 and 13) and Table 2 (column 7). The German cotton industry should, all the more, be intensively export-oriented; in other words we could perceive its principal characteristic in export orientation, although this industry could hardly be expected to balance its trade deficit alone. Therefore some reference to the foreign trade statistics of the German Custom Union or the German Empire is required to

explore the "business climate" of Germany. I have prepared
several tables on foreign trade in this industry as complements to
Professor Adelmann's five tables which, themselves give us very
valuable data.

4)   Now I would like to summarize the principal external-struc-
tural conditions given to the German cotton industry as I see them.

(1)   Necessity of raw cotton imports (lack of domestic
producing areas or colonies), to which Professor Adelmann
has referred too.

(2)   Lack of a raw cotton market within the German Custom
Union or the German Empire until the 1880s (Bremen)
and extreme dependence on the Liverpool market for raw
cotton supplies.

(3)   Speculative transactions in raw cotton and violent
fluctuations of its price.

(4)   Strong competition by more developed cotton industries
in Britain, Switzerland, Alsace and Belgium, to which
Professor Adelmann has referred too.

(5)   Possibility of technology transfer, i.e., relative ease of
import of advanced textile machinery from Britain,
Switzerland and Belgium, to which Professor Adelmann
has referred too.

(6)   Relatively abundant supply of cheap and good finishing
material from the domestic chemical industry, which was
historically in particular interdependence with the
German textile industries.

(7)   Well-developed railway and channel network, to which
Professor Adelmann has referred too.

Under such conditions there were several possible choices of the
"export strategy"—if such a term is available here—which German
cotton entrepreneurs could follow:

(1)   Raw cotton import, spinning (substituting for imported
yarn on the domestic market), then export of coarse yarn.

(2)   Raw cotton import, spinning, weaving or knitting, then
export of unfinished fabrics.

(3)   Raw cotton import, spinning, weaving or knitting,
finishing, then export of finished fabrics.

(4) Yarn import, weaving or knitting, then export of unfinished fabrics.

(5) Yarn import, weaving or knitting, finishing, then export of finished fabrics.

(6) Import of unfinished fabrics, finishing, then export of finished fabrics.

Choices actually made were different in periods, regions and stages of growth. It seems, however, that the export strategy of the German cotton entrepreneurs gradually converged into the third way and, to some extent, the fifth way. In any case, the finishing process was indispensable, or rather of strategic significance for the German cotton industry. Professor Adelmann, however, referred only to the printing of Alsace by the way. Therefore I would like now to ask you to refer to three tables I have compiled which show the following:

(1) From 1889 to 1905 cotton fabrics ranked between 1 and 4 (in the 1890s mostly 3 and in the 1900s mostly 1) among the most important export articles on a value basis (Table 2, column 1).

(2) Germany constantly exported more cotton fabrics than it imported on a value basis after 1880, at the latest since the 1830s, also on a weight basis (Table 1, column 13, and Table 3, columns 3 and 4).

(3) On the other hand, Germany constantly imported more cotton yarn than it exported on a value basis since 1880, and on a weight basis at the latest since the 1830s (Table 1, column 2 and Table 3, columns 5 and 6).

(4) Among ten groups of exported cotton fabrics, only four groups (c. tight fabrics dyed, printed etc.: 27%; h. hosiery: 26.3%; g. embroidery: 16.9%; f. lace: 14.4%) accounted for 85.4% of the total in 1905 (Table 1, columns, 5, 8, 9 and 10).

(5) Among ten groups of exported cotton fabrics, imports of only two were greater than exports, and one group of lower processed fabrics (a. tight fabrics, raw) comprised 28.5% of the total imported in 1905 (Table 1, columns 3 and 11).

From these figures we can now perceive that strategic export articles of the German cotton industry were fabrics of higher added value or specialized articles (group i: tulle, which was a special fabric of France, made the single exception). Through the efforts of export-oriented entrepreneurs at differentiation and specialization, the German cotton industry could only partly cover the deficit in its balance of trade. Thus it is easy to understand that the shift of entrepreneurs' concerns to higher production steps consequently limited the scale of investment, because large-scale enterprises were often too risky under unstable market conditions caused primarily by changing modes; this was one of the reasons that medium and small-scale firms in the German cotton weaving/finishing survived persistently.

5) Now one may question why German cotton entrepreneurs chose this export strategy. In this connection we cannot forget that most of them came from the merchant stratum or were the successors of such entrepreneurs, e.g. J. G. Brügelmann and his heirs. From the very beginning they were intensively export-oriented. In this regard I would like to refer further to the regional splitting of the "German" cotton industry, which Professor Adelmann mentioned too. It seems to me, however, that he described these characteristic circumstances from a rather negative viewpoint (at least concerning the development of spinning). I do agree totally with his opinion that "we mention a decisive structural element," when "speaking of the regional splitting of the German cotton industry." I would like to ask him, however, what he means by "traffic," when he says that "regional splitting . . . was caused by political and *traffic* reasons." Can we understand that not only non-economic but also economic factors, i.e., the market mechanism, have disturbed integration of the locations of the cotton industry within the German custom line? From my viewpoint the regional splitting of the cotton industry was not only a result of the regional disintegration of the so-called "German national economy" but also one of the *rationales* of the latter; i.e., development of the cotton industry itself was one of the factors which maintained or even strengthened the regional structure of that economy. Regional integration in Germany, in my opinion,

followed the industrialization process only to a certain degree. In the regional dynamism influenced by industrialization we can observe a certain trend of convergence to some unit spaces—to four units, as I see it, each of which included as an outstanding feature a cotton industry area or even "a Manchester of Germany" (Mönchengladbach, Augsburg and Chemnitz [now Karl-Marx-Stadt]). This economic regionalism, despite the foundation of the German Custom Union or the German Empire, was strengthened by intensive export orientation of the cotton entrepreneurs in each area, and the latter was partly caused by the former. I call each of these unit spaces a "Proto-economic-space" (*Urwirtschafts-raum*). Now I would like to ask Professor Adelmann how he interprets and evaluates the interdependence of *regionalization* on the one hand and the *industrialization* on the other hand in the growth of the "German" cotton industry.

6) Several small questions still remain.

(1) Professor Adelmann divided the regional structure of the German cotton industry into three districts: north-western, southwestern and central. In my opinion, how-ever, Lower Silesia historically made up an independent fourth district with its own tradition of linen industry, even though the Silesian cotton industry itself was the weakest regional component.

(2) With regard to the position of the Silesian cotton industry I have another question about Professor Adelmann's Table 5. Among various regions only Silesia shows a de-clining trend in absolute number and distribution ratio of people working in spinning as well as in weaving. How are the causes of this trend explained?

(3) In Table 4, columns 6, 8 and 12, the trend of Prussia on the one hand and that of Alsace-Lorraine and Baden on the other hand are in sharp contrast. What were the causes of this relatively declining trend of Alsace-Lorraine and Baden?

(4) In Table 1, column 9 the ratio of national self-sufficiency exceeds 100% after 1898. As my Table 1, column 2, shows, however, yarn import exceeded yarn export on

TABLE 1　　Import and Export of Raw Cotton, Cotton Yarn and Cotton Fabrics

	Raw cotton		Cotton yarn		a) Tight fabrics, raw		b) Tight fabrics, bleached		c) Tight fabrics, dyed		d) Purl	
	I.	E.	I.	E.	I.	E.	I.	E.	I.	E.	I.	E.
1905	398.2	36.1	65.3	34.1	11.9	4.3	2.4	13.0	4.1	104.7	0.2	18.3
04	471.0	51.3	66.8	29.8	12.1	3.1	2.1	11.7	3.7	95.1	0.2	19.2
03	395.1	40.4	60.1	32.5	11.5	3.0	2.0	13.7	3.6	94.2	0.2	18.9
02	319.7	35.1	51.2	31.7	11.0	1.8	1.9	11.0	3.4	81.2	0.2	18.4
01	296.2	27.7	48.6	28.5	10.3	1.9	1.7	8.6	2.9	69.5	0.2	19.8
1900	318.0	34.9	62.9	29.1	11.5	2.1	1.9	9.0	3.0	79.7	0.3	22.0
99	228.5	25.3	55.6	22.9	10.3	1.8	1.6	6.8	3.0	67.9	0.2	19.8
98	237.5	23.0	53.9	19.7	10.5	1.3	1.3	6.2	2.6	61.1	0.2	20.0
97	231.0	22.8	59.3	21.0	15.9	1.3	1.3	6.4	2.2	62.7	0.2	18.8
96	226.9	32.1	56.9	16.2	2.3	0.9	1.0	5.7	1.6	57.2	0.2	21.7
95	220.7	25.2	56.7	16.7	2.1	0.7	0.9	6.1	1.6	57.5	0.2	23.4
94	191.7	16.5	45.3	15.7	1.5	0.7	0.6	5.3	1.4	49.2	0.2	21.1
93	210.5	18.4	47.2	18.2	1.6	1.0	0.6	5.7	1.4	63.6	0.2	20.1
92	187.5	17.3	41.6	20.9	1.1	1.0	0.5	5.4	1.1	61.8	0.3	18.4
91	226.0	19.5	42.3	22.2	0.9	0.7	0.5	5.7	1.2	50.6	0.4	19.0
1890	280.6	28.9	52.3	19.9	0.9	0.7	0.6	5.8	1.4	51.0	0.3	19.0
89	270.9	23.5	58.1	19.2	0.8	0.9	0.5	5.8	1.2	48.2	0.4	15.2
88	206.1	17.7	55.0	17.4	0.8	1.4	0.4	6.0	1.1	49.5	0.3	13.9
87	218.4	16.1	51.3	17.7	0.7	1.5	0.3	6.2	1.0	53.3	0.2	15.3
86	170.3	11.9	52.2	18.2	0.7	1.5	0.4	5.7	0.8	44.7	0.2	14.3
85	181.8	11.2	50.4	18.5	0.8	1.5	0.4	6.4	0.8	40.1	0.2	12.7
84	202.4	22.5	57.9	22.6	0.8	1.3	0.5	7.6	1.0	46.9	0.2	13.5
83	208.0	24.7	57.2	25.6	0.8	1.3	0.5	7.5	1.0	44.0	0.2	13.3
82	179.2	21.8	51.8	32.3	0.6	1.6	0.5	7.7	1.0	48.0	0.2	14.6
81	172.8	21.4	43.5	33.0	0.6	2.1	0.5	6.7	0.9	37.8	0.3	10.8
1880	178.4	14.3	37.8*	51.4*	0.7	2.6	0.5	8.0	0.8	30.9	0.3	8.7

Source: *Statistisches Handbuch für das Deutsche Reich*, Part 2, 1907, pp. 28–
I: Import, E: Export.
*: Misprint?

(a~k) 1880–1905 (Mill Mark).

e) Velvet		f) Lace		g) Embroidery		h) Hosiery		i) Tulle		k) Loose fabrics, dyed		Fabrics, total	
I.	E.	I.	E.	I.	E.	I.	E.	I.	E.	I.	E.	I.	E.
1.2	5.1	4.6	54.1	6.6	63.8	0.4	99.0	7.2	0.1	3.2	14.6	41.8	377.0
1.0	5.5	4.7	41.0	5.4	55.0	0.4	88.4	5.6	0.1	3.0	15.2	38.2	334.3
0.5	5.4	4.5	35.6	4.7	34.7	0.3	82.0	3.0	0.1	3.1	11.3	33.4	298.9
0.7	5.6	3.6	30.2	4.0	25.2	0.3	72.9	3.4	0.1	2.8	9.8	31.3	256.2
0.6	5.2	2.3	24.6	3.8	19.5	0.2	59.6	4.8	0.1	2.3	8.7	29.1	217.5
0.5	5.1	2.1	20.8	4.8	24.2	0.3	71.1	5.8	0.0	2.2	8.1	32.4	242.1
0.5	3.9	2.5	17.5	4.6	18.0	0.3	61.9	6.0	0.0	1.6	6.3	30.6	203.9
0.4	3.2	2.6	17.7	3.8	12.1	0.3	52.2	6.3	0.0	1.4	5.2	29.4	179.0
0.4	3.4	3.2	13.9	3.9	10.1	0.3	53.6	9.0	0.0	1.5	5.2	37.9	175.4
0.2	1.7	2.9	5.6*	3.0	8.4	0.4	58.5	5.5	0.0	1.1	4.6	18.2	164.3
0.2	1.5	4.0	20.6 ⎫			0.4	67.9	3.6	0.0	0.8	4.1	13.8	181.8
0.2	1.2	2.6	11.7 ⎪			0.4	47.5	3.8	0.0	0.6	3.2	11.3	139.9
0.2	1.3	2.6	9.3 ⎪			0.3	48.4	2.7	0.0	0.4	3.1	10.0	152.5
0.2	1.2	2.6	12.8 ⎪			0.3	51.8	2.5	0.0	0.3	2.9	8.9	155.3
0.2	1.1	3.7	21.6 ⎪			0.3	42.9	3.8	0.0	0.3	2.8	11.3	144.4
0.1	1.1	4.2	27.4 ⎪			0.3	57.9	3.2	0.0	0.4	3.0	11.4	165.9
0.2	1.2	4.5	27.3 ⎬			0.3	58.3	4.1	0.5	0.3	2.9	12.3	160.3
0.2	1.5	4.3	40.3 ⎪	included		0.4	67.0	4.2	0.8	0.3	2.5	11.7	182.9
0.1	1.8	5.9	50.4 ⎪			0.4	71.8	5.7	0.1	0.4	2.5	14.7	202.9
0.1	1.9	7.6	40.6 ⎪	in		0.4	70.5	7.9	0.1	0.4	1.9	18.5	181.2
0.3	1.9	12.3	25.2 ⎪			0.4	59.8	6.0	0.1	0.4	2.2	21.6	149.9
0.3	3.2	11.3	13.2 ⎪	lace		0.4	61.5	5.5	0.1	2.6	5.6	22.6	152.9
0.2	2.9	11.8	9.7 ⎪			0.5	59.8	3.0	0.3	3.2	5.0	21.2	209.9
0.1	2.7	12.1	5.7 ⎪			0.5	59.3	1.9	0.1	3.7	5.6	20.6	145.3
0.1	2.5	8.7	3.9 ⎪			0.5	48.8	2.2	0.1	3.2	4.5	17.0	117.2
0.2	2.3	6.0	4.7 ⎭			0.4	36.2	1.1	0.0	3.9	4.5	13.9	97.9

51, 142–147.

TABLE 2   Share of the Most Important Six Articles in the German Foreign Trade 1889–1905 (on value base). (%)

	Export						Import					
	Cotton fabrics	Wool fabrics	Ma-chinery, all sorts	Coal	Sugar	Silk fabrics	**Cotton raw**	Wheat	Wool, raw	Barley	Coffee bean	Copper, raw
1905	① 6.5	5.0	5.0	4.0	3.1	2.6	① 5.4	4.4	4.4	2.6	2.3	2.0
04	① 6.3	4.7	4.7	4.3	3.4	2.7	① 6.9	4.1	4.2	2.1	2.4	2.0
03	① 5.9	4.8	4.5	4.3	3.6	3.2	① 6.2	4.0	4.6	2.6	2.3	1.6
02	② 5.4	5.5	4.1	4.3	3.3	3.0	① 5.5	4.7	4.7	2.2	2.5	1.5
01	① 4.9	4.7	4.4	4.6	4.5	3.0	① 5.2	5.0	4.1	1.8	2.6	1.5
1900	① 5.2	5.0	4.8	4.6	4.6	2.9	① 5.3	2.8	4.3	1.5	2.6	2.1
99	② 4.7	5.0	4.3	4.1	4.7	3.3	② 4.0	3.1	5.7	2.2	2.2	1.8
98	③ 4.5	5.0	3.7	4.0	5.3	3.2	② 4.4	4.3	4.4	2.4	2.5	1.4
97	③ 4.7	5.5	3.4	3.5	6.1	3.0	① 4.7	3.6	4.5	2.5	3.3	1.4
96	③ 4.4	5.7	3.1	3.2	6.3	3.3	② 5.0	4.3	5.2	2.4	4.2	1.2
95	③ 5.4	6.5	2.7	3.1	5.6	3.7	② 5.2	3.4	5.8	2.1	4.8	1.0
94	③ 4.7	6.1	2.6	3.3	6.9	3.4	③ 4.5	2.8	5.2	2.4	4.7	0.7
93	③ 4.8	6.7	2.0	3.2	6.8	4.7	③ 5.1	2.1	5.6	2.3	5.2	0.9
92	③ 5.0	7.0	2.0	3.2	5.7	4.5	④ 4.4	4.7	6.0	1.7	4.6	0.7
91	③ 4.4	6.8	2.0	3.6	6.8	4.4	② 5.1	3.7	5.6	2.4	5.0	0.8
90	④ 4.9	7.4	2.0	3.4	6.3	5.5	① 6.6	2.4	5.7	2.3	5.2	0.9
1889	④ 5.0	7.6	1.9	2.9	5.0	6.0	② 6.6	1.8	6.8	2.2	4.9	0.7

Source: *S.H.f.D.R.*, Part 2, pp. 498–505.

TABLE 3 Import and Export of Raw Cotton, Cotton Yarn and Cotton Fabrics 1836–1879 (Zentner).

	Cotton, raw		Cotton fabrics, all sorts		Cotton yarn	
	I.	E.	I.	E.	I.	E.
1879	3,772,786	1,204,466	55,535	330,858	431,279	216,455
75	3,200,548	822,168	52,503	258,944	417,582	175,852
70	2,167,776	482,652	26,117	207,950	285,783	67,839
61	2,002,681	469,425	9,887	200,567	463,855	68,193
52	669,235	213,755	7,589	129,838	467,559	36,302
46	352,740	32,579	9,853	70,156	634,382	54,813
36	187,858	35,494	16,505	84,322	318,434	39,797

Source: *S. H. f. D. R.*, Part 2, pp. 458, 462.
I: Import,   E: Export.

a value basis until after 1898. The ratio in the former table, therefore, may be regarded as valid only if yarn export exceeded yarn import on a weight basis in the period at issue. I would like to know how Professor Adelmann has calculated the self-sufficiency ratio in the German yarn demand.

Reply to the Comments

Gerhard Adelmann

I fully agree with M. J. Oates' comment on my paper pointing out "that in explaining the expansion of firms and the adoption of new equipment and production methods" or, in other words, in explaining the underlying entrepreneurial decisions, "political and social [cultural] as well as economic forces," [i.e., the business environment/business climate] "must be explicitly considered" too.

With regard to H. Watanabe's comment, I am very sorry to

reject his opinion that the pattern of behavior of management, e.g. the decisions of investors and managers to invest, or to direct their sales strategy from domestic to export markets or vice versa, are elements of the "business climate." The project leader of the conference, S. Yonekawa, stated that the behavior of the management and to a lesser degree that of the employees "reflects the business climate, but is not the business climate itself." The business climate is the cultural, social, [political] and economic environment which is external to the enterprise itself.

The entrepreneur is the changing agent on whose decisions depend to a large extent which of these external influences are transformed into internal business activities. Of course there are "perpetual interactions of subjective and objective conditions of business activities," between external business environments and internal business activities. Having published several essays on the German entrepreneurs, I am far from overlooking the influence of the business environment or business climate on the behavior of these individuals. But the simple finding that almost everything interacts with everything else does not justify the widening of the expression "business climate" to a definition which would cover the whole "development of the cotton industry" or even the "pattern of management of the German cotton industry." According to my understanding of the definition of "business climate," most of the information given in H. Watanabe's comment from his first point 3 to the end does not belong to the topic "business climate." It is valuable additional information on the history of the German (especially the M. Gladbach) cotton industry, but there are some obvious misunderstandings or one-sided statements which only apply to the Gladbach area where the scale of investment was, in fact, limited, while in other regions, e.g. Westphalia and Bavaria, large-scale enterprises were dominating.

By no means did I almost exclude the subjective element of the entrepreneur, as H. Watanabe asserts, when he writes that I only dealt with the attitude of the cotton entrepreneurs towards the tariff reform of 1879. This is an obvious misunderstanding on his part, for M. J. Oates' comment concentrates on my efforts to show how the firms, i.e., the entrepreneurs, reacted to structural changes in the business environment by internal decision-making: investment, modernization, etc. As to the tariff reforms, it was my special concern to point out that it was not the tariff reform itself which fostered the remarkable growth of the spinning sector of the German cotton industry. To answer M. J. Oates' question: the reform of 1846 which was followed by upswing times had the effect of partly holding back modernization, but during later downswing periods the tariff reform of 1879 had hardly any protective effects on ineffective producers. On the contrary, it indirectly stimulated the modernization of the German cotton industry by means of the growing internal concurrence. By the way, modernization in downswing times also meant some Darwinistic selection within the industry, i.e., a growing rate of bankruptcies. I am fully aware of the fact which M. J. Oates mentioned, that not only changes in the production factor "capital" but also in the *quality* of the labor force had important effects on productivity. That is a separate topic, however. In several German mixed industrial areas occupation in textile firms was often regarded as a transitory stage for male workers to higher skilled and better paid jobs in other industries and for females to marriage.

Regarding H. Watanabe's remark, "Generally speaking, the cotton industry has been a strategic sector in the process of industrialization of most countries," I have to remind him of the tendency even in British economic history to doubt the "leading sector" or "strategic sector" function of the this industry.

My 1966 paper, reprinted in "Essays in European Economic History," London 1970, disproved that opinion for the Rhenish cotton industry. Kirchhain's quantitative research on The Growth of the German Cotton Industry fully confirmed my view in 1973 which is now generally accepted in the latest "Handbuch der deutschen Wirtschafts- und Sozialgeschichte," II, ed. by Aubin/Zorn 1976.

As to H. Watanabe's very interesting question on the stagnation or even declining trend of the Alsatian cotton industry, at this time I can only refer to the political separation from the old French market, which was partly compensated by the founding of some Alsatian subsidiary firms in France and by the emigration of entrepreneurs and workers to France after 1871.

With regard to Table 1, column 9, the self-sufficiency ratio of the German weaving industry is calculated from the figures of Kirchhain: yarn production divided by output of cotton cloth. Even with a ratio above 100 the German yarn import did exceed yarn export because yarn was also used for products other than fabric.

The Business Strategy of Japanese Cotton Spinners: Overseas Operations 1890 to 1931

Tetsuya Kuwahara
Kyoto Sangyo University

Introduction

The Japanese cotton spinners depended on overseas markets for their growth almost from the initial stages of development. From 1890, when thirty-one bales were first exported, the export of yarns gradually increased reaching a peak in 1915 of 575,891 bales (equivalent to 33% of production).[1] Eighty-one percent of the export that year was for Chinese markets. After the First World War, however, Japanese spinners were forced to substitute for exports local production in China, where existing and potential competitive threats had been increased by the new protective tariff. Thus their overseas operations became for many years a defensive process in maintaining their already established position in the export market.

The overseas operations of Japanese spinners reflect the varying quality of their entrepreneurship. This can be understood by tracing how the management of each Japanese spinning firm perceived the needs brought on by changing conditions in the Chinese markets and how and with what alternatives they responded to those needs.

The entrepreneurial quality of Japanese spinners reflects the business climate as well as the unique personality of the management. Taking such cultural and personal factors into consideration, we analyze the entrepreneurship in formulating strategies for the Chinese market from 1890 to 1931.

I. From Import Substitution to Export Strategy

The volume of domestic production of Japanese cotton yarn first surpassed that of imported yarn in 1891, and in 1897 the export volume of Japanese cotton yarn surpassed that of imported yarn.

In April 1895 the Shimonoseki Treaty between Japan and China was signed. It contained a clause that permitted Japanese nationals to engage in manufacturing activities in the treaty ports, but it was the Westerners who quickly began to build local plants based on the most favored nation clause. Japanese spinners saw a threat by four Western trading companies, which had invested in China, and they perceived they would lose the Chinese market. Though they were exporting a negligible volume of cotton yarn to China, nevertheless that market was regarded as one indispensable for their prospective growth. As their response to this threat, the Japanese spinners established two direct foreign investment projects in Shanghai; these were the Towka Cotton Spinning and Weaving Co. and the Shanghai Cotton Spinning Co.[2]

These initial plans were given up in a few years; in the process of furthering the project the investors got more precise information concerning the realities of spinning mills in China. The production capacity was smaller than expected and the growth potential was also small, since the management was ineffective and the organizational climate was not appropriate to the operation of a large modern mill. Research showed that the competitors on the Chinese market were not local spinners but Indians from Bombay. The Japanese investors came to the conclusion that they must first of all improve their own operations in Japan and then acquire the Chinese market by export strategy. Towka was liquidated in 1897, and the Shanghai Co. had reconstructed its mill in Kobe by 1898.

In formulating export strategy, Japanese spinners had to solve various problems in their operations to strengthen international competitiveness. Cotton blending techniques, a labor management system based on traditional values, and speculation techniques in markets of raw cotton were developed. Large-scale operations and mass production were possible through frequent mergers.

The Japanese spinners had increased their export of yarn to China from 100,884 bales (77% of total exports) in 1897 to a peak of 463,921 bales (81% of total) by 1915. The Indian spinners, on the other hand, were unable to increase their exports to China after the peak year of 1899. They had been surpassed in these exports by Japanese spinners by 1912.

The Chinese spinning industry could not compete effectively with imported yarn until the First World War. Until that time two Japanese trading companies and one cotton spinning company had local cotton spinning plants in Shanghai; these were Mitsui & Co., Japan Cotton Trading Co. and Naigaiwata Co. The Shanghai mill of Naigaiwata was the first overseas mill owned by Japanese spinners. It was the only spinning firm which chose local production for the Chinese market while the Japanese export of cotton yarn was increasing.[3] Other spinners such as Kanegafuchi, Amagasaki and Mie Cotton Spinning had ideas of establishing local plants in China after the Russo-Japanese War, but they remained only plans except that Mie undertook a bank revêtement in Shanghai in 1913.[4]

II. Development of Direct Foreign Investment

1. Changing Conditions in the Chinese Cotton Yarn Markets during the First World War[5]

The Chinese cotton spinning industry, which had been retarded since its beginning, began expansion of its production capacity during the First World War. Spindles increased from 800,000 in 1913 to 2,400,000 in 1922. Cotton yarn production had surpassed imported yarn in China by 1916.

On the other hand, Japanese export of cotton yarn to China reached a peak of 462,921 bales in 1915, but declined sharply after that. Exports of cotton yarn (86 mil. yen) to China were surpassed by those of cotton cloth (88 mil. yen) in 1918. Of the cloth imported by China, that from Japan amounted to 55%, exceeding that of the British that year.

As a result of a sharp increase in wage rates in Japan, the wage gap between the two countries was enlarged. Though the physical productivity (output/man-hours) increased, [the wage increase

Investors ② \ year	1917	1918	1919	1920	1921
〔Spinning Firms〕					
Dainippon	May ●	△—△ T.	Mar. ~Apr. Sept. Nov. Mar. □—○ S.,T. T. T.	□ S.	July □ S.
Osaka Godo's stockholders	May July ●—△ S. Golden Rd.	Mar. July □——□ S. Yangzepoo		May Oct. ☆—○ Dong Shing Cotton Spinning & Weaving Co. (authorized capital 15 mil. yen, paid up copital 3.75 mil. yen) S.,Golden Rd.	
Nisshin		Oct.-Dec. Feb. Mar. △—△—□ S.,T. T. T.		Mar. ○ T.	
Kanegafuchi ③			Latter Half □— S.	First Half May △—○ S.	
Fuji Gasu ④			●	May Dec. △—□—□ Tientsin T.	Oct. ○ T.
Toyo			Apr. May △— China, Manchuria, Korea		Oct. ○ S.
Nagasaki					
Fukushima					
Kishiwada					Sept. Oct. △— S.
Kurashiki					May ● T. and Tientsing

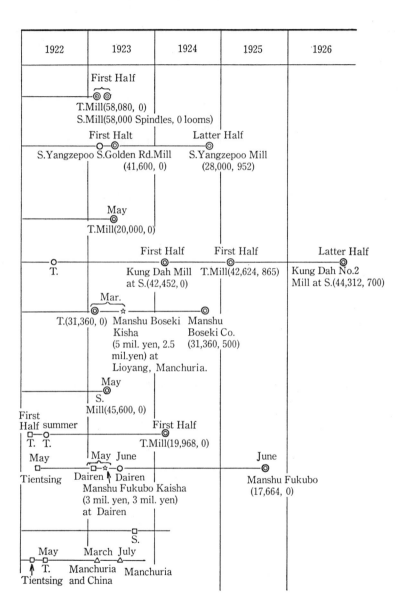

Investors ② \ year	1917	1918	1919	1920	1921
[Others] Japan Cotton Trading Co., C. Itoh & Co., S.Kawasaki and T. Wada		July, ☆◎ (61,500, 500) Japan China Pootung Mill Co. at S. (10 mil. yen, 4 mil. yen)⑤			
Toyoda, Sakichi and mangers of Mitsui & Co.		Oct. △ S.	1919 or 20 ○	Toyoda Boshoku Sho at S. (10 mil. Taels, 5 mil. Taels)	Nov. ☆
C. Itoh and others in Osaka				Apr. ☆ Tokwa Spinning Co. at S. (20 mil. yen, 5 mil. yen)	Apr. ◎ (10,000, 0)
Japan Cotton Trading Co.					

Fig. 1   Construction Process of Local Mills in China during and after the

Remarks

① Symbols:
   • planning, △ initial investigation, □ acquisition of mill sites, ○ beginning of construction, ◎ completion of construction, ☆ organizing local subsidiaries, T. at Tsingtao, S. at Shanghai.

② Investors are put in order of the date of beginning of construction.

③ Kanegafuchi carried out the projects through the existing local subsidiary, Shanghai Silk Spinning Co. It was acquired in 1911 when Kanegafuchi merged with the parent company Nihon Kenshi Boseki Kaisha in Japan. Kung Dah No. 2 Mill was bought in May, 1925.

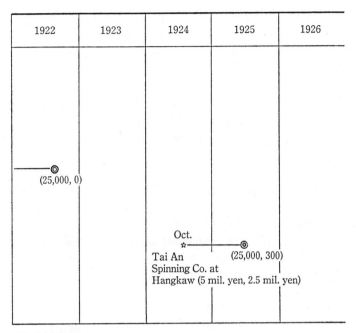

1922	1923	1924	1925	1926

(25,000, 0)

Oct.

Tai An   (25,000, 300)
Spinning Co. at
Hangkaw (5 mil. yen, 2.5 mil. yen)

First World War.

Kaisha in Japan. Kung Dah No. 2 Mill was bought in May 1925.
④ Fuji Gasu held 31% of shares of Manshu Boseki.
⑤ The mill was initially bought by S. Kawasaki from the British in May, 1918. Then he sold it to the Japan China Pootung Mill.
Source: T. Kawahara, Senzen ni okeru Nihon Boseki Kigyo no Kaigai Katsudo (The Overseas Operations of Japanese Cotton Spinning Firms in the Pre-Second World War Days: Case of Kanegafuchi Cotton Spinning Co.) in *the Rokkodai Ronshu*, Vol. 22, Nol. 1, Apr. 1975.

offset this, and decreased the cost performance (output/wage) by more than 50%.[6] Since the market price of cotton yarn was booming, the decrease of cost performance did not cause a decrease in profit for Japanese spinners. But it eroded cost competitiveness vis à vis the Chinese counterparts. Moreover the upward revision of Chinese customs cut the price competitiveness of Japanese cotton yarns in China. The revision took place in August 1919,[7] and was only the first step toward the Chinese customs autonomy of 1930.

2. Direct Foreign Investment in China by Japanese Spinners
A) General Survey
Immediately after the First World War, most of the major Japanese cotton spinners embarked on the establishment of local plants in China as a response to the threat brought on by the self-sustaining process of the Chinese cotton yarn market. All the ten largest spinning firms had investment projects, and seven of them completed these;[8] the twelfth largest firm also completed such a project. The other four investment groups completed local mills. In total, twelve investment groups established local production bases in China, and on a local unit thirteen firms were newly established. The construction process of local mills is shown in Figure 1.[9]

From this beginning until the outbreak of the Sino-Japanese War in 1937, no additional Japanese firms entered the spinning industry in China.

The overseas strategy of Japanese spinners is next studied by looking at the cases of the Big Three companies.
B) Dainippon Cotton Spinning Co.[10]
Amagasaki Cotton Spinning Co. had established a strong position in medium count yarns in the import substitution process of Japan. It accounted for 75% of the total domestic production of 42 count yarns in 1903. When other spinners began the production of medium count yarn by the outbreak of World War I, Amagasaki had shifted its market to overseas. While increasing export of the medium counts, it entered into fine count yarns by merging two firms in 1914 and 1916. As a result, it assumed a production share

of 30% of medium count yarns and 45% of gas burned yarns. Weaving began in 1909, and by 1914 it had become the third largest company in weaving capacity with 2,671 looms. Amagasaki stood first on the product market in growth potential.

Settsu Spinning Co., a major producer of coarse yarns, had been one of the leading exporters since around the time of the Sino-Japanese War. It exported 60% of its production in 1904 and accounted for 21% of the total exports of the Japanese spinning industry in 1905. Settsu's export reached a peak of 72,123 bales in 1914, but it began declining sharply after 1915. The company took up weaving with 400 looms in the year 1915. Given the product market structure, only the domestic coarse yarn market was left as a major market for the firm.

Kikuchi, the president of Amagasaki since 1901, assumed the presidency of Settsu in 1915, and merged it with Amagasaki on June 1, 1918. At that time, Amagasaki took the new name of Dainippon Cotton Spinning Co.

Kikuchi had already had the idea for local production in China around 1910, and employed necessary personnel for the purpose. When the Japanese government affirmed the Chinese tariff revision of August 1917, he began the project of local production on the Amagasaki side. Immediately after merging with Settsu, he sent a mill manager to China for investigation and the following March went there himself. With a little delay due to some difficulties in the process of construction, Dainippon Spinning Co. completed two mills in Shanghai and Tsingtao during the first half of 1923.

Dainippon's foreign direct investment policy was formulated as a response to the needs brought by Settsu. Kikuchi recognized the strategy as a mandatory alternative to defend Settsu's share of the coarse yarn market in China.

C) Toyo Cotton Spinning Co.[11]

The Osaka Cotton Spinning Co. was the leader in underscoring the export role as the proper role for the Japanese spinning industry as a whole. It exported 74% of its production in 1899. After the Boxer Rebellion however, export declined, and it could export only 2% of production in 1908.

While losing the export market of cotton yarns, Osaka shifted its

major export item to cotton cloths, in line with the expansion
program of its weaving capacity. After the war with Russia, it
moved with large quantities into the wider market area of Korea,
Manchuria and North China, where cloth from Britain and the
United States had had a monopoly. Osaka Spinning organized two
pools for exporting cloth there with the Mie Cotton Spinning Co.
and a few others facing stiff competition from Western cloth.
These firms played a role in Japanese exports of yardage surpassing
imports in 1909. Osaka's weaving section consumed 60% of the
yarns in 1911. The main product line and major export item had
been yardage before the merger with Mie in June 1914.

Before the merger with Osaka the major export product of Mie
had already been cotton cloth. It expanded its weaving capacity
after the Boxer Rebellion. The weaving section consumed 47%
of the yarns in 1905, and had begun export marketing to Korea and
China by 1906. In these export markets of cloth Mie encountered
stiff competition from Osaka and a few other Japanese firms as well
as from Westerners. This condition in the export market was the
reason for the merger of Mie and Osaka.

Toyo Cotton Spinning Co. was established as a result of this
merger. At the time, Toyo held 17% of the nationwide spindles
and 40% of the looms. In the year before the merger, Osaka and
Mie in total exported 44% of their production. Seventy-seven
percent of this was cotton cloth, and the rest was yarn. Toyo increased cloth exports and expanded into ever further market areas
during the First World War.

Toyo reached a peak in export rate of yarns with 18% in 1915,
but this declined to 3% in 1918. Conditions did not affect Toyo
as much as others, since it had large export markets for cloth, and
therefore this company did not soon take action to defend its share
of the yarn market in China. But it did need to maintain competitive balance with other Japanese spinners and so began to draw up
blueprints for the Shanghai mill in 1921. The mill was relatively
small compared with its rivals. Toyo began to expand its local
production base after 1930, when the exports of Japanese cotton
cloth to China began declining. This was caused by the self-sustain-

ing process in the Chinese cloth market under the conditions of Chinese restoration of customs autonomy.

D)   Kanegafuchi Cotton Spinning Co.[12]

Kanegafuchi had been the largest exporter of cotton yarn from 1898 to 1913, except for 1912. Kanegafuchi's exports of yarn reached a peak of 93,688 bales, equivalent to 32% of production, in 1914. But this declined to 8,776 bales, or 3% of production, in 1921. Sanji Muto, the managing director of the company, was developing new divisions with big potential in exports such as cotton weaving, finishing and silk spinning in those days. But Muto could not perceive the exigencies of the cotton yarn market in China. He thought that without the upward revision of Chinese tariff rates, Japanese spinners could continue to export yarns. Even after the revision, he opposed the construction of local plants in China since he deemed it would only cause a decrease of exports from Japan. These recognitions were supported by his business ideology that direct foreign investment was a deterrent to the Japanese economy as it would result in elimination of employment opportunities, decline of related industries, decay of local communities and so on.

While other Japanese spinners were proceeding with the construction of local production bases, Muto saw it as a threat to the satus quo. Seeing Kanegafuchi losing its position relative to Japanese competitors, he at last emulated them and began construction in 1921. The Shanghai mill was completed in 1924 and the Tsingtao in 1925. In the process of construction, Muto recognized the meaning of the local production of cotton yarns in China, and he even purchased an English-owned mill in Shanghai in May, 1925. As a result, the company then held mills with 129,288 spindles and 865 weaving looms. These were the largest local production facilities established by Japanese spinners after the First World War.

3.   Comparative Analysis of Direct Foreign Investment

A)   Procedures for Comparative Analysis

We next analyze the direct foreign investment strategy of

TABLE 1　Scale of Activity in China.

Company (order by no. of spindles in 1918)	Construction begun		Percentage of local spindles to total (at completion)	Characteristics
Dainippon	Autumn,	1919	17% (1923)	Aggressive
Toyo	Oct.	1921	7% (1923)	Fairly conservative
Kanegafuchi		1921	20% (1926)[1]	Fairly aggressive
Fuji Gasu		1921	14% (1924)[2]	Fairly aggressive
Osaka Godo		1920	19% (1924)	Aggressive
Fukushima	June	1923	8% (1925)	Fairly conservative
Kishiwada			0	Conservative
Kurashiki			0	Conservative
Nisshin	Mar.	1920	9% (1923)	Aggressive
Wakayama			0	
Nagasaki	Summer	1922	17% (1924)	Fairly aggressive

Source:　The percentage is based on the figures in Dainippon Boseki Rengo-kai, "Menshi Boseki Jijo Sankosho," the first half of 1923 to the second half of 1926.

Remarks:　1.　Lao Kung Mow Mill which was bought in 1925 is included.
　　　　　2.　Manshu Boseki Kaisha is included. Considering the 31% stock share of Manshu Boseki owned by Fuji Gasu, the rate of local spindles is 10%.

Japanese spinners from the point of view of their product market structure and entrepreneurship. The firms to be analyzed are Dainippon, Toyo, Kanegafuchi, Fuji Gasu, Osaka Godo, Fuku-shima, Kishiwada, Kurashiki and Nisshin Cotton Spinning Cos. and Nagasaki Cotton Spinning and Weaving Co.

　① Product Market Structure

It can be measured by the following three factors:

　a. the degree of integration with the weaving section; i.e., how much each company is dependent upon the cotton cloth market. This can be measured by the consumption rate of yarns for weaving cloths within the firm.

　b. the dependent rate of cotton yarns on export markets; i.e., whether the company depends for the growth on export or on the domestic market.

　c. the ratio of medium and fine yarns to total export.

While the export of coarse yarn was decreasing, the medium and fine yarns reached a peak of 169,866 bales (58% of exported

TABLE 2   Consumption of Weaving Yarns in 1917.

Company	Consumption rate of cotton yarns for weaving (1917)	Characteristics
Toyo	43%	Fairly conservative
Kanegafuchi	25%	Fairly aggressive
Amagasaki (Dainippon)	17%	The same as Settsu
Fuji Gasu	9%	Fairly aggressive
Osaka Godo	6%	Aggressive
Settsu	2%	Aggressive

Source: Based on the figures in "Menshi Boseki Jijo Sankosho," first and second halves of 1917.

yarn) in 1925. The export pattern of medium and fine yarns is distinctive from that of coarse yarn.[13]

② Entrepreneurship of Spinners

This is a subjective condition of firms, meaning the ability of perception and recognition of business opportunities and needs and the positiveness of responses to these needs. It is also the business ideology of an entrepreneur and his personal interest in China.

③ Characteristics of Direct Foreign Investment Strategy

These can be categorized as aggressive, fairly aggressive, fairly conservative and conservative. Categorization is based on two factors: the timing of beginning construction of mills and the size of completion scale. The timing is measured by the date of beginning construction. The size is measured by the local spindles out of total spindles of the firm. Characteristics are shown in Table 1.

④ Firms for Major Analysis

We next analyze the overseas operations strategy of the five largest spinning firms, as there is a big gap on the scale between the five largest and the other five. The five largest had 64% of all spindles in Japan and 66% of the looms.

B) *Product Market Structure and Direct Foreign Investment Strategy*

① Vertical Integration to Weaving Section

The 1917 consumption rate of cotton yarn for weaving was studied, when the export of cotton cloth surpassed the export of cotton yarn in money value. Table 2 shows the different attitudes of firms towards local production.[14]

Toyo and Kanegafuchi delayed more than other firms in building

TABLE 3   Export of Yarns in 1915.

Company	Export rate of yarns produced (1915)	Characteristics
Settsu	39%	Aggressive
Kanegafuchi	24%	Fairly aggressive
Osaka Godo	23%	Aggressive
Amagasaki (Dainippon)	19%	The same as Settsu
Toyo	18%	Fairly conservative
Fuji Gasu	15%	Fairly aggressive

Source: Based on the figures in "Menshi Boseki Jijo Sankosho," first and
second halves of 1915.

plants. As Toyo could approach the Chinese market with its cotton cloth, local production of coarse yarn was not as critical as for others. Kanegafuchi had a similar strength in weaving capacity. Dainippon and Osaka Godo were more aggressive in building local plants since they had smaller weaving capacity and hence it was more critical to defend their share of cotton yarns in China. Though Fuji Gasu had only a small weaving capacity, it was not as aggressive in local production. This point must be explained in another aspect of product market structure. We find that usually the smaller the weaving capacity, the more aggressively did the firms embark on building local plants.

② Dependent Rate of Yarns on Export Market

The rate studied is as of 1915, when the export volume of Japanese cotton yarns had reached a peak.[15] In Table 3 we fine the following facts:

Settsu had grown with large exports of coarse yarns. Immediately after it was absorbed by Amagasaki, Kikuchi embarked on building local plants in order to defend Settu's share in China. Though Kanegafuchi was a large exporter of cotton yarns, it delayed in embarking on a local production projects; this was due to Muto's misperception. But the company ultimately did establish a larger local production capacity than any of its Japanese competitors; the scale reflected Kanegafuchi's experience as a large exporter. With a relatively low export rate of yarns, Toyo was fairly conservative towards investment. The main purpose of local production was to maintain competitive equilibrium with its Japanese competitors. In spite of President Toyoharu Wada's strong interest

TABLE 4   Export of Medium and Fine Yarns by the Five Largest Firms, 1918.

Company	Export rate of medium and fine yarns to total exports (1918)	Characteristics
Osaka Godo	77%	Aggressive
Dainippon	64%	Aggressive
Fuji Gasu	63%	Fairly aggressive
Kanegafuchi	42%	Fairly aggressive
Toyo	33%	Fairly conservative

Source: Based on the figures in "Menshi Boseki Jijo Sankosho," first and second halves of 1918.

in direct foreign investment itself, Fuji Gasu was not very aggressive, hence its low export rate of cotton yarns. We find that firms with a higher export rate of cotton yarn were more aggressive in local production than others.

③   The Rate of Medium and Fine Count Yarn Exports to Total Yarn Exports

The rate taken is as of 1918, when the Japanese export of medium and fine count yarn reached its first peak of 123,711 bales. Table 4 shows the records of five big spinners; the ten top spinners are shown in Table 5. In both tables we find that firms with a higher rate of export of medium and fine count yarn were more aggressive in local production than others. While increasing their exports of higher count yarn, these exporters undertook the building of local production bases for the coarse yarn. On the other hand, the firms whose main export item was coarse yarn were more reluctant to invest.

This fact is contradictory to the inference of our fact-finding in former sections. This point may be explained from the point of view of entrepreneurship. The spinners whose major export item was medium and fine count yarn could perceive the market environment ahead of the others. They began exports of finer count yarn before decreasing exports of coarse yarn. Then, at the time when the Japanese export of yarn began declining, they saw that they would lose even the share of finer count of yarn in China soon thereafter.

C)   Entrepreneurship and Local Production in China

The product market structure of a firm is an objective condition of that firm. It does not automatically lead to a firm's optimal

TABLE 5　　Export of Medium and Fine Yarns by the Ten Largest Firms, 1918.

Company	Export rate of medium and fine yarns to total exports (1918)	Characteristics
Nisshin	86%	Aggressive
Osaka Godo	77%	Aggressive
Dainippon	64%	Aggressive
Fuji Gasu	63%	Fairly aggressive
Kanegafuchi	42%	Fairly aggressive
Toyo	33%	Fairly conservative
Fukushima	25%	Fairly conservative
Kishiwada	0	Conservative
Kurashiki	0	Conservative
Nagasaki	0	Fairly aggressive

Source:　Based on the figures in "Menshi Boseki Jijo Sankosho," first and second halves of 1918.

response to the needs brought on by changes in the market. The strategy is formulated by management, and is dependent upon that entrepreneurship. We have categorized the spinners into pioneers, followers and conservatives based on their entrepreneurship in the investment project in China.

① Pioneers

Amagasaki had a product market of big growth potential. On the contrary, Settsu relied on its coarse yarn. Taking over the presidency of Settsu, Kikuchi had to solve Settsu's problems of growth. Local production in China was a mandatory step for Settsu to defend its shares in Chinese markets. After the merger Kikuchi embarked on building local plants.

Though Osaka Godo's main product line was coarse yarn, it was also one of the largest exporters of medium count yarns.[16] Taniguchi had switched its major export item from coarse yarns to medium count yarns earlier than the others, i.e. by 1914. In June 1917, while opposing the upward revision of Chinese customs duties, Taniguchi sent his manager, Hirota Akiyama, to investigate the local production project. In 1923 and 1924 two local mills were established. They produced 42 count yarns and shirtings, which had not yet been produced in China at that time. As a result he could preoccupy the shares of those products in the market. It is obvious that he was getting ahead of other Japanese spinners in overseas strategies.

Nisshin Spinning Co. was not always in a good position to perceive the changing conditions in the Chinese market, having concentrated on the production of medium count yarns.[17] But Kiyojiro Miyajima, the managing director, was aggressive in the local production plans. He had had a strong interest in business in China since his college days. He had planned to work in China first after college graduation and then a second time when he resigned as director of Tokyo Cotton Spinning Co. This interest in China thus helped him to respond with aggressive alternatives to changes taking place in Chinese markets.

②　Followers

Wada had the business ideology that capital exports were necessary for the national benefit of Japan.[18] This helped him perceive changing conditions in the Chinese market and their effects on Japanese spinners. He insisted earlier than other spinners that the Japanese spinners should be engaged in production of coarse yarns in China and the finer count yarns in Japan. As early as the autumn of 1916 he went to China and investigated a mill proposed for sale in Shanghai and also researched the prospective location of local mills. He bought a mill in Shanghai as his personal business in 1918. But Fuji Gasu's construction of local mills was not done early in spite of Wada's early perception of the needs; this was due to its strength in exporting medium and fine count yarns.

Toyo delayed slightly in embarking on construction of a local plant, since with large weaving capacities it could approach cloth markets not only in China but in other nations. Nevertheless, Saito, the president of Toyo, built the local plant in Shanghai in order to maintain a competitive equilibrium with other Japanese spinners.

Muto of Kanegafuchi was still an export-oriented entreprenuer, even in such matters as the self sustaining process of export markets. He believed the export policy to be justified from the point of view of Japanese national economy. But he could not persist in his ide-

ology when other Japanese competitors embarked on building local
plants. Kanegafuchi finally built two plants and bought one mill
in order to defend its share from other Japanese investors.

Fukushima Cotton Spinning Co. was the largest exporter of
coarse yarns during the First World War.[19] Although the company
declined in the export of cotton yarns, President Yashiro did not
take any quick action to respond to the changing situation. In 1922
he bought a construction lot for a local plant in Tientsin but abandoned construction due to the unfavorable political and social
situation there. Then in 1923 he again began to build a local plant
in Dairen (Talien), but the completed plant proved too small to
defend the company's established share in China.

③   Conservatives

Kishiwada exported more than 90% of its yarn every year from
1910 to 1918.[20] Its strength lay in its mill management. President
Jinyomo Terada was effective in cutting costs in production processes; he avoided risky speculation and established a strong financial
position. But he had a misperception of the needs brought on by
changing conditions in the Chinese market. Emulating his competitors, he went to Shanghai for investigation in 1921 and bought
a mill site there in 1923, but the construction was not carried out.
As a result, Kishiwada had lost almost all of its established share
in the Chinese market by 1926.

Kurashiki concentrated on production of coarse yarn, and
exported 55% of it during the First World War.[21] In spite of the
sharp decline in exports after 1918, President Ohara did not take
any immediate action. Emulating his Japanese competitors, he
began the project of building local plants in China after 1921.
After unsuccessful attempts to establish local mills in Tientsin,
Tsingtao and then Manchuria, and after the Great Kanto Earth-
quake of 1923, he gave up investment plans. As a result, Kurashiki
was to suffer the same fate in China as did Kishiwada.[22]

D)   Summary

We get the following picture:

a.   Firms with relatively small weaving capacity responded
more aggressively than those with the large capacity, since changes
in the Chinese market had a more critical impact on the former.

b.   Firms which were relatively heavily dependent on the overseas yarn market responded more aggressively than those with small markets overseas, since changes in the export market affected the former more critically.

c. Firms which had a relatively strong position in medium and fine count yarns responded more aggressively than those with a heavy dependence on the coarse yarn. This must be explained from the point of view of entrepreneurship.

We conclude that Japanese cotton spinning firms as a whole brought forth positive and proper responses to the needs brought on by their product market structures, hence defending their established shares in Chinese markets.[23] Furthermore, in tracing the response of each firm, we found their strategies to have developed distinctively differently from each other due to these market structures and to their varying entreprenurial quality. Kikuchi, Taniguchi and Miyajima perceived the needs promptly and responded aggressively by establishing local production bases. As a result, Dainippon, Osaka Godo and Nisshin became pioneers in local production in China.

Wada assumed the role of pioneer as an individual in local production in China, but because of the nature of its product market structure Fuji Gasu delayed in beginning to build plants. Toyo's management recognized the needs brought on the firm less critically than others because of its strength in weaving capacity and also began construction in China only after some delay. Muto and Yashiro either had a misperception or showed a lag in perception, but they were active in emulating other Japanese competitors. Fuji Gasu, Toyo, Kanegafuchi and Fukushima became the followers.[24]

Terada and Ohara simply failed to perceive the needs and were, moreover, too conservative to emulate the movement of their competitors. Kishiwada and Kurashiki thus took the less risky alternative, which resulted in their losing their shares in the Chinese market.

4. Competitive Advantages of Japanese Local Plants in China over Chinese Spinners

As long as the Chinese market was self-sustaining, Japanese spinners had no alternative but to defend their share by local production. Thus, to keep their local plants competitive the Japanese had to have advantages over Chinese spinners with which they could compensate for the disadvantages of foreign operation.

Japanese spinners found the Chinese-owned cotton spinning mills inefficient for the first time in 1898.[25] The Chinese mills had been little improved even at the time of rapid expansion during the First World War.[26] They were operated on short-term perspectives, had little capital surplus and were always short of working capital. The management of processes and machines was poor, and materials and facilities were in disorder inside the mills.

When Japanese spinners evaluated the advantage of local operations over the Chinese spinners, Naigaiwata's Shanghai plants helped in this evaluation. Naigaiwata was more efficient in operation than the Chinese-owned mills.[27] Japanese spinners recognized their managerial resources for mill operation as their strength, having developed these during the days of export strategy.[28]

Conclusion

Japanese cotton spinners developed their overseas operations in three stages from 1890 to 1931. The years from 1890 to 1896 were the preliminary stage of exportation of cotton yarns. In the second stage, from 1897 to 1918, the Chinese coarse yarn market was acquired by export strategy. In the later period of this stage cotton cloth was added to their export items. After the First World War, to defend their established share in the Chinese cotton yarn market, the Japanese spinners undertook the establishment of local production bases.

Even in the first stage, Japanese spinners had two initial direct foreign investment projects in Shanghai as a response to the threat of losing Chinese markets. But the projects were given up when the investors could evaluate more precisely their positions in international competition. As a strategy for the Chinese cotton yarn market, export strategy was given priority over local production at that time.

In the second stage, the Japanese spinners cultivated export competitiveness by developing efficient mill management and operations, and realizing economies of scale merit through frequent mergers. The strategy was effective in taking over the already established positions of advanced spinners in the Chinese markets. But when the export of Japanese cotton yarns declined sharply in the process of self-sustainment of the Chinese markets during the First World War, Japanese spinners had to go into the third stage by adopting new strategies. Among these strategies were the local production of cotton coarse yarns in China as well as the expansion of weaving capacity and of production of fine and medium count yarns, the integration of a finishing division, and diversification towards the silk spinning and rayon industries. The Japanese companies chose from among these options in a manner distinctive from each other. These investment policies could be formulated on the basis of strong financial position built during the First World War.[29]

We have focused on the direct foreign investment processes in China by nine major spinning firms. Out of the nine, Dainippon, Osaka Godo and Nisshin have been defined as pioneers in local production as their management perceived the needs promptly and led in executing the proper strategies. The other four firms were defined as the followers. Though the management perceived the needs in time, Fuji Gasu and Toyo took on the projects only after some delay; this was due to the nature of their product market structure. The management of the other two, Kanegafuchi and Fukushima, failed to perceive the needs or showed lags in perception, but were still aggressive enough to emulate the pioneers in taking the path of strong resistance. The other two, Kurashiki and Kishiwada, have been defined as conservatives. While they needed local production to defend their shares in China, the management chose less risky alternatives.

As the result, most of the major Japanese spinners never lost their established shares in the Chinese market. This aggressive entrepreneurship in developing overseas operations reflects the business climate of Japanese spinners in those days. Their high devotion to their profession, with an ideology of one life for one business, cultivated keen perception and aggressive responses to market opportunities. Furthermore, in the face of a general conviction that the development of overseas markets could contribute to a national goal of enrichment and strengthening, the Japanese spinners as the leading industrialists at that time, were expected to conduct aggressive overseas operations.

NOTES

1. Source of statistical data: Koda, Yudo, *Hompo Mengyo no Tokeiteki Kenkyu* (Statistical Study of Japanese Cotton Spinning Industry), 1931, pp. 209–212. The All Japan Cotton Spinners' Association, *Cotton Statistics of Japan 1903–1949*, 1951. Seki, Keizo, *The Cotton Industry of Japan*, 1956, pp. 304–305.

2. Concerning Towka and Shanghai Cos., refer to: Kuwahara, Tetsuya, "Nisshin Senso chokugo no Nihon Bosekigyo no Chokusetsutoshi Keikaku" (The Direct Foreign Investment Project of Japanese Spinners after the Sino-Japanese War: Case of Towka Cotton Spinning and Weaving Co.) in *Keizai Keiei Ronshu*, edited by Kyoto Sangyo Univ. Keizai Keiei Gakkai, Vol. 14, No. 2, Sept. 1979. Kuwahara, T., "Nisshinsenso chokugo no Nihon Bosekigyo no Chokusetsutoshi Keikaku" (The Direct Foreign Investment Project of Japanese Spinners after the Sino-Japanese War: Case of Nakamigawa, Hikojiro and Shanghai Cotton Spinning Co.) in *Keizai Keiei Ronshu*, Vol. 15, No. 1, Sept. 1980.

3. This unique position of Naigaiwata could be explained by its managerial characteristics.

4. The Osaka Mainichi, May 2, 1905. Kodera Gengo Ou Denki Kankokai, *Kodera Gengo Ou Den* (The Biography of Gengo Kodera), pp. 185, 250–251. Kinukawa, Taichi, *Ito Denshichi Ou Den* (The Biography of Denshichi Ito), 1936, pp. 212–213.

5. Refers to Kuwahara, Tetsuya, "Senzen niokeru Nihon Bosekikigyo no Kaigaikatsudo" (The Overseas Operations of Japanese Cotton Spinning Firms in the Pre Second World War Days: Case of Kanegafuchi Cotton Spinning Co.) in *the Rokkodai Ronshu*, Vol. 22, No. 1, Apl. 1975, pp. 3–5. Concerned with statistical data, refer to: Imura, Shigeo, *Boseki no Keiei to Seihin* (The Management and Products of Cotton Spinners, 1926, pp. 53–54. 厳中平 (Yen Chungping), 中国棉紡織史稿 (Draft History of China's Cotton Textile Industry), 1963, (Japanese version, 1966, pp. 480–481). Takamura, N. "Chugoku niokeru Nippon Bosekigyo no Keisei"

(The Formation of the Japanese Cotton Spinning Industry in China), *The Socio Economic History*, Vol. 45, No. 5, 1980. p. 109. Cotton Statistics of Japan 1903–49, 1951.

6. Day wages of female workers increased from 0.32 yen before the war to 1 yen after the war in Japan. In Shanghai, they increased from about 0.2 yen to 0.4 yen. The decrease in cost performance of the five largest spinning firms in Japan is shown in the following table.

Cost Performance of the Five Largest Spinning Firms   (June 1915 and June 1919)

Spinning Firms	Dainippon	Toyo	Kanega-fuchi	Fuji Gasu	Osaka Godo
	kwan/yen	kwan/yen	kwan/yen	kwan/yen	kwan/yen
Cost performance, June, 1915[1]	8,350	6,243	6,486	6,045	6,119
Cost performance, June, 1919	2,714	3,120	3,207	2,560	2,504
Difference	−5,636	−3,120	−3,279	−3,485	−2,503
Attributed to physical pro-ductivity[2]	−0.5894 (−10%)	0.7235 (23%)	0.7463 (−23%)	1.5482 (44%)	0.1937 (8%)
Attributed to wage increase[3]	−5.0464 (−90%)	−3.8462 (−123%)	−4.0254 (123%)	−5.0278 (−144%)	−2.6967 (−107%)

Source: Dainippon Boseki Rengokai, *Dainippon Boseki Rengokai Geppo* (Monthly Report of the Japanese Cotton Spinners Association), July 1915, July 1919.

Remarks:
Concerning the revaluation rate of counts of yarn, refer to Nagai, M., Boseki Hyojun Genka Keisan (The Standard Cost Accounting of Cotton Spinning), appendix, p. 23.

[1] Cost performance is obtained by the formulation below:

$$CP=\frac{O}{(Lf+aLm)\cdot D\cdot Wf},\ O\cdots\cdots\text{output},\ Lf\cdots\cdots\text{number of female workers},$$

$Lm\cdots\cdots$number of male workers, $a=\dfrac{Wm}{Wf}$, $Wm\cdots\cdots$day wage of male worker, $Wf\cdots\cdots$day wage of female worker, $D\cdots\cdots$working days.

[2] $\dfrac{A}{A-B}(Cp_5-Cp_9)$, Cp_5: cost performance of 1915, Cp_9: cost performance of 1919, $A=\dfrac{X_5-X_9}{X_5}$, $X=\dfrac{O}{(Lf+aLm)D}$, $B=\dfrac{Wf_9-Wf_5}{Wf_5}$

[3] $\dfrac{B}{A-B}(Cp_5-Cp_9)$

(I am grateful to Prof. Miyamoto at Osaka Univ. for his advice on the analysis in this part).

7. As a result of upward revision of Chinese customs duties, the rate

per bale (400 pounds) of 20 count yarn increased from 2.85 Taels
to 4.14 Tales. Source: *The Chugai Shogyo Shimpo*, May 17, 1919,
Shina Kanzeiritsu Shinkyu Hikaku (Chinese Tariff Rates: Old
and New).

8. The spindles and looms of the ten largest spinners at the end of
    1918 were as follows: Dainippon Cotton Spinning Co. (569,114
    spindles, 3,561 looms). Toyo (511,512, 12,961). Kanegafuchi
    (484,608, 7,323). Fuji Gasu (297,888, 1,642). Osaka Godo (208,152,
    1,338). Fukushima (161,240, 1,048). Kishiwada (143,560, 460).
    Kurashiki (126,632, 0). Nisshin (86,962, 284). Wakayama Cotton
    Spinning and Weaving Co. (59,944, 856). Nagasaki Cotton Spinning
    and Weaving Co. (38,800, 0) is the twelfth largest. Source: Dai-
    nippon Boseki Rengokai, *Menshi Boseki Jijo Sankosho* (Half Year
    Statistics for Cotton Spinning), second half of 1918.

    Kishiwada, Kurashiki and Wakayama abandoned the invest-
    ment projects in the processes.

9. The facilities of Japanese owned local mills at the end of 1925 are
    shown in the table below.

	Spindles	Looms
New investors		
8 spinning firms	483,312	2,515
other 4 investment		
groups	371,376	900
Existing 2 firms	449,128	3,469
	1,303,816	6,884
	(39% of total spindles in China)	(31% of total looms in China)

Source: Dainippon Boseki Rengokai, *Menshi Boseki Jijo Sankosho*, second half
          of 1925.

10. Main references: Nichibo Kaisha, *Nichibo Shichijugo Nen Shi (The
    Seventy Five Years of Nichibo)*, 1966. Nitta, Naozo, *Kikuchi Kyozo Ou
    Den* (The Biography of Kyozo Kikuchi), 1948. Kodera Gengo Ou
    Denki Hensankai, *Kodera Gengo Ou Den* (The Biography of Gengo
    Kodera), 1960. Takamura, Naosuke, "Amagasaki Boseki Kaisha"
    and "Settsu Boseki Kaisha," Yamaguchi Kazuo ed., *Nihon Sangyo
    Kinyushi Kenkyu: Boseki Kinyu Hen* (The Historical Studies in Finance
    of Japanese Industries: Cotton Spinning Industry), 1970.

11. Toyo Boseki Kaisha, *Toyo Boseki Shichiju Nen Shi* (The Seventy
    Years of Toyo Cotton Spinning Co.), 1953. Kinukawa, Taichi,
    Ito Denshichi Ou Den (The Biography of Denshichi Ito), 1937.

Takamura, Naosuke, "Osaka Boseki Kaisha" (Osaka Cotton Spinning Co.), Yamaguchi, Kazuo ed., *Nihon Sangyo Kinyushi Kenkyu: Boseki Kinyu Hen*," 1970, pp. 325–392.

12. Refers to Kuwahara, Tetsuya, "Senzen niokeru Nihon Bosekikigyo no Kaigai Katsudo," Apr., 1975, pp. 5–18.

13. There were three peaks of exports of medium and fine count yarns. The exports reached the first peak with 125,711 bales in 1918, the second peak with 128,162 bales in 1922, and the third peak in 1925. Source: Koda, Yudo, *Hompo Mengyo no Tokeiteki Kenkyu*, 1931, p. 38.

14. The consumption rate of cotton yarn for weaving of 1918; Toyo, 48%, Kanegafuchi, 29%, Fuji Gasu, 10%, Dainippon, 9%, and Osaka Godo, 7%.

15. Applied to the rate of 1914, when the export volume of Japanese cotton coarse yarns reached a peak, Settsu is 48%, Kanegafuchi 32%, Osaka Godo 18%, Toyo 17%, Fuji Gasu 15%, and Amagasaki 8%.

16. Sakata, Kanta, *Taniguchi Fusazo Ou Den* (The Biography of Fusazo Taniguchi), 1931, pp. 150–160. Tachikawa, Danzo, *Watashi no Ayunda Michi* (My Path), 1970, pp. 136–158.

17. Nisshin Boseki Kaisha, *Miyajima Kiyojiro Ou Den* (The Biography of Kiyojiro Miyajima), 1965, pp. 41–43, 69, 81, 89, 92, 125, 128. Nisshin Boseki Kaisha, *Nisshin Boseki Rokuju Nen Shi* (The Sixty Years of Nisshin Cotton Spinning Co.), 1969, pp. 144–145.

18. Kita, Teikichi, *Wada Toyoharu Den* (The Biography of Toyoharu Wada), 1916, pp. 370–382, 426–427. Fuji Boseki Kaisha, *Fuji Boseki Goju Nen Shi* (The Fifty Years of Fuji Cotton Spinning Co.), 1947, pp. 178–181, 315–319. Wada, Toyoharu, "Shanghai Bosekigyo Shisatsu" (Report on Observations of Cotton Spinning Mills in China), in Dainippon Boseki Rengokai, *Dainippon Boseki Rengokai Geppo*, Vol. 294, Feb. 1917, pp. 4–8.

19. Fukushima Boseki Kaisha, *Fukushima Boseki Goju Nen Shi* (The Fifty Years of Fukushima Cotton Spinning Co.), 1942, pp. 154–164.

20. Fujioka, N., *Kishiwada Boseki Kabushiki Kaisha Goju Nen Shi* (The Fifty Years of Kishiwada Cotton Spinning Co.), 1942, pp. 52–55.

21. Kurashiki Boseki Kaisha, *Kaiko Rokujugo Nen* (The Sixty-five Years' Memoire), 1953, pp. 296–304.

22. On the other hand Kurashiki entered the rayon business by organizing a subsidiary, Kurashiki Kenshoku Kaisha, in June 1926, and began operations in 1930. This was successful and contributed to

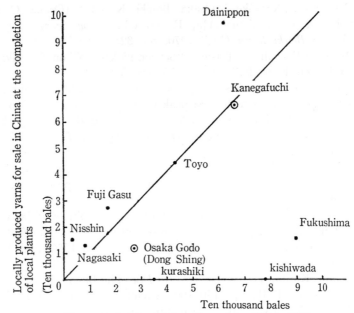

FIG. A.

Remarks
  1. Symbols:
       • firms producing yarns only for sale at local mills
       ⊙ firm having weaving section at local mills
  2. In the case of Fuji Gasu, the yarn for sale by Manshu Boseki Kaisha
      (Manchuria Cotton Spinning Co.) is not included.
  3. In the case of Kanegafuchi, the yarn produced by Lao Kung Mow Mill
      is included.
  4. Estimation was made to ascertain locally produced yarns.
  Source: Concerning export amount, Dainippon Boseki Rengokai, *Menshi*
           Boseki Jijo Sankosho, 1913–1919.
           Concerning local production of yarns, Hoshiyama, S., "Shanghai
           niokeru Hojin Bosekigyo" (The Japanese Cotton Spinners in
           Shanghai) in Kobe Kosho, *Kaigai Ryoko Chosa Hokoku* (Report of In-
           spection Trip Abroad, Summer 1924), 1925, pp. 230–235. Sasaki T.,
           "Tsingtao Bosekigyo nitsukite" (On the Cotton Spinning Industry in
           Tsingtao), in *Kaigai Ryoko Chosa Hokoku*, 1925, pp. 258–259. Urano,
           S., "Tsingtao niokeru Bosekigyo" (The Cotton Spinning Industry
           at Tsingtao), in Kobe Kosho, *Kaigai Ryoko Chosa Hokoku*, 1926,
           p. 131. Imura, S., *Boseki no Keiei to Seihin* (Management and Products
           of Cotton Spinner in China), 1926, pp. 342–367.

Kurashiki's growth. Kurashiki Boseki Kaisha, *Kaiko Rokuju Nen*, 1953, pp. 335–352, 413–415.

23. The relationship of export volume of yarns of Japanese spinners and their local yarns for sale is shown in Figure A.

24. Nagasaki also could be defined as a follower.

25. Muto, Sanji, "Fukumeisho (Report on Research of Cotton Spinners in Shanghai), 1898, in *Muto Sanji Zenshu* (The Complete Works of Sanji Muto), Vol. 1, 1963.

26. Wada, Toyoharu, "Sina Bosekigyo Shisatsu," Vol. 294, Feb., 1917, pp. 4–8. Moriyama, H., "Sina Bosekikojo no Dassenteki Arisama ni tsuite" (The Erratic Situation of Chinese Cotton Spinning Mills), *Dainippon Boseki Rengokai Geppo*, Jan., 1919, pp. 20–32.

27. Naigaiwata's Shanghai mills produced 1.24–1.32 pounds of 16 count yarn per one spindle each 24-hour day, while the Chinese mills produced 0.87–1.0 pound. Hioki, Fujio, "Naigaiwata Kaisha Kojo Shisatsu Hokokusho" (Report of Inspection of Shanghai Mills of Naigaiwata Co.), Apr. 1913. Toa Dobunkai, *Sina no Kogyo* (Manufacturing Industries in China), 1916, pp. 152–158.

28. After the local operation of local mills, the Japanese spinners found their evaluation of competitive advantages correct.

　　1) Production cost per bale of cotton yarn (20 counts) of Chinese and Japanese cotton mills in China is 43.70 yuan and 20.40 yuan each in the early 1930s. The major reason for the cost difference between them is taxes and interest, and wages. The Chinese paid 15 yuan as taxes and interest and 10.50 yuan as wages, while the Japanese paid 2.70 and 5.80 each. Sources: Yen Chungping, 1963, Japanese version, 1966, pp. 282–284. Ching-ming Hou, *Foreign Investment and Economic Development in China*, 1840–1937, 1965, pp. 143–44.

　　2) Capital-labor ratio and productivity in 1929 is shown as follows: Spindles per worker are 15.33 in Chinese mills, 25.33 in Japanese mills in China and 34.69 in Japanese mills in Japan. Bales per worker a year are each 8.86, 18.89 and 34.52 (1 looms = 15 spindles, 1 bale = 1,000 yard). Source: Kiyokawa, Y., Chugoku Mengyo Gijutsu no Hatten niokeru Zaikabo no Igi (On the Japanese-owned Cotton Mills as a Transferred Technology to China), Institute of Economic Research at Hitotsubashi Univ., *Keizai Kenkyu* (The Economic Review), Vol. 25, No. 3, July 1974, p. 256.

29. When we consider the spinners' propensity for internal capital accumulation and the attitude toward the direct foreign invest-

ment, the following table is relevant:

The Reserve Rate and the Direct Foreign Investment Strategy, 1914–1918.

	Firms	Reserve rate (amount of reserves), 1914–1918[1]	Characteristics of direct foreign investment strategy
The five largest	Kanegafuchi	65% (50,138,495 yen)	Fairly aggressive
	Osaka Godo	55% (12,838,502)	Aggressive
	Toyo	52% (38,861,123)	Fairly conservative
	Fuji Gasu	43% (12,324,032)	Fairly aggressive
	Dainippon[2]	42% (17,654,372)	Aggressive
Sixth to the tenth largest	Kishiwada	55% (7,184,835)	Conservative
	Nisshin	49% (3,036,784)	Aggressive
	Kurashiki	46% (4,298,999)	Conservative
	Fukushima	42% (4,096,949)	Fairly conservative
	Wakayama	41% (3,462,756)	Conservative

Source: Dainippon Boseki Rengokai, *Menshi Boseki Jijo Sankosho*, first half of 1914 to second half of 1918.

Remarks

[1] Reserve Rate = (Depreciation + Earning Surplus + Balance Incrementals)/(Net Profits Depreciation).

[2] Settsu's reserve rate and the reserve amount is 57% and 9,278,750 yen each.

COMMENTS

1

Jong-Tae Choi
Seoul National University

This research paper has permitted us to understand Japanese entrepreneurship in formulating strategies for the Chinese market during the period from 1890 to 1931 and the modern business strategy of the Japanese industry in relation to cotton spinners. From this presentation the following two facts are clear.

First, Japanese cotton spinners developed their overseas operation in three stages during the period from 1890 to 1931 in relation to a market-oriented strategy. The years from 1890 to 1896 constituted the preliminary stage of exporting cotton yarns. In the second stage, from 1897 to 1918, the Chinese coarse yarn market was acquired by export strategy. In the later period of this stage cotton cloth was added to their export items. After the First World War, in order to defend their established share in the Chinese cotton yarn market, the Japanese spinners established local production bases.

Second, most of the major Japanese spinners never lost their established shares in the Chinese market. This aggressive entrepreneurship in developing overseas operations may reflect the business climate of Japanese spinners in those days. An awareness that developing overseas markets contributed to the national goal of enrichment and strengthening of the nation could foster the business climate which prevailed among those who had led the industrialization of Japan.

This research paper was written using the following characteristic analytical approaches:

(1)   Horizontal and Vertical Analyses

By analyzing the Japanese entrepreneurship in formulating strategies for the Chinese markets, this study offered not only vertical analysis through the case study of each firm, but also horizontal analysis through the firms' comparative study.

(2)   Subjective and Objective Analyses

By analyzing the business strategy, this research paper provided not only subjective analyses through the entrepreneurship of spinners, but also objective analyses through the structure of the product market.

The Environmental Variables of Business Strategy

When we talk about business strategy we always think of the interaction between business and its environment. The strategic decision-making of business depends strongly upon technical, economical, political and social environmental variables. In analyzing the business strategy of Japanese cotton spinners in relation to Chinese markets, it is necessary to examine the main variables of the technical, economical, political and social situation at that time. The particular situations in relation to technical accumulation is one of the most important factors for business strategy to analyze.

What about the variables of technical, economic and political environment for business strategy at that time?

Subsidiary Variables of Entrepreneurship: Financing and Organizing Factors

In order to formulate a successful strategy of entrepreneurship, it is necessary to supplement the entrepreneurs' abilities of financing and organizing with the abilities of innovation and risk-taking.

What about the entrepreneurs' abilities of financing and organizing at that time? How could we create the challege culture of the business climate? How could we have changed the production-oriented culture into a market-oriented culture at that time?

Imperialistic Viewpoints of Approach Attitude

This paper has pointed out only the advantages of Japanese local plants in China over Chinese spinners. There are always disadvantages as well as advantages and dysfunctions as well as functions of the overseas operations of industrial countries over developing countries; we know of many of these disadvantages in the various fields. Therefore it is necessary to analyze such disadvantages and dysfunctions of overseas operations over developing countries. Through such analyses, we can achieve long-term and real cooperation between industrial and developing countries. If we analyze only the advantageous side, we are likely to indulge ourselves in a so-called imperialistic approach.

What about the disadvantages and dysfunctions of Japanese local plants in China over Chinese spinners at that time?

Interrelationship with Korean Spinners

By analyzing the Japanese entrepreneurship in formulating strategies for the Chinese market from 1890 to 1931, we should not neglect the Japanese policy over Korea. What about the interrelationship with the Korean market in order to promote the Chinese market at that time?

2

Matao Miyamoto
Osaka University

T. Kuwahara's paper is an attempt to shed light on the characteristic features of the business climate among Japanese cotton spinners before the Second World War, through an analysis of their strategies of direct investment in China. Based on a detailed empirical study, his argument is well proved and very persuasive. Before commenting, I would like to express my respect for his great efforts. As I found few faults in his paper, what I would like to ask him is to give us some additional explanations on the following points.

1) The most important and the most interesting part of his paper is, I think, the third section. Here he made a comparative analysis of direct investment strategies of Japanese spinners. He

found (a) that the smaller the weaving capacity, the more aggressively the firms embarked on building local plants in China; (b) that the firms with a higher export rate of cotton yarn were more aggressive in local production; and (c) that the firms with a higher rate of export of medium and fine count yarn were more aggressive in local production because the spinners who exported such product could perceive the market environment ahead of the others. He concluded that Japanese cotton spinning firms as a whole brought forth positive and proper responses to the needs brought on by their product market structures. Moreover, he discussed the difference in entrepreneurial qualities as another factor which has accounted for the difference of foreign investment strategies among Japanese spinners.

Preceding studies on this subject have been somewhat aggregate in approach and have focused mainly on determining the general background which drove Japanese spinners to embark for China. According to these earlier studies, the rapid increase in direct investment in China by Japanese spinners was considered a defensive move when those spinners confronted increasing difficulties in exporting their product to China because of the upward revision of Chinese customs tariff and the sharp increase in wage rates in Japan. T. Kuwahara added a new insight to these conventional views from his viewpoint of business history. According to him, it was the differences in product market structure and entrepreneurial quality among Japanese spinners that brought on behavioral differences among them in approaching China. I quite agree with him in this; however, I do not think that the behavioral differences can be attributed solely to the factors that he mentioned. Other variables should be taken into account. The financial condition of each spinner may have been an important factor. In T. Kuwahara's classification, Kishwada, Kurashiki and Fukushima were the "conservatives" in direct investment in China; however, we have to recall that these firms were not so large in scale. Kishiwada was ranked as No. 7 in 1914, Kurashiki as No. 12 and Fukushima as No. 9 in terms of holding spindles. This may imply that these firms were inferior in financial power to larger firms such as Amagasaki, Osaka Godo and Settsu which he classified as "aggressives." I wonder whether these relatively small firms had enough funds for overseas direct investment even if they had wanted to do so.

Next, let us examine the financial conditions of the Big Six, Toyo (Osaka and Mie), Kanegafuchi, Amagasaki, Fuji Gas, Osaka Godo and Settsu. In Table 1 (attached), which shows the disposal of gross profit of each firm in 1912–1914, we see that in the cases of Amagasaki, Osaka Godo and Settsu which were classified as the "aggressives," proportions of dividends were lower and other proportions, especially of depreciation, were higher than in the cases of Osaka, Mie, Kanegafuchi and Fuji Gas, which belong to the "fairly aggressives" or the "fairly conservatives." This may imply that the "aggressive" firms such as the former three had a stronger propensity to accumulate owned capital than the others, although the data shown are limited. Can we not say that the different financial conditions among spinners probably affected the direct investment policy of each spinner?

I would like to ask T. Kuwahara for his opinion in this regard.

2) The condition of the labor market of each firm may be important as another factor which explains the behavioral difference among spinners. Although it has been said that Japanese spinners as a whole began to suffer from the increase in wages after World War I, I suppose different spinners faced different degrees of difficulties. Table 2 (attached) shows the labor productivity of each firm per 1 yen of wage in 1914. We find in this table that labor productivity was lower in Settsu and Osaka Godo, which are characterized as "aggressives" by T. Kuwahara, than in Kanegafuchi, Fuji Gas, Kishiwada and Kurashiki, the "follower" or "conservative" types. If the figures in Table 2 shows the relative labor cost of each firm correctly, we might assume that Settsu and Osaka Godo had more necessity to escape from the Japanese labor market than others. I would like to ask T. Kuwahara for his explanation about market conditions of cotton laborers in those days.

3) My third point is related to the definition of business climate. According to T. Kuwahara, Japanese spinners as a whole

responded to the changing market situations after World War I by adopting new strategies: direct foreign investment, expansion of weaving capacity, shift of production from coarse to fine and medium count yarns, the integration of a finishing division as well as diversification towards silk spinning and rayon industries. In this sense, I suppose that T. Kuwahara considers the rational behavior as a characteristic feature of Japanese cotton spinners or of the Japanese business climate. However, I wonder if rationality can be called business climate. It seems to me that rational behavior is a universal attitude of firm managers rather than one peculiar only to Japanese spinners. The matter to be looked at is not the rationality itself but to what directions or to what strategies this rationality led Japanese spinners. In this connection, it seems very important to ask the reasons why Japanese spinners followed the strategy of direct investment in China, instead of other alternatives such as full integration or expanding the domestic market.

4)   My final question is related to his fourth section. Here he argues that Japanese cotton mills in China had advantages over Chinese mills. I have heard that Japanese cotton spinning firms succeeded in reducing the cost of cotton by their traditional know-how of buying cotton, while Chinese firms were suffering from the situation described as a "simultaneous rise in price of raw cotton and fall of that of yarn." I would like to hear some additional explanations of in what respect Japanese could have had an advantage. I would appreciate it greatly if T. Kuwahara would show us some examples which illustrate these advantages.

TABLE 1   Disposal of Gross Profit (1912–1914).

	Dividend	Depreciation	Reserve	Balance carried forward to next term	Classification by Prof. Kuwahara
Toyo					
Osaka	49.4%	29.8%	16.4%	4.6%	Fairly conservative
Mie	43.4	24.8	21.5	10.2	
Kanegafuchi	57.6	16.0	16.5	10.0	Fairly aggressive
Amagasaki	30.5	52.0	6.8	9.6	The same as Settsu
Fuji Gas	67.2	12.5	10.7	9.5	Fairly aggressive
Osaka Godo	36.2	47.5	12.1	4.1	Aggressive
Settsu	47.6	38.3	13.6	11.1	Aggressive

Source: Naosuke Takamura, *Nihon Boseki-gyo-shi Josetsu*, Vol. 2, p. 250.

TABLE 2   Labor Productivity per 1 Yen of Wage (1914).

	Labor productivity per 1 yen of wage
Toyo	5,985 momme of yarn
Kanegafuchi	6,260
Fuji Gas	6,555
Amagasaki	8,859
Osaka Godo	5,949
Kishiwada	10,389
Settsu	5,214
Fukushima	8,910
Kurashiki	6,881

Source: Naosuke Takamura, *op. cit.*, 212–213.
1 momme is an unit of weight, equivalent to 3.75 gramme.

Innovations in the Indian Textile Industry: The Formative Years

Dwijendra Tripathi
Indian Institute of Management, Ahmedabad

The modern Indian cotton textile industry, as is well known, has developed during the last century and a quarter. Even though India had a long tradition of cotton manufacturing before British domination, the traditional method of production could not withstand the challenge of a new technology generated in the wake of the Industrial Revolution in England. The traditional manufacturing processes and techniques, symbolized by small companies in the large British colony, gradually yielded to large factories using sophisticated machines and equipment imported from the mother country. The process began in 1854 and made rapid progress in spite of a series of adverse factors, including the unsympathetic attitude of an alien government. That India by 1913 had come to possess as many as 259 mills with about 6,600,000 spindles, 94,000 looms, and more than 250,000 workers[1] is a tribute to the Indian entrepreneurial initiative and determination. Before the First World War gave an unexpected, though bloody, boost to the fortunes of the Indian industry, Bombay and Ahmedabad had already emerged as the major centers of textile production; a few mills had been set up in some other parts of the country as well.

The growth of the Indian industry is sometimes referred to as a case of "adaptive innovation."[2] There is no denying the fact that the textile industry in India originated and developed under inspiration from England, that the Indian entrepreneurs during the formative years of the industry were wholly dependent on British suppliers for plants and machinery, and that the physical layouts and technical features in the early Indian factories were closely patterned after those in Lancashire. Placed as they were in a colonial set-up,

175

and having easy access to a sophisticated technology, it was neither possible nor necessary for the Indian entrepreneurs to commit their resources and skills to technological discovery or advancement. But the considerable entrepreneurial courage and wisdom that they displayed in adopting a new and rather unfamiliar technology in an uncertain environment for their own use should not be overlooked. In the absence of more sophisticated and now familiar techniques to gauge the profit potential of a new venture, they had nothing but their intuitive judgment to guide them; the hope of any positive help from an alien government would have been unrealistic; and the threat of stiff competition from Manchester, with the enormous political leverage that the British manufacturers enjoyed, could have daunted the most determined of spirits.[3] Under these conditions, the introduction of a new method of production had all the risks and dangers inherent in what is considered to be a "primary innovation." In fact, inasmuch as the adaptation of a new production function to a milieu different from the one which gave it birth is an act of innovation, the distinction between the "primary" and "adaptive" innovation, to my mind, is meaningless. It is even more so in the case of the Indian experiment in textile production.

It is also worth mentioning that the early Indian entrepreneurs did not always emulate Lancashire in the choice of technology. The introduction of ring spinning is a case in point. Even though the Rabbeth ring spindles had been invented in the United States a few years before the birth of the Indian industry, they had received at best a cold reception in Lancashire when J. N. Tata decided in 1883 to give a fair trial to the new device in the face of general British disapproval. A number of experiments were carried out at his Empress Mills at Nagpur and several improvements had been effected by his technicians before the superiority of the new spindles over the mules was established, at least for spinning the coarse counts on which most of the Indian mills concentrated. It was an accomplishment of no mean significance as the ring method had not until then given sufficiently promising results, even in the United States where it had been invented. Though the English firms continued to remain skeptical about the suitability of the ring spindles, and Tata had some difficulty in persuading the Platt Brothers of Oldham, the principal machinery supplier to India, to manufacture the necessary plant, he went ahead with his plan to equip his mill wholly with the new machines. The Empress Mill thus was among the first textile companies in the world to make large-scale commercial use of a technology with revolutionary consequences for the industry.

Several other Indian producers followed Tata's lead, with the result that more than a million ring spindles were in use in various Indian mills at the turn of the century. The output of the new machines was substantially larger than that of other types, their technical features were less complicated, and labor requirements less exacting. They were thus more suitable to Indian conditions and labor efficiency. The introduction and large-scale application of the new device was no insignificant factor in giving the kind of advantage to the Indian mills which they so badly needed in their unequal fight against Lancashire.[4]

The easier acceptance of the ring method, or at least the less resistance against it, in India than in Lancashire was one of the very few departures made by the Indian entrepreneurs from the prevailing British practices relating to technology. By and large, they followed Lancashire. In several other spheres, however, they displayed a remarkable sense of independent judgment. And in assessing the innovative ability of the Indians, or for that matter any group of entrepreneurs, technological matters alone should not be the only data. Innovation in other managerial functions and processes must be given due attention, for technology alone cannot determine the future of an enterprise.

In this context it is important to point out that the form of ownership that the Indians chose for their textile enterprises had nothing in common with the system under which the British textile companies had developed or were then operating. When India's debt to Britain is analyzed, it is scarcely noticed that at the time of the birth of the Indian textile industry most of the British companies were partnership firms and continued to be so until well after the First World War.[5] In contrast, the very first Indian textile mill, founded by Cowasjee Nanabhoy Davar and inaugurated in 1854, had several elements usually associated with a joint stock concern. It was not a full-fledged joint stock company, but with more than fifty shareholders with limited liability, it was more than a partnership; S.D. Mehta has called it a "co-partnership." The third Indian mill, established in 1858, was converted into a joint stock company within a year after its birth, and joint stock became the basis of establishing practically all subsequent undertakings in the field. A few which started as partnership were soon converted into joint stock firms.[6]

Statistics bear this out. In 1860, out of 5 cotton textile companies in existence, all were registered as joint stock firms. In 1880, there were 62 mills operating in various parts of the country, out of which only 9 were private mills. Two decades later, the number of companies had grown to 198, but the net addition to the private companies was limited to 2 since as many as 179 of the total were operating as joint stocks. Precise figures of the registered companies in the entire country immediately before the beginning of the First World War are not readily available, but out of 33 Ahmedabad concerns for which details are known, only 3 were under partnerships or sole proprietorships in 1914. On a rough reckoning, a similar situation seems to have prevailed in Bombay, the other principal textile center.[7]

The full significance of the adoption of the joint stock principle by the Indian textile manufacturers would be still more clear if we remember that joint stock was yet to become the widely accepted basis of business organization in India when the modern industry made its beginning. Indubitably, the Indians were aware of the joint stock principle and had, in fact, practised it on a limited scale and at least in a few regions in the 17th century. Some scholars have drawn our attention to the "joint stock associations" formed in the last quarter of the 17th century by Indian merchants on the Coromandel coast "for the purposes of managing the supply of textiles to the European Companies" trading with India.[8] These, most probably, were associations of brokers or middlemen who organized themselves into ongoing concerns at the instance of the trading companies, wishing to minimize the danger of frequent increase in prices resulting from competition among individual bidders. These quasi-joint stock organizations had fallen into disuse by the end of the 18th century. Perhaps the sole *raison d'être* of their existence was the need of the buyer companies, and as the need declined, so did the organizations satisfying it. It is no surprise, therefore, that these associations failed to advance to the next logical stage of evolution. In any case, there is no evidence of such business formations existing in other parts of India.

The Indian business horizon in the last quarter of the 18th century and the first quarter of the 19th was dominated by the operations of British free merchants and agency houses on one hand, and Indian traders and indigenous bankers on the other. The free merchants operated either individually or in partnership with their compatriots, and Indian traders and moneylenders were the sole proprietors of their businesses. When the agency houses came to grief following the financial crisis of 1829, the organizations that emerged from their ruins were all partnership firms. We know of at least 17 such partnerships emerging in Bengal alone between 1832 and 1847. Simultaneously the Indian traders and bankers continued their operations on an individual basis as the general environment offered them little incentive to come together.[9] True, a few banking and insurance companies were formed on joint stock lines, but they lacked some of the essential features of joint stock undertakings. The Union Bank of Calcutta, for instance, could not sue or be sued through its officers until 1845. The concept of limited liability was absent, and the failure of a company could cause consternation in the entire share market as it actually happened when the Union Bank of Calcutta failed in 1848.[10] For all practical purposes, there was little difference between a partnership firm and a joint stock company during this period.

Among the factors that inhibited the growth of joint stock companies in the first half of the 19th century was the absence of a company law. There was no legislative sanction to back up the concept of limited liability, and a single shareholder could be considered liable for the debts of a company. It was not always possible for the companies to raise finances on the basis of their own credit and there were occasions when a company had to raise funds against the guarantee of individual shareholders. Preference shares and debentures could not be issued as they were hardly compatible with the concept of unlimited liability. Above all, there was no provision in the law requiring the registration of a company, and without registration a company could not enjoy the privileges which a handful of companies, incorporated under special and separate acts, enjoyed.[11]

The Indian Company Act of 1850 removed some of the disabilities from which the companies suffered. But it was the act of 1857 that introduced the system of limited liability and made registration compulsory for a certain class of companies. While the act of 1850 was based on the existing English laws, the 1857 legislation was patterned identically after the company law passed in England a year before. The idea behind a common legal framework governing company operations in the mother country as well as the colony was to ensure that those "desirous of carrying on either the whole or a portion of their business in India might know that the law in both countries was substantially the same, and that they would incur no greater risks in India than they would in England."[12] And yet while the new legal provisions encouraged an unmistakable shift in the approach to company formation in India, in England they made little impact, at least on the textile manufacturers.

Why the English manufacturers chose to cling to the older form of ownership even after the legislation of 1856 is not my concern, nor is it easy to discern the motive behind the adoption of the joint stock system by the Indian producers. Perhaps the partnership pattern was too deeply entrenched in England to be easily disturbed merely by legislative changes. And it is possible that the Indian pioneers, unencumbered by any indigenous precedence of ownership pattern in large factory establishments, found it easier to embrace a system which had the potential to attract investors who, with too small resources or too little ability or willingness to participate actively in floating or managing a large and complex system, would have been reluctant to join a partnership. That such investors did not come forward at the initial stages to acquire shares in the joint stock textile companies is beside the point. It is well known that early promoters distributed the shares of their concerns among their own close relatives and friends. But what is pertinent is that the pioneers might have calculated that once their manufacturing enterprises would register progress, the initially cautious and hesitant parties would feel encouraged to join their capital structure. At later stages of the development of the Indian industry, a number of cotton companies in fact did dilute the family holdings of the promoters in their share capital.[13]

Embarking on the joint stock system rather than the partnership so successfully tested by the British producers was, thus, an act of some foresight on the part of Indian pioneers. It was also consistent with the Indian environment in which both capital and managerial ability were scarce. Undoubtedly, the promoters of industrial companies in other fields also adopted the joint stock concept for their own purposes, but it was the cotton manufacturers who were the first to make use of it on a large scale and, thus, establish its viability as an instrument of industrialization. The idea of joint stock was by no means new when the first mills came into being, but the credit for applying it effectively in the industrial field at a scale sufficient to win for it a general acceptability must belong to the early promoters of factory-based textile production. It is in this sense that the Indian departure from the time-honored British convention was an innovation.

The Indian approach to management structure also differed radically from that in vogue in the British mills when the Indians started their own industry. While the Lancashire mills were managed by salaried managing directors who worked under the overall control of the board of directors,[14] the Indian pioneers, on the other hand, adopted for their purpose a structure almost unique to India. The concept of the managing agency system of management under which the Indian cotton textile developed, like that of the joint stock principle, was not unknown when the first mills were born, and some scholars trace it as far back as the 18th century. But the origin of the system is still shrouded in mystery.[15] One thing, however, is certain: the system as a form of corporate management was yet to establish itself when the early Indian pioneers embarked on textile ventures. A few companies in Bengal were all that could be deemed to have come, by any stretch of logic, under the managing agency structure.[16] Thus, without any meaningful precedence, whether in India or abroad, the adoption of the new form of management involved some degree of risk and required a great deal of imagination.

The managing agency structure facilitated the promotion and management of one or several companies, though separate and independent legal entities, by a single controlling firm which, in turn, was usually controlled by a single family. The *modus operandi* was simple. A family with considerable financial strength would launch a company and allot to its own members or near relatives and close friends a sufficient number of shares necessary to control the new concern. Simultaneously, those holding the controlling interests in the new company joined to form a managing agency firm, usually a partnership or sole proprietorship, to which the management of the new company was entrusted under an agreement stipulating the terms and conditions between the shareholders and the managing firm. The remuneration of the managing agency was usually fixed in terms of a certain percentage of annual sales or profits. Technically speaking, thus, the managing agents did not own the company; they only managed it, for which they were remunerated. But in practice all critical and strategic decisions about the managed company were taken by the managing firm. Even though the company in question did have a board of directors, but its members, handpicked by the managing agents, were no more than a mere decoration.

The Indian pioneers of textile ventures were the first to embrace the managing agency system for managing industrial concerns. This is clear from the earliest extant deed of agreement between the shareholders of a company and its promoters, which anticipated several essential features of such agreements of later dates. Significantly, this agreement relates to the first cotton mill company in India. Written originally in Gujarati (an English rendering is enclosed as an appendix to this paper) the document makes it clear that the managing agency system was still in an infant stage. It does not use the phrase "managing agent" even once and refers to the appointment of Cowasjee Davar, the promoter of the mill; as the *arhatiya* or "broker." But the right and privileges conferred on him were those which became the usual features of all managing agency agreements in later years.

Other mills that were established in the 1850s followed the pattern of Davar's company, and in 1860 an agreement signed between the shareholders of the Oriental Mills and the firm of Messrs. Merwanji Framji & Company used the word "agent" for the latter. This, according to a competent contemporary observer, was the formal inauguration of the agency system of management in Bombay.[17] The system proved so effective that, barring a few stray cases, all mills in Bombay as well as in the upcountry centers were started and developed under the agency structure. The companies producing other industrial goods also emulated the examples of the textile manufacturers.

The development of the managing agency system was due to "the peculiar circumstances prevailing in India."[18] Among the factors often considered responsible for its origin and gradual evolution was the scarcity of capital and managerial ability.[19] Sociological factors, however, were no less significant. The managing agency framework was nothing but the adaptation to industrial management of the time-honored family system which was still a prominent feature of the Indian social structure. The head of the family controlled the purse, exercised authority over the junior members, and had a dominant, almost decisive, voice in matters affecting the family. Prior to the emergence of the industrial organizations in India, there was little qualitative difference between the role played by the heads of commercial families and those of non-business families in managing their respective affairs. In other words, the business management structure was coterminous with the family management structure. Since in a majority of the cases it was the commercial families which initiated the industrial concerns, they found it easier to adopt the managing agency framework for managing their industrial undertakings; the system entailed little or no threat to the authority of the head of the family, forming the managing agency firm, in managing the industrial undertaking floated by it. Whatever the origin of the system, there is no doubt that it flourished because of the economic and social realities in the 19th century India.[20]

The role of the managing agency form of management in the industrial development of India has been commended by a number of scholars. True, the system was open to abuses, and some of the managing agents actually did misuse their powers and privileges, for which they came under vigorous attack in the Indian press—particularly in the two major centers of textile production—during the closing years of the 19th century.[21] The attack intensified in the 20th century and recently led the government of free India to abolish this system of management. During the initial stages of India's industrialization, however, the system undeniably provided an effective instrument to promote and manage industrial undertakings in the Indian milieu. A government report published in 1888 unhesitatingly conceded that the management of the Bombay mills was in no way inferior to that of Lancashire factories, and about that time Japan recognized the same fact by sending a delegation "to study and learn from management and technical practices" in the Indian mills.[22]

The ability of the Indian cotton producers to innovate did not remain confined to the forms of ownership, control, and management. They displayed some degree of originality in the functional areas as well. Their approach to raising working capital through public deposits is a case in point. Some features of the Indian strategy, of course, were similar to the methods adopted by the Lancashire manufacturers. In both cases, for instance, the quantum of total public deposits in a mill was usually much higher than its total paid-up capital. But the Indians made significant departures from the British practice, and it was due to those departures that their method acquired a greater endurance quality than was the case in England. One of these departures lay in the fact that whereas in Lancashire a person buying shares of a mill could pay off only a part of the value of the shares and leave the balance as deposits with the company, in India this kind of combination was not possible. Since the *sine qua non* of the deposit system was public confidence, the Lancashire method was fraught with danger, as partial shareholders were likely to withdraw their deposits to pay for the unpaid portion of their shares when the company found it necessary to call for additional capital to meet a sudden financial crisis. This is actually what happened during the crisis of 1922–23. The withdrawal of deposits during difficult times was a phenomenon in the Indian mills too, but their suffering was nowhere as acute as that of the Lancashire mills on this account.[23]

A major factor in the relatively greater success of the deposit strategy in India, at least during the formative years of the industry, was the underdeveloped state of modern banking. The Indians had not adopted this strategy in imitation of Lancashire, but because of the age-old tradition of indigenous bankers who used to accept public deposits at rates of interest lower than the ones on which they gave loans to needy parties. As most of the promoters of the Indian mills were either merchants or bankers (or both), in whom the public had come to place a great deal of confidence, they adapted this traditional custom to raise industrial finance. The Report of the Indian Central Banking Enquiry Committee rightly pointed out: "In its origin, the system of deposits with industrial concerns was undoubtedly a reflex and transformation of the old system of money being kept in safe custody with the Mahajans."[24] As modern banking developed, the system of deposits declined in Bombay where the deposits were mostly for short periods and where no steps had been taken to retain its attractiveness for the public.

The Ahmedabad industrialists had already insulated the system of deposits against these dangers, perhaps because the tradition of indigenous banking in their city was much longer. Not only did they accept deposits for longer duration, usually for five to seven years, but they also introduced a system under which the depositors could share a small part of the agency commission. Through these methods they precluded, or considerably reduced, the possibility of sudden withdrawals of deposits to which the Lancashire and Bombay mills were exposed. It is not precisely known when and by whom these innovations were made. It is possible that Bechardas Laskari, the founder of the second textile company in the city, initiated the practice. He was a partner in a banking firm before he branched off into the mill industry. But it is more likely that the Jain and Vaishnava bankers of Ahmedabad, who took to textile production in a big way after 1877, perfected the system.[25] In any case, the Ahmedabad method of raising industrial capital had been firmly established by the end of the century and remained in vogue even after the deposit system had declined in its vigor in Bombay and elsewhere in India.[26]

The Ahmedabad innovation was partly due to the fact that almost from its very inception the mill industry in the city employed a small amount of equity capital. In fact, the most common pattern in Ahmedabad before the First World War was to start a mill with a paid-up capital of Rs. 500,000. The strategy of raising working finance through deposits enabled the Ahmedabad industrialists, as elsewhere, to pay higher dividends on the equity capital than would have been the case if additional finances were raised through new issues, for the rates of interest paid on deposits were lower than the rates of and not on dividends. If the policy of low equity investment was to be enduring, it was necessary for the Ahmedabad mill magnates to devise a method of retaining the depositors' interest in keeping their savings with the textile companies, and discourage them from withdrawing their money at will. The system of long-term deposit along with the depositor's privileges to share in the agency commission was the answer.

The Ahmedabad industrialists showed greater imagination in yet another area of management. In the matter of maintaining industrial peace in their city, they were much more successful than their counterparts in Bombay. This is evident from the fact that whereas Bombay witnessed a series of labor strikes in the 1890s, there was only one strike in Ahmedabad. Also, attempts to organize textile labor in Bombay preceded those in Ahmedabad by at least two decades.[27] It is possible that the difference in the behavior pattern of the labor force in these two cities was partly due to the difference in the character of the labor market and the nature of the work force. At the same time, there is no doubt that a very long trading tradition had created a certain kind of ethos in Ahmedabad which abhorred conflict. In comparison to Ahmedabad, Bombay had a much shorter history as a center of trade and commerce. The Jain and Vaishnava values of peace were deeply entrenched in the former city; the business life was much less complex in Ahmedabad than in Bombay; and the textile magnates, most of whom came from the Jain and Vaishnava stock, were a more cohesive group. Traditionally the Ahmedabad millowner had been, by and large, more accessible to his employees of all categories than in Bombay, and this generated much better personal rapport between the employers and the employees.[28] It was, perhaps, due to these factors that the industrial life in Ahmedabad was generally peaceful during the formative years of the city's cotton textile industry. It lay in the logic of history, however, that the industrial culture would eventually overpower the trading ethos, paving the way for greater conflict between capital and labor. Before this could happen, however, the Ahmedabad industrialists devised a novel system to settle labor disputes peacefully, which is sometimes referred to as the "Ahmedabad experiment."[29] Under an agreement effected in 1918, to which the millowners and the labor union are bound in perpetuity, all disputes between them are referred to arbitration. The agreement institutionalized, as it were, the peaceful approach that characterized the industrial relations in the city before the First World War. And it is because of this that the Ahmedabad mills have never been closed on account of grievances of employees against their employers. Much of the credit for establishing the system belongs, of course, to Gandhi's initiative and leadership, but its continuance even after the industrial environment in Ahmedabad became much more complex than in the early decades of this century is largely due to socio-cultural factors.

I do not propose to discuss in this paper why the Ahmedabad methods of raising working capital and dealing with labor disputes did not inspire similar experiments elsewhere in the country. I also do not wish to dwell on the imaginativeness of the Indians to produce goods like *dhotis* and *saris* suited to the Indian market, or their marketing aggressiveness which resulted in wresting a sizable share of the China market in the last decade of the 19th century. What I have tried to point out are some of the distinctive methods adopted by the Indian textile manufacturers in a few crucial areas of management. Their inability to invent new technological processes during the formative phase of their industry is understandable, but their ability to look for and adapt for their own purpose technologies developed elsewhere, and to evolve distinctive managerial processes consistent with their needs and environment, is in no way unimpressive. Technology is not the only index of innovation, and the innovative ability of a community cannot be properly assessed without reference to the possibilities of innovation in a given milieu.

Appendix: Deed of Agreement between Cowasjee N. Davar and the Shareholders of the Spinning and Weaving Company

To Parsee Cowasjee Nanabhoy Davar. We who have placed our signatures below address you that you have decided to open here a factory for the manufacture of yarn and cloth with the help of machinery and that you have named the said factory as Spinning and Weaving Company. It has been decided to make 100 shares thereof so that each share is of Rs. 5,000 (Rupees five thousand). The document in connection with these arrangements is penned by us in accordance with the undermentioned details.

1. Firstly, for the above mentioned purposes, you shall secure the buildings or premises here and import machinery from England and arrange for its erection. You shall build the necessary buildings. You shall do all things necessary for the purpose and engage men for the same. Whatever expense has to be incurred for the purpose may be incurred by you. The entire management of these matters is entrusted by us, of our own will and pleasure, to you, and you will continue to do so in the course of your lifetime.

2. Secondly, against shares which we have taken up from the above-mentioned 100 parts or shares, we have placed our signatures and stated the number of shares taken up by each one of us. And all these who have signed this Agreement have paid Rs. 1,000 (Rupees one thousand) per share to you and have taken for the same a receipt bearing your signature.

3. Thirdly, whatever expenses are involved in the construction of the building and the erection of the machinery should be taken from us, the shareholders, in equal contributions according to shares held by each, and for that purpose, as and when necessary, you may make calls which we shall pay up within a period of 15 days there-

from. If, however, in that period of 15 days the amount called for by you is not paid, the defaulting shareholders shall use their rights on Rs. 1,000 per each share, or whatever other additional calls have been paid thereon, and the money already paid in by the shareholders shall be credited to the profit account of the above Company. Of those who have placed their signatures below, any shareholder might transfer his share or shares to any individual or make it over to any individual, but the subsequent owner or owners shall be regarded as being bound by the stipulations made herein.

4. Fourthly, we shareholders have, of our own will and pleasure, resolved that in recompense of the trouble taken by you in the floatation of the factory, you are appointed Arhatiya or Broker of the said factory during your lifetime, that is to say, that whatever cotton is required for the said factory should be purchased by you and whatever yarn and cloth are manufactured in the said factory should also be sold by you, and on whatever sales you effect on account of the said Company a commission of 5%, that is, five per cent, shall be taken by you in your lifetime; but on purchases you will not charge anything to the said Company. In the event of the Company selling goods directly you shall still be entitled to your commission of 5% on the sale proceeds in your lifetime.*

5. Fifthly, with regard to the purchase of any building or land on behalf of the Company and the importation and erection of machinery and the construction of any building you are entrusted with the sole managership thereof. So all partners hereby give it to you in writing that any damage caused in any manner to the abovementioned building and machinery shall be taken over by us as shareholders in proportion to our share or shares. Secondly, whatever deposit you make for bringing out machinery from England and if it entails any risks and results in any loss, we shareholders agree to take it up in the same way as mentioned above.

6. Sixthly, for the purposes of the above Company you shall circulate a circular a few days prior to and all shareholders shall

---

* One sentence at the end of Clause Four defies translation, even in a broad sense, partly due to illegibility of the document and partly due to lack of clarity in the framing of the sentence.

remain present on the appointed day. If however despite such warning any partner or partners, due to any reason whatsoever, is unable to attend the meeting, the absentee partner shall be bound by whatever resolution has been passed by those shareholders who were present at the meeting. Moreover, no other person shall be allowed to attend the meeting on behalf of the said partner or partners.

7.   Seventhly, if from among us the shareholders any sells his share or shares, then the purchaser shall give it to you in writing that all the terms of this Agreement are accepted by him and only then would the share or shares be transferred to his name.

8.   Eighthly, any partner who acts in contravention of the conditions and stipulations laid down in this document shall pay to you a penalty of Rs. 4,000 (Rupees four thousand) without any objection, which penalty you shall collect and credit to the profit account for the benefit of all the partners.

9.   Ninthly, all stipulations penned in this document have been read by us and considered by us by our own will and pleasure and we have agreed thereon with you and these are acceptable to us and to our heirs, assigns, executors and administrators.

Shri Bombay dated 7th in the year 1854 of the Christian era.*

(Quaintness of expression and oddities of style, which have disappeared even from Gujarati, the original language of the Deed of Agreement, have precluded a verbatim translation in the exact sense of the word. Maximum effort, however, has been made to preserve the tenor and tone of the original document).

NOTES

1.   S. D. Mehta, *Cotton Mills of India: 1854 to 1954* (Bombay, 1954), 233. Some other works give slightly different figures.
2.   Entrepreneurial theorists generally make distinction between "creative" and "adaptive" or "primary" and "derivative" innovations. See Yusif A. Sayigh, *Entrepreneurs of Lebanon* (Cambridge,

---

* Source: S.D. Mehta, *Cotton Mills of India, 1834* (Bombay, 1954), 26–27. The original
        in Gujarati is reproduced on the facsimile page.

Mass., 1962), 19–20; James J. Berna, *Industrial Entrepreneurship in Madras State* (Bombay, 1960), 6; I have also benefited from an unpublished paper, "On the Study of Entrepreneurship in India" by my colleague, H. N. Pathak.

3. For the difficulties of the early pioneers, S. D. Mehta, *Cotton Mills of India*, 1–25; M. J. Mehta, "Rauchhodlal Chhotala and the Ahmedabad Cotton Textile Industry: An Entrepreneurial History" (Ph. D. thesis, Gujarat University, Ahmedabad, 1979), 130–478. For government policy and Manchester's influence, Peter Harnetty, *Imperialism and Free Trade: Lancashire and India in the Mid-Nineteenth Century* (Vancouver, 1972); C. J. Hamilton, *The Trade Relations between England and India* (Calcutta, 1919); Dwijendra Tripethi, "Opportunism of Free Trade: Lancashire Cotton Famine and Indian Cotton Cultivation," *Indian Economic and Social History Review* IV (September 1967), 255–63.

4. F. R. Harris, *Jamsetji Nusserwanji Tata: A Chronicle of His Life* (Bombay, 1958), 31–32; S. S. Rutnagur (ed.), *Bombay Industries: The Cotton Mills* (Bombay, 1927), 19; S. D. Mehta, *Cotton Mills of India*, 43–45.

5. Textile Institute, *Management in the Textile Industry* (Manchester, 1969), 2.

6. S. D. Mehta, *Cotton Mills of India*, 13; Rutnagur, *Bombay Industries*, 9. Occasionally a joint stock company was converted into a partnership as was the case with the second mill in Ahmedabad. However it was again changed into a joint stock company. Another Ahmedabad mill, the Maneklal Harilal Spinning and Manufacturing Company established in 1888, started as a partnership but became a public limited concern at a later date. See Natverlal N. Desai, *Directory of Ahmedabad Mill Industry, 1929–1955* (Ahmedabad, 1958), 38–39, 98–99.

7. Radhey Shyam Rungta, *Rise of Business Corporations in India, 1851–1900* (Cambridge, 1970), 46, 153, 298. The figures of partnership firms in Ahmedabad in 1978 are based on information given in Desai, *Directory of Ahmedabad Mill Industry*. For Bombay data see, Rutnagur, *Bombay Industries*, 97–243.

8. S. Arasratnam, "Indian Merchants and Their Trading Methods (circa 1700)," *Indian Economic and Social History Review*, III (March 1966), 85. Also see John Irwin and P. R. Schwartz, *Studies in Indo-European Textile History* (Ahmedabad, 1966), 31–33.

9. Dwijendra Tripathi, "Indian Entrepreneurship in Historical

Perspective,'' *Economic and Political Weekly*, VI (May 29, 1971), M 59–M 62. For the career of a free merchant see Hilton Brown, *Parrys of Madras* (Madras, 1954), S. B. Singh, *European Agency Houses in Bengal* (Calcutta, 1966) is a comprehensive account of its subject matter. N. K. Sinha, ''Sources and Problems of Business History in India in the First Half of the 19th Century,'' Indian Historical Records Commission, *Proceedings of the 37th Session*, XXXVII (Delhi, 1966), 75–79, discusses the Bengal partnerships during 1832–47.

10. Rungta, *Rise of Business Corporations in India, 33.*

11. *Ibid,* 18–35.

12. Government of India, *Proceedings of the Legislative Council of India for the year 1857* (Calcutta, 1858), 603.

13. This observation is based on the perusal of the financial records of a number of mill companies in Ahmedabad. The dilution of the family holdings in the mill companies took place mainly after the First World War. Also, the companies which started after the war had much larger public participation than was the case previously.

14. Rutnagur, *Bombay Industries*, 1927, 49.

15. H. N. Sinha, *Early European Banking in India* (Allahabad, 1927), 4. While most writers trace the origin of the managing agency system to the British enterprise, Blair B. Kling, ''The Origin of the Managing Agency System in India,'' *Journal of Asian Studies*, XXVI (November 1966), 37–47 holds that an Indian firm, Carr Tagore Co., was the first example of the system.

16. In addition to the Carr Tagore Company, which Blair B. Kling thinks contained the elements of the managing agency structure, some insurance companies in Bengal, according to Rungta, were managed under a system similar to managing agency. See Rungta, *The Rise of Business Corporation in India*, 223–26. Rungta, however, stands on questionable ground.

17. Rutnagur, *Bombay Industries*, 9.

18. Vera Anstey, *Economic Development of India* (London, 1957), 113.

19. P. S. Lokanathan, *Industrial Organization in India* (Longton, 1935), 13–40; 214–233. Other works which stress this point are Raj K. Nigam, *Managing Agencies in India* (Delhi, 1957); S. K. Basu, *The Managing Agency System* (Calcutta, 1858); Andrew F. Brimmer, ''The Setting of Entrepreneurship in India,'' *Quarterly Journal of Economics*, LXIX (November 1955), 551–576.

20. For a fuller discussion see Dwijendra Tripathi, *The Dynamics of a*

Tradition: Kasturbhai Lalbhai and His Entrepreneurship (New Delhi, 1981).

21. For a sample see, "The Bombay Cotton Mills: Their Defects in Management and How to Remedy Them," *Indian Textile Journal*, V (November 1894 to June 1895); Between 1898 and 1903, *Prajabandhu*, published in Ahmedabad, published a number of articles alluding to the alleged misdeeds of the mill agents.

22. S. D. Mehta, *Cotton Mills of India*, 52.

23. Loknathan, *Industrial Organization in India*, 179–80.

24. Government of India, *Minority Report, Indian Central Banking Enquiry Committee* (Delhi, 1931), Vol. I, Pt. II, 329.

25. M. J. Mehta, "Ranchhodlal Chhotalal and the Ahmedabad Cotton Textile Industry," 148–251.

26. Most of the mills floated in the last quarter of the 19th and the early years of the 20th centuries were started by the old banking houses. For a fuller discussion see M. J. Mehta, "Ranchhodlal Chhotalal and the Ahmedabad Cotton Textile Industry," 148–251.

27. S. D. Mehta, *Cotton Mills of India*, 82; 133–35.

28. For a discussion on social—cultural ethos of Ahmedabad see. Kenneth L. Gillion, *Ahmedabad: A Study in Indian Urban History* (Berkeley, 1968).

29. A. K. Rice, *Productivity and Social Organization: The Ahmedabad Experiment* (London, 1958), 18–22.

COMMENTS

1

Douglas A. Farnie
University of Manchester

Professor Tripathi has examined the formative years in the history of the Indian textile industry when the country rapidly built up, during an era of free trade, the largest cotton mill industry in Asia. The magnitude of that achievement may be measured in the comparative statistics assembled in 1899 by F. von Juraschek, showing that India possessed in 1896 the sixth largest cotton spindle-age and the third largest average size of spinning mill in the world. Such an achievement cannot be explained simply in terms of a favorable conjuncture but must have been based upon a superior factor-endowment and upon a high quality of entrepreneurship.

Eschewing a purely technological interpretation of the process, Professor Tripathi sets the technical aspect in a wider perspective. Thus India became, through the medium of Tata, a pioneer of ring spinning and supplied Platt Brothers of Oldham with its third largest foreign market, after Russia and Germany, during the forty years 1873–1913. India also ranked as the largest single foreign market for British exports of textile machinery during the thirty years 1904–33 and so injected a new element into the Anglo-Indian economic symbiosis.

In emphasizing the respects wherein India deviated from the British pattern and made a series of significant and successful innovations, the author has tended to prefer a socio-cultural to a purely economic interpretation, relating the introduction of the managing agency from 1854 to the pervasive influence of the family system. Even the joint stock company, adopted from 1859, had initially to adapt to the strength of kinship links. Ahmedabad developed its mill industry in competition with that of Bombay under the influence of its established banking houses and on a distinctive basis of loan deposits ranking for a share in the agency's commission. It also maintained harmonious labor relations in a community deeply committed to the Jain and Vaishnava values of peace. The author's perceptive study of the differences between two great centers of production is one that might well repay imitation.

Professor Tripathi has clearly revealed the contrast between Britain and India as well as that between Bombay and Ahmedabad. He has thrown a searching light upon one of the greatest transformations in the world's economic history, by which India transformed itself, through indigenous enterprise and in its own distinctive style, from Lancashire's largest customer into a formidable competitor.

2

Shin-ichi Yonekawa
Hitotsubashi University

Professor Tripathi's paper was most stimulating mainly because he is interested not only in the technological but also in the institutional transformation of the industry, an area I have long been interested in. His mention of the family element in Indian business is also most suggestive to Japanese scholars.

As far as the birth of the Indian textile industry is concerned, I would like to repeat that barriers were tremendously high. What he pointed out was that despite this, the Indian cotton industry was able to become prosperous. In this regard I agree with his argument.

He mentioned five items of Indian entrepreneurship: (1) the early adoption of ring spindles, (2) the early prevalence of limited companies, (3) the introduction of a managing agency system, (4) the introduction of a loan system different from that in England, and (5) Ahmedabad's peaceful labor-capital relationship.

Although his references are very pertinent, I would like to add some facts not mentioned in his paper to make our discussion more productive.

(1)   In terms of the adoption of rings it is indeed true that a few Indian entrepreneurs were quick to use them. As I mentioned in my paper, the unanswered question remains why other managers were slow in following them, compared with those in Japan. Presumably this stemmed from Lancashire's influence.

(2)   As for the prevalence of limited companies, Dr. Farnie could comment more directly. It seems to me that, after all consideration, it occurred simultaneously with that in England, and not before. According to my survey, before the Companies Act of 1862 there were already around forty cotton spinning and/or weaving companies based on the Companies Act of 1856. Moreover, in the last century yarns exported to India were largely produced by public companies limited concentrated in the Oldham and Rochdale districts, although almost all of the weaving firms were partnerships.

(3)   I agree with Professor Tripathi that the agency system was an institutional innovation. However it would be difficult to say until what time this system was essential in introducing capital to industries. Although there is no definite evidence that ordinary company management was better in India than this system, a probable answer would be that sooner or later this system became instead a barrier to better company management. I have some evidence supporting this. My survey of company files stocked at the Company Registration Office of Bombay showed that among eleven companies established before 1880 whose records survive, Central India and Bombay Dyeing, two companies of superior performance, were not under a managing agency's control in the last century. The former introduced it with J. N. Tata's death and the latter when the firm set on the management of its spinning mill in 1906. This suggests that the system was necessary to attract

initial capital but was not necessarily good for company management.

(5)   It is certain that P. S. Lokanathan referred to public loans in the Bombay cotton industry. However I could not find such evidence supporting his argument in the last century, that is, during the formative period of the industry. I do not know whether or not my idea is right but I think that the loan system was characteristic of Ahmedabad in the period considered, just as was peaceful labor-capital cooperation.

Last of all, I agree with the author's opinion that it is meaningless to suppose that the spinning industry was a primary innovation in England while it was an "adaptive innovation" in India. I would like to say, however, that it is entirely different from my distinction between "innovative" and "imitative" firms. Through my survey of four countries I became aware that a number of spinning firms came into being as a result of floating booms, and at that time there were one or two firms on which other firms were modelled. Sun Mill and Osaka Spinning Company are the best examples. So the next important things to consider are the speed of diffusion and the continuance of an innovative firm's creativity or the emergence of a new innovative firm.

Of course, these points I have touched upon are rather trivial compared with what Professor Tripathi has contributed in his excellent paper, especially since I am almost entirely unfamiliar with the business climate of the Indian cotton industry about which he is a real expert. It would therefore be most appreciated if he could add a few points which he thinks are important in order to understand this.

Changing Patterns of Management
in the Lowell Mills

Heidi Vernon Wortzel
Northeastern University

Every now and then historians are exposed to a large and powerful organizing idea. The strength of this idea is that it can be used to explain disparate materials that would be hard to handle otherwise. For some time, the establishment and subsequent management of the textile industry in Lowell, Massachusetts, has piqued the interest of researchers, but placing its managerial changes in the context of the larger development of American business has presented problems of organization and analysis. In 1977, Alfred D. Chandler, Jr., wrote *The Visible Hand*, in which he describes how and why the visible hand of management replaced the invisible hand of market forces in American business. Using Chandler's paradigm, I have attempted to fit the changes that took place in the management of the Lowell firms to the larger picture of American business history. Although one is tempted to mold the data to fit into a construct as persuasive as Chandler's, there is no way to tuck in the ends and corners of the Lowell story. With this in mind, I have related events in the Lowell corporations to Chandler's work as carefully and closely as possible, while acknowledging that there are ragged bits of the story that must be explained in other ways.

Chandler outlines his big idea in a series of general propositions, one of which describes the process by which original entrepreneurs lost or relinquished control of the firms they founded and were gradually replaced by professional managers. Usually the pattern was this. A small group of investors, linked by family or business, formed an enterprise in which they held most of the stock. Meeting

informally, as well as formally, these men developed a strategy
for their firm that was based on common experience and goals.
Almost from the start, however, they were unable to devote enough
time and energy to the affairs of the fledgling company. Sometimes
they appointed a relative or younger protégé as manager, but
more often they hired an outside officer to share the decision-
making responsibility.

Soon independent investors, who cared only about regular and
generous dividends, bought shares. They did not want to assume
the task of managing, nor did they have the expertise or commitment to make decisions for the firm. Even though founders and their
families continued to serve on the board of directors and to hold
veto power, salaried managers made day-to-day decisions. As the
entrepreneurs became less involved, managers came to dominate
and, eventually, to control the enterprise.

When large amounts of capital were needed to operate the
firm, founders would often invite an outside financial institution
to invest, in return for a position on the board of directors. While
the principals of the institution might have participated in the
affairs of the firm in the beginning, their active involvement
diminished along with that of the entrepreneurs. Both groups
began to look upon the business as a source of income rather than
as an enterprise to be managed.[1]

At first the textile industry in Lowell followed Chandler's paradigm. Between 1821 and 1839, Boston-based merchant-importers
formed ten large textile corporations. By the 1840s, only a score
of years after the first company was incorporated, entrepreneurial
involvement in the firms had begun to diminish. Original investors
lost interest, retired, or died, and were replaced by inexperienced
family members or outside managers. Large blocks of stock were
sold by disinterested heirs to new investors whose only concern
was a regular and generous declaration of dividends.

In partnership with the corporations, selling agencies acted as
financial institutions to provide a variety of services. They secured
discounted bank loans that manufacturing companies could not
procure on their own. In addition, they furnished much of the
money for payrolls, dividends, and raw materials. In return, the

agents were given stock, directorships, and a monopoly on the sales of Lowell textiles. As time went on, selling agents also became less interested in participating in textile company management. They or their successors sold off much of their stock in the manufacturing firms, while retaining their monopoly on the sale of finished goods. No longer receiving payment through dividends, they began to take exorbitant commissions on the sales of the goods.

In the late 1850s and early 1860s, a diversion unique to Lowell sidetracked the smooth progression of Chandler's paradigm. Led by James C. Ayer, a group of Lowell stockholders tried to return management to the collegial, entrepreneurial pattern. This time, they, not the Boston group, would be in control. The American Civil War, which coincided with Ayer's attempt, brought the textile industry in Lowell to a complete halt. Financial losses that accompanied the work stoppages merely confirmed the Lowell group's conviction that Boston-based financiers had abrogated their responsibility toward the firms they managed.

In spite of the strife and discord generated by the efforts of the Lowell contingent, very little was actually done to retard the loss of control by entrepreneurs. The first part of Chandler's paradigm fits the Lowell experience, although the change to professional management was never completed while the corporations remained in the city.

I. From Harmonious Beginnings to Family Quarrels, 1810–1857

The manufacture of cotton textiles in New England began in a desultory fashion during the first decade of the nineteenth century. The mills that were scattered around the hinterland were poorly financed, used primitive machinery, and had almost no outlet for their finished products. Before 1812, most textiles sold in the United States were made of American cotton that had been woven in England. The goods were then imported by the same merchants who had sent the raw cotton across the Atlantic.

The outbreak of war between the United States and England

provided the stimulus for these merchant-importers to reassess their role in the textile trade. Even though the American government imposed heavy duties or embargoes on the textiles, most importers circumvented the restrictions by shipping to Canada or by placing their vessels under a neutral flag. Nevertheless, governmental policy cut deeply into their profits.

A group of merchant-importers led by Nathan Appleton began to plan a stable, large-scale American textile industry as a way of reducing its reliance on British imports. The major problem to be overcome was the woeful inadequacy of American technology. British manufacturers had successfully prevented the exportation of machinery plans abroad, although they stole processes and plans freely from one another.

Appleton had the foresight and good fortune to discuss his ideas with Francis Cabot Lowell, who was also fascinated by the prospect of starting an American textile industry. The two men travelled to England and Scotland, visiting as many factories as would let them in. Lowell spent many days studying the machinery of the Lancashire mills and memorizing the details of their operation. When he returned to Boston, Lowell and mechanic Paul Moody constructed a power loom very similar to the English model but with enough changes to warrant a patent.[2]

In 1813, the Massachusetts General Court accepted a petition to grant to Francis Cabot Lowell, Nathan Appleton, and their associates corporate status under the name of the Boston Manufacturing Company. According to Frances Gregory's exhaustive study of Nathan Appleton, the proprietors, who were also called the Boston Associates, thought of their corporation just as Chandler's paradigm suggests they would. The firm would be sort of an enlarged partnership in which they would "pursue a business at mutual risk and for mutual profit."[3]

It is interesting that the entrepreneurs formed a corporation rather than a partnership, the latter being by far the most prevalent form of legal association at the time. Gregory speculates that the incorporators were not greatly concerned about protecting themselves against risk and liability. The primary reason for choosing the corporate structure, she maintains, was that the associates hoped to obtain a banking license which would ensure financial support for the textile companies. Banks had to be incorporated under state law, and the entrepreneurs may have believed that their petition for the license would be granted more readily if the manufacturing establishments were also incorporated. Although the banking license was denied, Appleton felt that a corporation made potential investors feel more secure about the safety of their money in this speculative venture.[4]

The Boston Associates found a suitable site for their first mill on the Charles River in Waltham. By 1815, the company was making coarse sheetings, which it sold in a Boston shop. When the profits on the first lots of goods proved to be very poor, Appleton suggested that the next batch be sold through his newly-formed partnership with Ward and Company. Soon Ward was selling everything the Waltham mill could make, while realizing a substantial profit for both himself and the manufacturer.

By 1821, the flow of the Charles River could not produce enough water power to run the now-expanded manufacturing operation. The Associates began to search for a new site upon which they could build a complex of mills to make a variety of products.

The Merrimack River and connecting Pawtucket Canal had recently been turned into a backwater because of the completion of the Middlesex Canal, which was now the main waterway from Newburyport to Boston. After purchasing the Pawtucket Canal, river rights, and adjoining land in the fall of 1821, some of the principals of the Boston Manufacturing Company applied to the legislature for a new corporation, the Merrimack Manufacturing Company. This enterprise and the nine others that were built within the next eighteen years were organized and run in the form that Chandler terms entrepreneurial or family businesses.

The managerial structure of these new enterprises was unique in one respect. The corporations were linked horizontally by interlocking directorates. This structure appears to have been the outgrowth of the entrepreneurs' desire to make the textile business in Lowell a harmonious, friendly undertaking among peers. Together they could decide upon the product to be made by each company so that all would prosper. Because there were a limited number of participants in each venture, it seemed appropriate that they should sit on several boards at once.

The formation of all the companies followed the same pattern. After the Merrimack was incorporated and production was under way, promoters began to plan a second company to make a different kind of fabric. Those who had invested in the Merrimack were given first option to buy Hamilton Company stock. With the establishment of each subsequent company, the circle of investors grew, although most were still part of the Boston merchant-importer group. In each case, after the stock was sold, the principals adopted a set of by-laws that formally organized the firm's management structure and described the duties of its officers. Without exception, management was highly centralized and lines of authority were clearly delineated.

The board of directors was composed of seven men, two of whom were the treasurer and the selling agent. Although an elected president presided over meetings, his function was largely ceremonial and did not carry any special authority. Only the board could declare dividends and set company policy. The board had the final word on expenditures, salaries, and accounting procedures. In addition, it was legally responsible for the solvency of the firm.

As the chief operating officer, the treasurer had general care of bookkeeping and making up of the semi-annual accounts that were presented to the board prior to the declaration of dividends. Through a vast network of correspondence, the treasurer ordered raw cotton from his agents in the South, machinery from both domestic and foreign makers, and coal from Pennsylvania. Needles, dyes, oil, and other materials came from a variety of sources around this country and abroad.

The treasurer kept abreast of work in Lowell through daily correspondence with the resident manager or agent of the mill. Flood, drought, strikes, and a hundred other details were discussed in their letters. Once a week the treasurer boarded the Boston & Lowell Railroad for the nearly thirty-mile trip to Lowell. There, in the spartan mill office, he and the agent took care of matters they were unable or unwilling to resolve in their letters.

The treasurer also kept in touch with the selling agency to make sure that the company's goods were properly stored and sold. As compensation, this busy man received a salary and some stock, but it was clear that the directors were aware that the job had its seductive aspects. Each treasurer, no matter how great his personal wealth, was required to post a bond of $35,000 to protect the company against possible malfeasance.

The physical plant in Lowell was managed by an agent who hired and fired operatives, maintained equipment, and kept track of goods from the time they entered the mill yard until they were shipped to the selling agent. Although the agent had prestige and power in Lowell, he was really just a highly skilled, salaried technician so far as the Boston directors were concerned. He did not help them set policy, nor was he privy to their meetings. In fact, the only formal contact most agents had with the directors was during the semi-annual inspection trip to the mill. In all matters, the mill agent consulted the treasurer, at whose pleasure he served.

The marketing function was the responsibility of the selling agent, who determined where the goods were sold and how much of each kind the mill should make. Because B. C. Ward, the first selling agent of the Waltham Company, was unable to handle the quantity of goods that poured out of the new Lowell factories, Appleton dissolved their partnership. In 1829, he formed a new partnership with James W. Paige, a successful importer of British fabrics. J. W. Paige & Company took over the sales of the Merrimack, Hamilton, Appleton, and Suffolk mills, as well as some Lowell Company textiles. Preferring to spread his risks, in case the selling agent went bankrupt, Nathan Appleton formed a second partnership, this time with selling agents A. & A. Lawrence. The new agency handled the output of the Boott and Tremont mills and the remaining Lowell Company goods. In addition to conducting the actual sales, the agents provided money for operating expenses and took care of some bookkeeping chores for the mills.

Until the early 1840s, outwardly harmonious relations continued between the mill directors and the other stockholders. Management remained in the hands of the Appletons, Lowells, Jacksons, Lawrences, and other early investors, in spite of the participation of a growing number of small stockholders. But a fall in mill profits between 1840 and 1843 created some uneasiness among stockholders about the way in which their investments were managed.

For the first time, two factions of directors quarrelled openly over a variety of managerial issues. It must be stressed that this dispute was not part of the later movement away from entrepreneurial ownership. Rather, it was an internal struggle that was significant because it marked the first time that disagreement had publicly surfaced among the founders.

Henry Lee, Sr., a leader of one group of managing stockholders, charged that another group, gathered around Nathan Appleton, had mismanaged the affairs of the companies they both directed. Lee averred that friendship, rather than competitive bidding, determined who received contracts for raw materials. Accounting procedures were sloppy, he declared, and, worst of all, he and his friends did not receive salaries for their directorships, although Appleton and his group did.[5]

Lee's dissatisfaction may have been due in part to the long-lasting effect of the 1837 depression on the textile industry as a whole. The non-competitive climate among the mills had already begun to break down. Each company had adjusted its looms to manufacture whatever products it could sell. Lee seemed convinced that the companies in which both he and Appleton owned shares had not done well enough in the depression, when compared to other mills.

The essence of the conflict was that each group wanted the largest possible return on its investment. Lee's complaints about accounting and bidding were used as arguments to force Appleton to take less himself and to allot more to Lee. When Appleton and his coterie agreed to a salary reduction, that ended the strife. Neither group wanted to spoil their overlapping business arrangements and years of friendship.

Even into the early 1850s, the management of the Lowell corporations still fit comfortably into the first stage of Chandler's paradigm. Although changes were taking place, entrepreneurial founders who had enjoyed close personal and professional associations for many years still tried to sustain their cooperative control of the firms. Quarrels and misunderstandings, such as the Lee–Appleton affair, were resolved within the corporate family.

As the influence of the original investors waned in the late 1840s and 1850s, there was no cadre of well-trained personnel to assume responsibility for management. Neither the new stockholders nor the selling agents were willing or able to undertake the task of guiding the enterprises. Finally, in the period after the 1857 depression, a new Lowell-based group of stockholders began to gain in strength and influence.

II. New Critics of Old Policies, 1858–1859

Between the time of the so-called "Golden Age" of Lowell in the 1830s and the early 1850s, directors, stockholders, and selling agents, all of whom had significant influence on the way Lowell firms were managed, either lost or relinquished control. First-generation directors had each owned large blocks of stock when the companies were founded. When the Hamilton Company was incorporated, for example, only fifty-five people held the $600,000 in stock. Founders of other companies each owned between twenty-five and one hundred shares valued at $1,000 per share. In the 1840s, their successors owned only an average of three shares each.[6] As their amount of stock diminished, so did their interest in the companies.

New stockholders, who usually had one or two shares in a company, did not have the experience or the commitment to take part in management. By the late 1840s, their lack of interest and involvement was obvious. At an annual meeting of the Merrimack Manufacturing Company, no more than twelve of the two thousand stockholders bothered to vote. Knowing little about textile manufacturing and caring primarily about the income from dividends, they signed over their proxy votes to those few directors who were still active managers.

There was further deterioration of the entrepreneurial pattern as the directors of the sales agencies withdrew from the management of the manufacturing firms. When the marketing function had been closely integrated, even though legally separate, selling agents and manufacturing firms had operated together to ensure a mutual profit. As the original organizers and partners in the selling agencies died or retired, however, they were replaced by men who did not have business connections or personal ties with the mill directors. Moreover, these new men owned little, if any, stock in the manufacturing companies. The new managers of the sales agencies placed Lowell textiles wherever and however they could in order to make the greatest commission, regardless of what that meant to the manufacturer.

The 1857 depression was devastating for the textile companies, and even though business picked up in the spring of 1858, most of the companies did not have enough money to declare dividends. Although only the Middlesex Woolen Company actually went bankrupt, all the firms suffered financially. A new group of Lowell-based stockholders, who were irate over the way in which Boston entrepreneurs had guided the companies during the depression, began to criticize the directors openly. Chandler's paradigm suggests that small stockholders should not have been interested or powerful enough to try to make substantive changes in the way the firms were administered. Yet, for a time, these dissidents, with their strong-willed leader, did just that.

The coalition of Lowell stockholders that began to investigate the management practices of Boston-based directors and selling agents was motivated by more than reduced or cancelled dividends. Textile companies were the major industry in the city and the basis of its fiscal well-being. These stockholders owned a variety of non-textile businesses such as foundries, drug stores, dry goods emporiums, machine shops, and small mills. All of them were tied economically to their giant brick neighbors. When the corporations were healthy, the rest of Lowell prospered. Conversely, when the corporations suffered, as they did in the 1857 depression, the welfare of Lowell's small businesses was imperiled.

The leader of the Lowell group was an inimitable character named James Cook Ayer. When Ayer was eleven years old, his father, a Connecticut woolen manufacturer, died. After a short stint in the family mill, the young teenager came to Lowell to live with his uncle, James Cook, agent of the Middlesex Woolen

Company. Ayer graduated from Lowell high School but failed to persuade a local politician to sponsor his appointment to West Point. After his application to his second choice of college, Dartmouth, was turned down, Ayer decided to undertake his own program of education. Working as many as twelve hours a day as an apprentice apothecary, Ayer read every book in the Harvard University undergraduate curriculum.[7] While the reading program doubtless contributed to his intellectual development, Ayer's business acumen was already stropped to a fine edge. Within a few years he owned the apothecary shop where he had trained and had begun a patent medicine business. By the mid-1850s, Ayer's *American Almanac*, full of folksy wisdom and advice, advertised his remedies to ailing millions all over the world.[8]

There were probably a variety of reasons why Ayer bought stock in the textile firms of his adopted city. His uncle had been fired as agent of the Middlesex after the 1857 crash, and it is likely that Ayer was looking for some way to retaliate against the Boston owners of the company. Certain that the firms were being mismanaged, Ayer intended to participate in company affairs to restore what he considered the old and proper relationship between owner and manager.

Chandler interprets the dilution of stockholdings and the concomitant loss of director interest as a phenomenon that occurred in many industries over a long period of time and which presaged a new order of professional management. Ayer, whose experience was limited to one industry over a very short span, was convinced that this trend meant the end of prosperity of the textile industry in Lowell. The mills were in trouble, Ayer concluded, because their directors had abandoned their original concept of management. In the beginning, he maintained, the businesses had done so well because they were organized and run by a few men who worked together as co-owners. In the 1850s, however,

> the present stockholders, instead of having as the original owners did, a personal and intimate acquaintance, rarely know each other at all. They have bought their shares as an investment, and with the delusive hope that somebody is interested in it [the business] who can and will take care of it.[9]

Even if Ayer could have conceived of the concept of professional management, he surely would have rejected it. He was certain that unless one owned his firm, he would not have the interest or commitment to devote himself completely to its affairs. Doubtless, Ayer would have preferred to run the companies as proprietorships or partnerships rather than as corporations. Having shares in a firm removed the manager from the direct involvement Ayer deemed so necessary. But, while Ayer might have liked another form philosophically, he did accept the inevitability of the structure already in place. Purification, not elimination, became his key to responsible management.

After the 1857 depression brought on the collapse of the Middlesex, the company was reorganized and recapitalized with Ayer as a major stockholder. It was with this firm that he decided to begin his investigation of improper management. After inspecting the books, Ayer filed a formal complaint at the annual meeting in January 1859. Finding that he had insufficient support to force through an investigation, Ayer took his charges to the Massachusetts State Legislative Committee on Manufactures. In February, he testified that before the bankruptcy of the company, Samuel Lawrence, who was then treasurer, had tampered with the books to hide a deficit of over $100,000. Lawrence's defaulted bond had never been paid, even though it had been co-signed by his brother, selling agent Abbott Lawrence. Even after the reorganization and installation of new officers in 1858, no one made payment or took legal action against treasurer Lawrence. The legislative committee, which was probably packed with Lawrence family supporters, ignored Ayer's testimony. Ayer, always pragmatic, dropped his complaint in favor of investigating other issues.[10]

Reorganization of the Middlesex included the establishment of a new organizational structure that was unique in Lowell textile companies. The firm fired its selling agent and gave its own treasurer the task of placing the finished goods. The company was thereby able to tie the treasurer's compensation directly to the company's profits. Lowell historian Charles Cowley wrote later that "by this arrangement, the business of selling was kept under the company's control, and the interest of the selling agent made identical with those of the Company."[11] For the first time, the directors of a Lowell textile firm gave the operating officer a direct monetary incentive to increase the profits. Apparently it worked well. For many years thereafter, the percentage profits of the Middlesex exceeded those of any other company in Lowell.

It is tempting to speculate about why this arrangement, which worked so well for the Middlesex, was not copied by the giant cotton corporations. Generally, forward integration into marketing does not take place unless existing marketers cannot do the job efficiently. This was not the case in the sales of the Middlesex goods. Although the agency of A. & A. Lawrence had not sold the textiles advantageously and had defaulted on the treasurer's bond, there were other selling agents that were well qualified to conduct the business. Giving the task to the treasurer seems to have been a serendipitous experiment that the large cotton corporations would not have needed to emulate.

Cotton corporations shipped thousands and thousands of yards of material each week to their New York and Boston agents. No treasurer, however energetic, would have been able to add the duty of selecting buyers to the tremendous number of tasks for which he was already responsible. The output of the Middlesex was minuscule compared to that of the cotton companies, which was the only reason the arrangement was possible.

Even if forward integration were not applicable to the cotton corporations, reformer stockholders concluded that they still needed to find some way to align the interests of the selling agent more closely to those of the manufacturer. Their efforts led to a re-examination of the interaction between manufacturer and selling agent.

The relationship between the firms had changed over the years. As the close social and financial ties disappeared, so did their mutual aims. Chandler describes the process in the following paragraph:

> As the family- and financier-controlled enterprises grew in size and age they became managerial. Unless the owners or representatives of financial houses [in this case, selling agencies] became full-time career managers within the enterprise itself,

they did not have the information, the time, or the experience to play a dominant role in top-level decisions. As members of the boards of directors they did hold veto power. They could say no, and they could replace the senior managers with other career managers; but they were rarely in a position to propose alternative solutions. In time, the part-time owners and financiers on the board normally looked on the enterprise in the same way as did ordinary stockholders. It became a source of income and not a business to be managed.[12]

Ayer and his group, realizing that some profound change was taking place in the way in which selling agencies and manufacturing plants were relating, began to investigate conditions in the Lowell (Carpet) Company. They were more interested in the mechanism by which the goods were sold than in policies affecting the manufacture. At the annual meeting in January 1859, the directors appointed a committee composed of Ayer and his people to determine whether the goods could be sold more profitably and efficiently in Boston and Lowell by a salaried agent than in New York through a branch of A. & A. Lawrence.

For some time, A. & A. Lawrence had been in charge of marketing all of the Lowell Company's output and had gradually increased its commissions on sales. When the agency heard that an investigation was underway, it hurriedly lowered the commissions, although the commissions still remained higher than those of other selling agents. Ayer and his group, calling the commissions exploitative, attributed their high level to the withdrawal of the original founders of the Lawrence Company from policy-making positions. With the deaths of Amos and Abbott Lawrence, the committee charged, "we are paying our proportion of a tribute over twice as large as the house received when its able founders were living and active in it." Although more than five-sixths of the goods of the Lowell Company were sold in New York, only one of the five partners of the selling agency lived there, and he supervised the sales of seven firms in addition to those of the Lowell Company.[13] A. & A. Lawrence received its commissions based on the quantity of goods sold, rather than on a percentage of the price the textiles brought. The committee accused the agency of taking advantage of this mode of business by dumping the material in auction houses just to get rid of it.

The system could be eliminated, the committee suggested, by having the company appoint its own salaried agent to arrange the sales instead. This novel proposal for integration of the marketing function was flatly turned down by the directors, who thanked the committee for its report and ignored its recommendations completely. For the time being, Ayer did not have enough votes to push through his reforms. Frustrated but resolute, he determined to gather enough evidence of mismanagement so that it would be impossible for the directors to ignore him. The outbreak of the Civil War and subsequent strategy of the Boston-based directors provided Ayer and his band with ample data.

III.   Wartime Strategy and Managerial Reform, 1861–1863

As soon as war was declared in April, 1861, the Boston directors began to examine Lowell's competitive position in the New England textile industry. Several things were clear. Lowell's physical plants were nearly obsolescent, in spite of additions and repairs. New technology and buildings made textile manufacturing in other cities far more efficient. In any case, Lowell's mills were unsuited to the manufacture of military materiel. Because uniforms and blankets were made of wool or a mixture of wool and cotton, new machinery would have to be set up and new operatives hired to work it. Retooling would take six months to a year, about as long as everyone expected the war to last. Far better, the directors decided, to double the capacity of the mills and buy new cotton machinery in order to be ready for the expected post-war boom.

They agreed that construction of this magnitude would be very expensive, but, fortunately, they possessed a readily convertible asset. All of the mills had at least a six-months' supply of raw cotton in storage. When the treasurers had bought the cotton, they had paid ten cents per pound. Within eight months after the war started, the price per pound had risen to thirty-two cents. If they sold their cotton to other mills in New England better suited to wartime production, the Lowell companies would have more than enough cash to pay for buildings and machinery.

For many of the directors, the sales of their stored cotton meant little more than a rearrangement of their assets. Years earlier, numbers of the Boston group had become principals in cotton mills all over New England. If companies in Lawrence, Lewiston, and Biddeford could make material from Lowell cotton, they would make a handsome profit anyway. As a group, the managers of the Lowell mills decided to sell the staple and to close down the factories.

Within six months, it became apparent that the directors' plan was going away. In the summer of 1862, the war was just warming up, not concluding. Mills in Massachusetts, Maine and New Hampshire ran on Lowell cotton, switching from fabric to fabric as the public and army demanded. While Lowell looms remained silent, independent stockholders grew restive. A simple miscalculation in timing began to look like a grave error as cotton reached ninety-two cents per pound in January, 1863. This was nearly sixty cents more per pound than the price for which the staple had been sold. Now that the directors realized that the war would drag on far beyond their original expectation, it was too late to change their strategy.

The situation was quickly exploited by the same group of Lowell-based stockholders who had made such a commotion in 1858 and 1859. Although they were delighted to receive the large dividends that had been paid after the cotton sales, they were eager to use the faulty judgment of the Boston capitalists to effect real changes in administration. Calling the miscalculation of the directors only one example of long-term mismanagement, Ayer and his people launched a new attack. This time they were supported by local people, who now owned a substantial proportion of the total number of shares in some Lowell companies.

From the beginning, Ayer's plan had been to test issue after issue until he found one he could win. In 1858, when his censure of Samuel Lawrence came to nothing, he moved on to criticizing the sales practices of the Lowell (Carpet) Company. In 1862, Ayer again chose a cause. This time it was reform of the proxy voting procedures, a rallying point for local support. If Ayer could arrange for Lowell stockholders to take part in decisions concerning the companies, he could restore the original and proper relationship between stockholders and management.

Although annual meetings had been poorly attended in the late 1840s, a decade later stockholders were clamoring to take part. Worried about their shrinking or non-existent dividends, as many as six hundred stockholders tried to gain entrance to a room designed to hold between forty and sixty people. They were excluded and their proxy votes were collected in a very devious way. As each stockholder entered the treasurer's office to collect his dividends, he was instructed to sign two papers, which he would assume were both receipt forms. When he was unable to squeeze into the jammed meeting room, the stockholder would leave and the proxy vote, which he had unknowingly signed, would be voted by a director.

By 1860, proxy collection had become such a scandal that a bill for reform, supported wholeheartedly by Ayer, was passed by the state legislature. The new law stated that not more than twenty votes could be held by any one officer and that all stock would be divided into shares of $100, instead of $1,000 each. With the new law in effect, no one holding proxies could vote more than $2,000 worth of stock. Most treasurers ignored the new law altogether and quickly organized a campaign to have the law repealed. In the next session, legislators passed the repeal, leaving Ayer thwarted once again.

Frustrated but tenacious, Ayer turned his attention to what he charged was grave mismanagement by J. W. Paige and Company in its handling of Hamilton Company sales. Paige had been one of the entrepreneurs and board members who had invested heavily in the stock of the manufacturing companies when they were first organized. Through the years, the number of shares held by him and members of his firm fell sharply. By the time Paige was elected as a director of the Hamilton Company in 1832, he had only five shares. In 1851, when he became a director of the Merrimack, Paige owned three shares in that company. As his holdings in the companies decreased, his commissions rose. Nathan Appleton, who was still a partner in the sales agency and who held large blocks of stock in both companies, had been able to stifle any direct opposition to Paige. But when Appleton retired in 1860, his influence quickly waned. Although Paige remained on the boards until 1862, his direct involvement in decision-making was nominal, and his primary concern was profit for his sales agency.

The Lowell Citizen & News published an account of the Hamilton's annual meeting in June, 1862. According to the newspaper, Paige's commissions from the Hamilton amounted to $20,000 per year. Added to those of the eight other companies he represented in Lowell and in other cities, his income swelled to $180,000. If true, the paper pronounced, "it is evidence of gross mismanagement on the part of those who have the direction of affairs."[14] The stockholders asked for Paige's resignation from the board of directors and replaced him with Lowell Mayor Hocum Hosford. Paige was not asked to confess any wrongdoing in his relations with the manufacturer and was allowed to retire quietly.

Encouraged by this victory and goaded to further action by the continued economic stagnation of Lowell, Ayer decided to open a full-scale attack on what he regarded as a pervasive failure of the Boston directors to manage the firms responsibly. By 1863, Ayer was one of the largest stockholders in several of the corporations. He was determined to purge the boards of Boston financiers so that he and his friends would be able to take over and restore management to the ideal state—a close and cooperative interaction among friends for the profit of all.

Ayer's pamphlet, which was published in April, 1863, was entitled *Some of the Usages and Abuses in the Management of Our Manufacturing Corporations*. In it, Ayer enumerated the instances of mismanagement which he declared had occurred in the direction of the Hamilton, Merrimack, Boott, Lowell, Middlesex, and Massachusetts Companies. He deplored the conduct of the selling agents, citing case after case in which they dumped Lowell's textiles onto the public auction market for reduced prices. Excoriating A. & A. Lawrence for its handling of the Lowell Company carpets, Ayer charged that the compensation taken by the agency was "altogether excessive—entirely beyond what is reasonable . . . for the advantages afforded and the services rendered by the firm." Even in ordinary times, it would have been too much, Ayer declared, but "through the times of discouragement to manufacturing interests which we have had, it is intolerable."[15] According to Ayer, other sales agencies were anxious to do business for less than one-half the commission charged by A. & A. Lawrence.

Chandler mentions that from the beginning, the original founders of the firms were unable to devote enough time to the affairs of their firms. In order to keep the business in the family, Lowell mill owners appointed relatives or in-laws to take over some duties. Ayer condemned nepotism, calling it "thoroughly bad." It had, he declared, "demoralized . . . administrators until they can and do unblushingly perpetrate acts which would anywhere banish them from the fellowship of honorable men."[16] Allowing for Ayer's tendency to indulge in hyperbole, it seems clear that there were several instances in which nepotism resulted in serious monetary losses for the firms.

For example, Thomas G. Cary, the treasurer of the Hamilton, had, before the war, sent his young son to the South to buy cotton. The youth paid for the cotton without examining the bales, which were filled with sand and stones. When the rubble was separated from the staple, the company found it had paid $50,000 for trash. Compounding his bad judgment, Cary ordered the entire matter expunged from the company's records.[17]

In another instance, Boott Company President William Appleton offered to furnish the corporation with money and credit if his son-in-law, Thomas Jefferson Coolidge, were elected treasurer. Coolidge had had no previous experience in managing a cotton mill. In fact, the only job he had ever held was in a mercantile business that survived the depression only because, Coolidge admitted, "our connection with wealthy men helped out our credit."[18] Ayer's real ire at Coolidge's appointment was directed at the fact that Appleton never made good on his promise. Very possibly Ayer would have been less critical if financial aid had been forthcoming.

Ayer's pamphlet created such an uproar in the newspapers that stockholders demanded that investigatory committees, packed with Ayer's supporters, be formed. The findings of the committees did result in one substantive change in the way business was conducted.

Ayer finally realized that there was no hope of recreating the close ties between the manufacturing company and the selling agency because, by 1863, all the original founders and partners of the agencies had died or retired. The new men, who had no financial or family connections with the corporations, were only interested in making as much profit as possible for the selling agencies. Ayer reasoned that if he and his associates could not restore the old system, then they would have to develop a new relationship between agent and manufacturer.

The committees therefore recommended a complete split. The selling agents became employees of the textile companies. They did not own stock, nor did they have seats on the boards of directors. Using competitive bidding, each Lowell company hired its own selling agent, putting a formal end to the cooperative informal relationship that had long since passed in fact.

Apparently there was no discussion at this time of integrating the marketing function. Selling agents did an adequate job of placing the goods, and now the manufacturer could fire the agent if his commissions became exorbitant. Treasurers, wary of giving up too much responsibility to the selling agent, took more responsibility for determining style, quality, and fashion of the goods.

Ayer and his group did not try to reorganize the internal structure of command and responsibility in the manufacturing firms. Although they held large blocks of stock in several mills, they began to concentrate their energies on the complete takeover of the Tremont and Suffolk Companies. Once again, after testing and probing, Ayer settled for the attainable goal. Although his rhetoric may have sounded quixotic, he was an intensely practical man who did not waste his efforts on unachievable ends.

The Tremont and Suffolk, located side by side, had briefly been converted to woolen and worsted manufacture during the war. In 1867, when other Lowell companies were beginning to show a profit, these two firms were still working part-time and were losing money. At the annual meeting in 1868, Ayer took control of the board of directors, fired the treasurer, and replaced him with an experienced Lowell cotton mill agent.[19] Next, he and his group applied to the state legislature for permission to consolidate the two firms. Within a year, Ayer was elected president of this new company, and his supporters controlled the board of directors.

Their election signalled a clear and final break between the original Boston owners and the new Lowell-based management.

All the storminess of the post-war period quickly dissipated as the mills of Lowell settled down to weaving the cotton cloth for which the city had become so famous. Unhappily, competition from mills in other cities and increasing labor problems prevented Lowell from ever recapturing its prewar eminence in the textile business.

If Chandler's paradigm had been played out in Lowell, the firms would have grown in size, internalized their various activities, and developed a managerial hierarchy. Salaried managers would have taken on new services and products and encouraged further growth. Instead, the structure of the companies froze in their post-Civil War stage. They remained subject to the invisible hand of market forces long after newer industries had completed the transition to managerial capitalism.

During the early twentieth century, the corporations either closed, merged with other New England firms, or moved south. By the time foreign competition forced the American textile industry to respond in a modern sense, none of the original corporations were left in Lowell. Most had simply closed their gates and gone out of business. The great significance of Chandler's work in the Lowell saga is that it provides a structure for examining the establishment of the mills and the loss of control by the original entrepreneurs. It is somewhat disappointing and anticlimactic to realize that there was no neat conclusion or completion of the process so far as Lowell was concerned. Lowell's manufacturing companies were unable or unwilling to reorganize in ways that would enable them to compete in a modern business environment.

NOTES

1. Alfred D. Chandler, Jr., *The Visible Hand* (Cambridge: Harvard University Press, 1977), pp. 9–10.
2. Frances W. Gregory, *Nathan Appleton: Merchant and Entrepreneur* (Charlottesville: University Press of Virginia, 1975), pp. 145–46.
3. *Ibid.*, p. 151.
4. *Ibid.*, pp. 147–48.
5. Paul F. McGouldrick, *New England Textiles in the Nineteenth Century* (Cambridge: Harvard University Press, 1968), p. 23.
6. Gregory, *Nathan Appleton*, p. 262; Hamilton Manufacturing Company, Proprietors' Records, December, 1824.
7. Charles A. Cowley, *Reminiscences of James C. Ayer and the Town of Ayer* (Lowell: Penhallow Printing Company, 1879), pp. 43–44.
8. James Harvey Young, *The Toadstool Millionnaires* (Princeton: Princeton University Press, 1961), p. 138.
9. James C. Ayer, *Some of the Usages and Abuses in the Management of Our Manufacturing Companies* (Lowell: C. M. Langley & Company, 1863), p. 3.
10. Cowley, *Reminiscences*, pp. 43–44.
11. Charles A. Cowley, *Illustrated History of Lowell (rev.)* (Boston: Lee & Shepard, 1868), p. 54.
12. Chandler, *The Visible Hand*, p. 10.
13. *Report of a Committee of the Stockholders of the Lowell Manufacturing Company* (Lowell: Samuel N. Merrill, Printer, 1859), pp. 4–5.
14. *Lowell Citizen & Mews*, p. 2, June 25, 1862.
15. Ayer, *Some of the Usages*, pp. 6–7.
16. *Ibid.*, p. 7.
17. *Ibid.*, p. 24.
18. Thomas Jefferson Coolidge, *The Autobiography of T. Jefferson Coolidge, 1831–1920* (Boston: Houghton Mifflin Co.), p. 11.
19. *Lowell Daily Courier*, p. 2., March 4, 1868.

COMMENTS

1

Shin-ichi Yonekawa
Hitotsubashi University

Dr. Wortzel took recent trends of business history into consideration and wrote a most insightful paper. Her paper refers to managerial problems of the nineteenth century's cotton spinning firms and is thus most stimulating to our business historians.

I am pleased to say that I have learned much from the facts that she presented about the Lowell firms, because I have been working on the history of the Fall River cotton spinning firms. In the American cotton spinning industry, the figure of spindleage in Lowell ranked first until the third quarter of the last century, when Fall River caught up with it through the floating boom of the 1870s, and then later on New Bedford did too. Despite this, some of the Lowell firms remained competitive into this century. Tables 5 and 6 of my paper show that Massachusetts mills of Pepperell and Merrimack were located in the city of Lowell.

Wortzel's paper is very pertinent and is one of the best cases for comparative study. Although it has many implications I would like to sum up a few points which I think are particularly significant. (1) After the floating booms of the 1820s and 1830s large stockholders gradually lost their interest in the management of firms. (2) However, full-time and salaried professional managers never came to Lowell at that time. The stockholders did not want to have that sort of management; they simply wanted to get back to entrepreneurial control. (3) Apart from this managerial deviation, firms succeeded in a kind of informal integration of the marketing function.

I am confident that, generally speaking, integration, both process and functional, was achieved comparatively early in the American cotton industry. One of Dr. Wortzel's contributions was her illustration of the process in detail; a rare case, I think. The problem is the other side of Prof. Chandler's paradigm: the growth of modern managerial organization along with the birth of a managerial elite. In this regard I have not been able to obtain a general view so far of the organizational development of American textile firms. They seem for the most part not to have had complicated organizations, so we have to pay attention to the control of the managerial elite at the same time.

The development of firms in Fall River would be interesting to compare with those in Lowell. Founded during the same period, the firms had been controlled by general entrepreneurs through their concessions as landowners until the 1850s. The successful adoption of steam engines weakened their influence and a new sort of entrepreneur settled in the city, initiating the floating boom in the 1870s. This boom made the difference between these two cities, as Lowell never experienced such a boom. In the course of the great depression the cotton industry in Fall River was wielded by outside influences which were entirely beyond the power of local entrepreneurs. The Fall River Iron Works emerged as an integrated firm, though not in the legal sense of the word, and many of the firms which could not consolidate their production and marketing functions lost their positions afterwards. In this period many of them went into bankruptcy. As J. Shumpeter said, the existing firms' death was very important to make the industrial structure dynamic. Public companies in Lancashire on the solid foundation of cooperative management, having no close connection with banks, managed to survive the great depression, except in a very few cases, but it seems to have made the industrial structure rigid. Please give some suggestions on the Lowell industry during the depressed period of the 1870s–1880s, if possible.

Last of all I would like to mention what I think was most interesting: the commission of the selling agency and the existence of the mill agent. It was said that the commission was based on the quantity of goods sold. This is actually similar to the commission of the managing agency in India, and it seems that this Indian system was not as anomalous as it has sometimes been considered. Managing agents in India were both mill agents and selling agents, and mill agents in the U.S.A. were salaried managers. Indian managing agents and American selling agents gave financial support to spinning firms.

One of the things that interested the participants in this conference seemed to be the relationship between the spinning company and the selling agent. This relation may be measured as a percentage based on the price the textile brought, because the commission based on the quantity of goods sold can be roughly calculated into the above-mentioned figure. I have been researching the commission of Japanese trading companies for the export of cotton goods, but so far without success. A friend specializing in the history of the Indian cotton industry wrote in his book that 1/3 anna per pound commission in late nineteenth century India would be roughly 3.5% commission, and if I am not wrong, a yarn dealer's commission in England was 1–1.5%. So it will be most appreciated and interesting if the American case can be given in more detail.

2

Takeshi Yuzawa
Gakushuin University

Dr. Wortzel is to be complimented for having presented us with such a fascinating paper on the structural characteristics of the early stage of the cotton industry in New England. In her paper she has successfully tried to clarify, using Chandler's paradigm, the changing patterns of management as applied to Lowell mills.

Lowell was once called "the Manchester of America" (by J. Montgomery) in the middle of the nineteenth century in light of the large-scale agglomeration of the cotton industry. Therefore,

Lowell would be one of the best places for the study of the dynamic evolution process of the U.S. cotton industry, especially in the first half of the century. At that time, each cotton firm in Lowell was originally incorporated by Boston Associates, which had been formed through a special network of close human relationships among wealthy merchants. The board of directors of each firm had both a treasurer and selling agent among its members and was functionally carrying out management of the firm. But as time went on, some antagonisms grew up—in the 1840s among the directors, and between the directors and stockholders, particularly Lowell-based stockholders, after the 1857 crisis. Dr. Wortzel cited the case of H. Lee to analyze the substance of the former antagonism, while she considered the J. C. Ayer case as the latter parallel.

First of all I would like to point out that these problems took place due to the structurally built-in peculiarity of the form of the corporation. In contrast with the U.S., the nineteenth-century cotton industry in Britain, where partnership was a prevailing company form, did not seriously suffer from such problems. If we wish to compare the characteristics of management in the cotton industry from a historical point of view, I think we must reveal the main reasons why the U.S. cotton industry took a corporation form from its beginning. Dr. Wortzel attributes these reasons to the fact that the incorporators hoped to obtain a banking license, based on the study by F. W. Gregory. My suggestion is, however, that these reasons could perhaps be more reasonably discussed in terms of the business climate.

Secondly, I would like to focus my attention upon the relation between the cotton manufacturing company and the selling agent. We have been told that the selling agent played an important role in marketing and financing for the cotton company. Dr. Wortzel pointed out that the increasing control tendency of the manufacturing company over the selling agent led to Ayer's contention that company should appoint its own salaried agent. However, in the 1840s and 1850s a new kind of selling house (for example the firm of Mason and Lawrence), emerged to take advantage of the opportunity for profit which lay in the trade, succeeding such a firm as J. W. Page and Co. which had been organized in the 1820s by a group of manufacturers to further the interest of their business (C. F. Ware, *The Early New England Cotton Manufacture*, p. 183). How do we appreciate the role of this new kind of selling house? I think that, as the company grows, its forward integration into marketing is a prevalent trend among U.S. industries. But we can also argue that the product distributing system becomes more sophisticated and complex as this integration of an industrial company progresses.

According to the study of P. F. McGouldrick, there was no correlation between the profitability of a manufacturing company and the degree of control of the company over the selling house (*New England Textiles in the Nineteenth Century*, pp. 27–28). It was also pointed out that an overly-high commission of a selling house was only the second order of importance to the manufacturing company, whereas the selling house got a large return by managing sales of a number of companies (*ibid.*, p. 42). From these facts, I think it is difficult to generalize Ayer's complaint against the high commission of the selling house. I wonder what Dr. Wortzel thinks about it.

Lastly, we would like to discuss the changing roles of the treasurer which Dr. Wortzel referred to in her paper. The treasurer living in Boston controlled the agents residing at the mill site. This treasurer-mill agent system was established prior to the 1830s (*ibid.*, p. 21), and helped the growth of professional managers. I think in one sense this process is more important than the appearance of the salaried sales agent, because managerial hierarchies primarily depend on the smooth performance of the manufacturing function. Would you please give us your opinion on the implications of the transition from a treasurer to a professional manager?

Locational Patterns of Southern Textile Mills, 1880–1920

Mary J. Oates
Regis College

"The effectiveness of private enterprise is not a thing independent of time, place and circumstances, but depends on the surrounding conditions."
J. M. Clark, 1942

Studies of the American cotton textile industry have given much attention to the relocation of the industry from New England to the South.[1] After 1880, southern mills proliferated, and by 1925 the number of active spindles in the region exceeded that in the older textile center. The capacity of the Piedmont states of North and South Carolina, Georgia and Alabama for cotton manufacturing had long been acknowledged, and it has been widely accepted that mills could be opened almost anywhere and find ample water-power and productive resources and a business climate conducive to success. Evidence that southern mill expansion proceeded in accord with this description is drawn from impressionistic contemporary accounts or is based upon state-level data which do not allow analysis of actual patterns of intraregional mill settlement.

The southern experience with cotton manufacturing differed in several ways from that of the older New England region. First, southern mills were usually smaller in size and more numerous than were northern establishments. Table 1 indicates that although Piedmont mills increased in scale after 1880, they held in 1900 far fewer spindles than the typical northern mill. This differential could be observed in 1920 as well. Second, southern mills were dispersed over a large geographical area. In contrast, New England mills tended to be highly localized.[2] Third, within the South,

TABLE 1   The Southern Cotton Textile Industry, 1880–1900.

	Spindles and average mill scale	
	Total spindleage (000,000)	Spindles per mill
Four Piedmont states*		
1880	0.4	3,553
1890	1.2	6,358
1900	3.8	10,651
207 Piedmont counties		
1900	3.6	10,799
New England States		
1900	13.2	50,374

*North Carolina, South Carolina, Georgia, Alabama.
Source: Twelfth Census of the United States, Census Bulletin, No. 215,
          June 28, 1902, p. 12; U. S. Census of Manufactures (1927); *Davison's
          Textile Blue Book*, 1900.

important differences existed in mill size and degree of integration, variations not characteristic of the New England factories.

This paper maintains that the southern industry did not develop that diffused locational pattern which would be expected if plentiful resources were everywhere available. Nor did it concentrate in only a few centers in an evolution similar to that observed in New England. Disaggregated county-level data will be utilized to determine changes in spindle and mill concentration, mill size and product type, and explanations will be proposed for mill site decisions of southern entrepreneurs over the 1880–1920 period.

I.   Decentralization of Southern Cotton Mills

Emphasis by local press and politicians on southern advantages for cotton manufacturing in materials and labor supply and frequent comparisons of southern with northern mills motivated local efforts to begin mills in small agricultural communities in the years immediately following the Civil War. By 1880 a "mass recognition of possibilities" had developed, and community-sponsored mills were opening at a more rapid pace than formerly when they were small in number and widely dispersed.[3] About 1900 textile expansion accelerated in a "release of entreprenurial activity" following the success of many of the post-1880 mills. "There had been scarcely any interruption of the exceeding prosperity of Southern spinners . . . [They] sold all they could make at prices which gave their stockholders handsome dividends."[4] The 1880–1920 period was one of remarkable indigenous textile expansion, and for this reason our analysis of southern mill settlement and practice will focus on those years. After 1920, northern mills and financial interests became increasingly important in the textile industry of the region.[5]

Most southern mills were located in a relatively homogeneous, contiguous region of North and South Carolina, Georgia and Alabama. In 1900 these Piedmont states contained 89% of southern spindleage (Table 1). Of 207 counties in this "textile belt," 43% had at least one mill in 1900, and 60% had a mill in 1920.[6]

Early mills were established by local citizens and merchants. Since a cotton factory would provide a market for their cotton, surrounding farmers were eager to invest in it. Factors and tradesmen from commercial houses involved in cotton production, familiar with the raw material and possessing some marketing experience, were often hired manage the mill.[7] But the Piedmont was a rural area and local capital was scarce. Lumber, land and labor to construct the mill and mill village were accessible, but machinery purchased from northern manufacturers was expensive.[8] To acquire needed capital, local entrepreneurs sold stock on installment:

> The subscription to shares, usually $100 par value, was made payable in weekly installments of 50 cents to $1 a share without interest. Occasionally, a mill was built with a 25-cent installment. Purchasers paying cash were allowed a discount of about $10 on a $100 share.[9]

Many communities, unable to raise sufficient capital for a cloth mill, constructed instead a less costly spinning mill. Before 1900, $50,000 was sufficient to begin a small yarn mill while a coarse cloth mill required three times that amount.[10] The small spinning mill used local cotton and sold coarse yarns in local markets to knitting mills and to cloth mills unable to meet their immediate requirements.[11] Therefore, the freight as well as the machinery costs of

TABLE 2   Distribution of Southern Spindleage among Counties: 1900, 1920.

(207 Counties)

County spindleage:	Percentage of counties		Percentage of total regional spindleage		Average mill size (spindles per mill)		Percentage of spindleage in yarn mills		Spindle: Loom ratio in integrated mills	
	1900	1920	1900	1920	1900	1920	1900	1920	1900	1920
600,000 or more	0	1.9	0	26.1	—	25,538	—	22.2	—	46.7
300,000—599,999	0	1.9	0	12.1	—	37,222	—	7.8	—	42.0
100,000—299,999	4.3	15.0	41.6	42.7	18,827	20,750	22.8	20.5	28.3	39.3
60,000—99,999	3.4	7.3	15.8	9.0	8,410	15,220	23.8	35.6	25.2	48.5
20,000—59,999	14.0	14.0	31.1	7.0	9,155	13,130	31.2	40.7	32.8	34.7
1—19,999	21.3	19.8	11.5	3.1	5,293	8,113	61.0	55.8	31.8	44.5
No spindles installed	57.0	40.0								

Source: *Davison's Textile Blue Books,* 1900, 1920.

such mills were lower than those of the cloth mill. The advent of the ring spindle in 1870 eliminated the need for skill in spinning, making surplus labor from nearby farms adequate and cheap. The determination of local communities after 1880 to have their own mills gave rise to the yarn mill, a distinctive and enduring feature of the southern textile industry. By 1900, 40% of North Carolina spindles were in such establishments.[12]

Table 2 presents the distribution of spindleage in Piedmont counties after the first twenty years of industrial expansion. While more than 40% of counties in the region had at least one mill by that date, few could be termed textile centers. Nearly three-fifths of the region's spindleage was scattered among counties with fewer than 60,000 spindles. Yarn mills were most prominent in counties with the least investment in the industry. A majority of the spindles in counties with fewer than 20,000 spindles were located in such establishments. The small plant scale in isolated textile counties is, in part, a result of the dominance of the spinning factory. Of counties which had only a single mill in 1900, if the mill was a yarn mill it held on average only 5847 spindles, while if it was integrated it contained twice as many spindles. Such county differences in textile investment support our contention that capital and productive resources were not evenly distributed within the region.

Northern commission houses stood ready throughout the period to provide credit for cloth mills as well as to function as their selling agents in national markets. Southern producers were charged relatively high commissions and, if loans were not repaid, the houses assumed control of mill operations:

> A southern manufacturer pays his selling agent three and one-half or four percent, a northern manufacturer, one and one-half or two percent. The commission on southern goods includes two percent for selling and two percent for guaranteeing the payment of the purchaser's accounts.[13]

Given the inadequacies of the southern banking system, such a method of financing new mills was inevitable.[14] But southern managers made every effort to reduce production costs and their financial dependence upon the selling houses. In the earlier years of mill growth, used machinery was purchased from New England

mills. This practice was soon recognized as a mistake, and after
1890 new mills were furnished with the latest models of spindles
and looms.[15] Managers justified night work in spinning by citing
the rapid obsolescence of cotton machinery. "Improvements in
machinery have come so rapidly that a machine can seldom be run
until it is no longer capable of effective work."[16] Despite a 13%
higher equipment cost for a new mill furnished with Northrop
looms rather than with conventional power looms, southern mill
men were quick to install the new loom, marketed by the Draper
Co. in 1894, because of its potential for reducing labor costs. The
loom was automatic, demanding less skill of the weaver, who could
operate sixteen Northrups instead of only four to six common
looms. "It has reduced the labor cost of weaving one-half . . . [and
this] constitute[s] one-half the entire labor cost of manufacturing
cotton cloth."[17]

The sustained profitability of many southern mills allowed them
in time to progress to greater autonomy. Since numerous New
England mills which produced standard plain cloths were able to
sell direct, southern managers endeavored to increase plant size,
using profits after dividends to finance additional capacity.[18] Unlike the small yarn mills which sold direct in local markets, few
cloth mills could dispose of their entire output in such markets.
Those that did were small mills producing such coarse goods as the
heavy ducks used in harvesting cotton.[19] Despite their efforts,
most integrated establishments were not large enough in 1920 to
achieve financial independence from commission houses.

For the Piedmont region as a whole, average plant scale increased
by 77% over 1900–1920, but the typical 1920 mill held only 19,085
spindles, a scale much smaller than that of the New England
cotton factory of over 69,000 spindles. We note in Table 2 a variation among counties in average mill size. Those with relatively
higher concentrations of spindles also had larger plant scale. This
was a result of their lower representations of small yarn mills,
found more often in counties with low spindle densities. But even
in these counties, the average scale did not approach that of the
older region in 1920.

Although the southern business climate was receptive to the

introduction of cotton enterprises after 1880, there existed in the region a serious shortage of managerial and technical skill. A cotton mill expands by adding more rather than different equipment, with operatives and looms increased proportionately with spindleage. In this sense, it is said that the small cotton mill can operate as efficiently, from a technical standpoint, as a larger mill.[20] But more managers, engineers and mechanics are required for large mills than for smaller ones, and in the agricultural South of 1880–1920 it was difficult to find individuals with the necessary managerial and technical talent. Southern mill engineers tended to be northerners, or southerners trained in New England.[21] A general shortage of managerial experience in the region slowed its movement toward larger scale cotton mills.

This deficiency is related as well to the heavy concentration of southern mills on coarse and medium grade yarns and cloths. While national and export demand continued strong for these staples,[22] this does not fully account for the unwillingness of southern mill managers to engage in production of finer grades. In 1900 only one southern state reported any fine spinning at all.[23] The reluctance arises from the small supply of experienced managers since production of finer grades demanded more proficiency of the entrepreneur. He needed "a capacity for forecasting styles, getting on to them early, and getting off in time to dispose of the goods before the styles have changed."[24] The decision of most southern mill men to produce coarse and medium grades was also related to the availability of skilled operatives needed in finer goods production. While in the production of coarse and medium grades no significant differences could be observed in the efficiency of northern and southern workers, southern labor in this period was less effective in finer grade cloth production.[25]

Textile machinery for goods of all degrees of fineness tends to be similar in type. But for finer cloths, the ratio of spindles to looms is higher than it is for lower quality products. At least 50 spindles per loom are needed to produce fine goods, 40 for medium goods and 30 for coarse cloths.[26] Table 2 demonstrates that southern cloth output increased in quality over 1900–1920 in integrated mills located in isolated areas as well as in those counties with

TABLE 3   Proportions of Workers by Age and Sex: Massachusetts and
Three Piedmont States, 1900.

State	Average number of persons employed	Men, 16 years and over (%)	Women, 16 years and over (%)	Children, under 16 years (%)
Massachusetts	92,085	48.98	44.59	6.43
Georgia	18,283	39.98	35.52	24.50
North Carolina	30,273	42.22	34.23	23.55
South Carolina	30,201	44.43	28.72	26.85

Source: Massachusetts Bureau of Statistics of Labor, *Cotton Manufactures in Massachusetts and the Southern States*, Part II of the Annual Report for 1905 (Boston: Wright & Potter Printing Co., 1905): 94.

higher levels of spindleage. Little systematic variation can be observed in either year by level of county spindleage. Nevertheless southern cloth output remained on, average, of coarse/medium grade in both years.

The dispersion of mills over a wide geographical area may be explained not only by early efforts of many local communities to open their own mills but also by entrepreneurial searches for low-cost factors of production. Land needed for mills and mill villages was cheaper in the more rural locations and southern mills preferred to own large areas of land.[27] T. Jefferson Coolidge, Treasurer of the Amoskeag Manufacturing Co. for much of the 1876–1898 period, describes with some awe a prosperous mill of the period:

> I lunched with a man named Smythe, who is at the head of the best mill in the South, I believe, in the Alleghany foothills in South Carolina. He owns the whole county, sees to the schooling of the children and really regulates the expenditures and taxes.[28]

Textile labor, while adequate throughout the region before 1900, was acknowledged to be cheaper in the more remote counties.[29] While in New England little variation in wage rates could be observed among mill towns after 1865, significant differentials persisted among the scattered southern mills.[30] The region's labor force was assembled in mill villages from the tenant farms of the surrounding countryside, and included considerable numbers of children[31] (Table 3). Managers recruited children by giving pref-

TABLE 4   Clustering and Dispersion of Southern Mills: 1900, 1920.

(207 Counties)

	In "clustered counties" (8 or more mills)		In "dispersed counties" (only one mill)	
	1900	1920	1900	1920
Number of counties*	13	24	28	45
Percentage of total regional spindleage	40.7	61.9	6.9	6.2
Percentage of regional mills	44.4	59.1	8.6	7.1
Average mill size (spindles per mill)	9,467	21,340	8,308	17,760
Spindle: Loom ratio in integrated mills	30.4	42.0	34.2	48.2
Percentage of spindleage in yarn mills	15.9	19.3	35.4	23.9

	1900	1920		1900	1920
*North Carolina	8	13	*North Carolina	8	8
South Carolina	4	8	South Carolina	2	2
Georgia	1	3	Georgia	11	23
			Alabama	7	12

Source: *Davison's Textile Blue Books*, 1900, 1920.

erence in mill village housing to families with children old enough to work.[32] Rural mills, in particular, reduced their labor costs by using child labor in spinning. In 1909, 40% of South Carolina spinners were children, a sharp contrast with 7.2% in New Hampshire.[33]

Propinquity to a raw cotton supply was a concern voiced before 1900 by some managers in choosing a mill site. An abundant supply of "back-door cotton" meant lower transportation costs for the rural mills selling locally. The importance of this factor in mill location is difficult to assess since the mill purchased its cotton through brokers and it is impossible to determine the origin of a given mill's supply.[34]

II.   Concentration of Southern Mills and Spindles

After the early period of mill expansion, southern textile growth became more concentrated in location. Table 4 indicates the growing propensity of managers after 1900 to locate in counties already populated with mills. Six percent of Piedmont counties had eight or more mills in 1900. By 1920, 12% could, by this standard, be termed "clustered counties," with approximately 60% of regional mills and spindleage within their borders. At the same time, the number of counties with only one mill also increased considerably after 1900. Despite such apparent dispersion, the share of regional mills and spindleage in these isolated locations did not increase. New factories tended to be placed in counties already having at least one mill, although mills in more remote locations continued to compete throughout the period. Not much divergence between the two groups of counties can be perceived in quality of cloth produced in integrated mills.

The extent of the movement toward localization in a span of only twenty years was impressive. Among the "clustered counties" considered in Table 4, fourteen had by 1920 become preeminent. Forty percent of the region's mills and 50% of its spindleage were concentrated in these counties by that date. Over half of the highest-ranking counties were in South Carolina.[35]

Why did some locations become more attractive than others to entrepreneurs considering a new mill or a mill expansion? Contemporary writings abound with examples suggesting the presence of an "imitation effect." The development of Piedmont, South Carolina, into a major textile center has been attributed to the success of its first mill. "The example of its success was contagious and there have clustered about it . . . mills by the score."[36] Although it is likely that some element of imitation was part of the location decision, noting that cotton manufacturing is "essentially gregarious"[37] is not sufficient explanation for changing location patterns of southern mills and spindles.

Developments after 1900 in power and transportation provide some explanations for these trends. Early mill decentralization was possible only because the Piedmont region was well endowed with water power resources. Entrepreneurs considering textile manufacturing had many more options than they would have had in early New England. Yet even in the 1880s the relative merits of steam and water power were discussed and steam was introduced

on a wide scale. Although locational choices were restricted somewhat by the need to be near coal supplies, steam power allowed
communities without water resources but wanting a mill to open
one.[38] Despite the fact that power costs amounted to only about
5% of total costs in a plain goods mill,[39] the availability of adequate
power resources strongly affected the choice of mill site. The early
concern about power continued among mill managers, indicated
most clearly by their interest in using hydroelectric power upon
its introduction in the late 1890s. While steam was still the source
of two-thirds of the power in southern cotton mills in 1905, by
1930 Piedmont states were producing "a greater proportion of total
power by water than . . . any states east of the Rocky Mountains."[40]
Costs relative to other power sources were similar, and electric
power allowed greater uniformity in speed with a resulting increase
in output of about 10%.[41]

The new technology was introduced in the South more quickly
than other parts of the country but it was not adopted uniformly
by the region's cotton mills. Notwithstanding the varied locational
options provided successively by the introduction of water, steam
and electric power, post-1900 mills were more often being placed
in or near established towns. In 1900 most mills were still building
their own power plants. But with the development of electric power,
it became more efficient to purchase power for mill additions and
for new mills from public utility companies. "Plain mills of moderate
size can probably purchase current cheaper than it can be generated by an isolated plant at the mill."[42] Suppliers of electric
power in the early years of its development were unable to transmit
it over long distances without incurring transmission losses and
higher costs.[43] For example, the electric power sold by the Columbia
Water Power Co. (S.C.) was praised not only for being the cheapest
power available but also because it could be delivered "anywhere
in or near the city."[44] Such a constraint on distribution encouraged
a clustering of new mills in established towns. In addition, electric
power lines were frequently erected along Southern Railway
routes.[45] This served to reinforce an earlier concentration of mills
along railroad tracks. Where cheap electric power was supplied,
cotton mills were soon constructed. But in the 1900–1920 years this

power tended to be more accessible near the industrial and commercial centers of the region.

The critical factor affecting mill location decisions after 1890 was the adequacy of transportation facilities. A postwar improvement and expansion of southern railroad lines began about 1880, " . . . roads in financial difficulties being reorganized and narrow gauge being changed to broad gauge."[46] Mills opened after 1890 were drawn to railroad lines, so that by 1920, 77% of all southern spindles were in factories on the Southern Railway System.[47] The best shipping services were provided mills located in areas of concentrated spindleage. A description of railroad service in Columbus, Georgia, provides a good example:

> A belt railroad takes cars from any one of the seven roads entering the city and switches them up to the door of any factory or jobbing house. New tracks are laid to accommodate new establishments.[48]

Rate discrimination by location was common within the South in this period. Adjustments were occasionally made, based upon complaints from businesses located in more remote points on railroad lines, but they were not always satisfactory. It was not until after 1920 that rates fostering concentration near older manufacturing and shipping centers were eliminated in favor of rates determined uniformly by distance.[49]

III. Conclusion

This paper has presented a disaggregated examination of cotton textile expansion in the Piedmont region of the American Southeast between 1880 and 1920. An unusual pattern of mill settlement has been identified and an explanation of entrepreneurial decisions about mill sites based upon the distinctive features of the local economic climate has been offered.

Mills located in remote rural communities coexisted with those clustered in growing textile centers. Yarn mills became an established feature of the southern industry. Choosing sites giving cost advantages in labor and land, concentrating production on coarse yarns and cloths requiring few skills of operatives, and selling direct in local markets allowed small country mills to compete with larger mills in the region throughout the period. As the pool of managerial talent in the region expanded after 1900, average scale of mill rose and output quality improved. In time the small mills became less important in numbers and spindleage relative to larger mills in the region as new mills clustered more often in counties with higher spindle density.

NOTES

1. Recent studies include: Gavin Wright, "Cheap Labor and Textiles before 1880," *Journal of Economic History* 39 (September, 1979): 655–680; and John S. Hekman, "The Product Cycle and New England Textiles," *Quarterly Journal of Economics* 94 (June, 1980): 697–717.

2. Hekman, 704–706, demonstrates the great concentration of New England mills around Boston during the 1840–1880 period.

3. Seth Hammond, "Location Theory and the Cotton Textile Industry," *Journal of Economic History* 2 (December, 1942): 109–110. See also Senate Document No. 126, *Cotton Textile Industry*, 74th Congress, 1st Session (Washington, D. C., 1935): 115. Some continue to disagree with the choice of 1880 as the beginning of a modern textile industry in the South. See, for example, Dwight B. Billings, Jr., *Planters and the Making of a "New South"* (Chapel Hill: University of North Carolina Press, 1979): 60–61; and Tom E. Terrill, "Eager Hands: Labor for Southern Textiles, 1850–1860," *Journal of Economic History* 36 (March, 1976): 84–99.

4. Twelfth Census of the United States, 1900, Census Bulletin No. 215 (Washington, D. C.: June 28, 1902): 5; E. B. Alderfer and H. E. Michl, *Economics of American Industry* (New York: McGraw Hill, 1957): 346.

5. A 1922 survey determined that 83.8% of southern spindles were owned and managed by southerners. (Massachusetts Department of Labor and Industries, Report of a Special Investigation, *Conditions in the Textile Industry in Massachusetts and the Southern States*, August, 1923, pp. 17–18.)

6. For a description of how these 207 counties were chosen, see Mary J. Oates, *The Role of the Cotton Textile Industry in the Economic Develop-*

ment of the American Southeast, 1900–1940 (New York: Arno Press, 1975): Appendix I, 166–177. In the South, the county has always been the key local unit.

7. Hammond, 111; Twelfth Census of the United States, 1900, Census Reports, Volume VIII, Manufactures, Part II, "States and Territories" (Washington, D. C., 1902): 133.

8. Richard W. Griffin, North Carolina: The Origin and Rise of the Cotton Textile Industry, 1830–1880 (Unpublished Ph. D. Dissertation, Ohio State University, 1954): 159.

9. Holland Thompson, From the Cotton Field to the Cotton Mill (New York: Macmillan, 1906): 82–83.

10. Hammond, 112. Footnotes 12 and 13.

11. Melvin T. Copeland, The Cotton Manufacturing Industry of the United States (Cambridge: Harvard University Press, 1912): 150–151.

12. Twelfth Census of the United States, Volume IX, Manufactures, Part III (Washington, D. C., 1902): 51.

13. Copeland, 210. Selling houses often loaned between 75 and 90% of the value of a mill's products. Machinery manufacturers also invested in new mills by accepting shares in the company instead of cash. They sold the shares as soon as possible. (Copeland, 50). See also Solomon Barkin, "The Regional Significance of the Integration Movement in the Southern Textile Industry," Southern Economic Journal 15 (April, 1949): 396.

14. Gustavus G. Williamson, Jr., Cotton Manufacturing in South Carolina, 1865–1892 (Unpublished Ph. D. Dissertation, Johns Hopkins University, 1954): 100.

15. Massachusetts Bureau of Statistics of Labor, Cotton Manufactures in Massachusetts and the Southern States, Part II of the Annual Report for 1905 (Boston: Wright and Potter Printing Co., 1905): 43; New England Cotton Manufacturers Association, Transactions 63 (1897): 384–385; Thompson, 65, 78–79; and Marvin Fischbaum, An Economic Analysis of the Southern Capture of the Cotton Textile Industry to 1910 (Unpublished Ph. D. Dissertation, Columbia University, 1965): 213.

16. Thompson, 135–136.

17. Melvin T. Copeland, "Technical Developments in Cotton Manufacturing Since 1860," Quarterly Journal of Economics 24 (November, 1909): 146. See also, W. Paul Strassman, Risk and Technological Innovation (Ithaca: Cornell University Press, 1959): 98; William H. Chase, Five Generations of Loom Builders (Hopedale, Mass.: Draper

Corp., 1950): 18; and Massachusetts Bureau of Statistics of Labor, 88.

18. "Profits [were] . . . almost certain. Mills, though not always economically managed, paid good dividends, and the best were phenomenally successful." Thompson, 67. See also, Barkin, 397, and William Hays Simpson, *Some Aspects of America's Textile Industry with Special Reference to Cotton* (Columbia: University of South Carolina, 1966): 55–57. Ownership of establishments in larger mill towns became more concentrated. In Gaston County, North Carolina, control of many mills passed in three decades "from a relatively broad community base into the hands of less than a dozen families." Liston Pope, *Millhands and Preachers* (New Haven: Yale University Press, 1942): 143.

19. Chen-Han Chen, *The Location of the Cotton Manufacturing Industry in the United States, 1880–1910* (Unpublished Ph. D. Dissertation, Harvard University, 1939): 203.

20. If only technical operations are taken into account an integrated plant scale of about 10,000 spindles allowed efficient production. When managerial constraints are considered, this figure rises to 20,000 spindles. (Oates, 62–63). Doane found no significant relationship between firm size and average cost. David P. Doane, "Regional Cost Differentials and Textile Location: A Statistical Analysis," *Explorations in Economic History* 9 (Fall, 1971): 8.

21. Simpson, 55. Copeland (1912), 144, describes the managers of small southern mills as usually inefficient. Hekman, 716.

22. "Almost 3/4 of the yardage of all woven goods reported falls under the classification of coarse or medium goods—print cloths, sheetings, and shirtings, drills, ticks, denims and stripes, duck and bagging." Department of Commerce and Labor, Bureau of the Census, Manufactures, 1905, Part III (Washington, D. C., 1905): 35. In 1926, 90% of southern output was still of coarse and medium grades. Charles T. Main and Frank M. Gunby, "The Cotton Textile Industry," *Mechanical Engineering* 48 (October 1926): 1001.

23. Department of Commerce and Labor, Bureau of the Census, Manufactures, 1905, Part III. "Special Reports on Selected Industries" (Washington, D. C., 1908): 38–39. This comprised 1% of national output.

24. Main and Gunby, 1001. See also, Robert Robson, *The Cotton Industry in Britain* (London: Macmillan and Co., 1957): 111. Footnote 1.

25. Chen, 170; Doane, 22.
26. Oates, 99–100.
27. August Kohn, *The Cotton Mills of South Carolina* (Columbia: South Carolina Department of Agriculture, 1907): 66.
28. Cited in Daniel Creamer and Charles W. Coulter, *Labor and the Shut-Down of the Amoskeag Textile Mills*, Work Projects Administration, National Research Project, Report No. L–5 (Philadelphia, November, 1939): 164.
29. Hammond, 115–116; Melton Alonza McLaurin, *Paternalism and Protest: Southern Cotton Mill Workers and Organized Labor, 1875–1905* (Westport: Greenwood Publishing Corp., 1971): 27–28.
30. Thomas Russell Smith, *The Cotton Textile Industry of Fall River, Massachusetts* (New York: King's Crown Press, 1944): 68; Wright, 679; Hammond, 116.
31. Jefferson Bynum, "Piedmont North Carolina and Textile Production," *Economic Geography* 4 (July, 1928): 238. In the four Piedmont states, 95% of the local white population in 1910 were natives of white parentage. Thirteenth Census of the United States, 1910, Volume I (Washington, D. C.: 1913): 140. See William N. Parker, "The South in the National Economy, 1865–1970," *Southern Economic Journal* 46 (April, 1980): 1042–1043.
32. Broadus Mitchell and George S. Mitchell, *The Industrial Revolution in the South* (Baltimore: Johns Hopkins University Press, 1930): 136. See also Broadus Mitchell, *The Rise of Cotton Mills in the South* (Baltimore: Johns Hopkins University Press, 1921): 44–45.
33. Thirteenth Census of the United States, 1910, Volume X, Manufactures, 1909, "Reports for Principal Industries" (Washington, D. C., 1913): 42. Six percent of South Carolina *weavers* were children.
34. Chen, 171.
35. Calculated from Davison's Textile Blue Book, Office Edition, 1920 (Redgewood, N. J.: Davison Publishing Co., 1920).
36. Frank Presbrey, *The Empire of the South* (Washington, D. C.: The Southern Railway Co., 1898): 88.
37. Twelfth Census of the United States, Census Bulletin No. 215 (Washington, D. C. June 28, 1902): 12.
38. Chen, 237.
39. Charles T. Main, "Power for Textile Mills," *Mechanical Engineering* (1926): 125.
40. Thorndike Saville, "The Power Situation in the Southern Power

Province," *Annals of the American Academy of Political and Social Science* 153 (January, 1931): 95–96. See Selby Haar, "Transmission Systems of the World Operating at or above 70,000 Volts, Ranked According to Operating Voltage," Supplement to *Electrical World* (April 25, 1914): 147.

41. Haar, 147; Department of Commerce, Bureau of the Census, "Central Electric Light and Power Stations," and "Street and Electric Railways, 1912" (Washington, D. C., 1915): 113.
42. Main, 127; Saville, 114.
43. Main, 126.
44. Presbrey, 86. See also, Department of Commerce and Labor, Bureau of the Census, Special Reports, "Central Electric Light and Power Stations, 1907" (Washington, D. C., 1910): 42.
45. Pope, 8–9.
46. Mitchell, 74. Hammond, 110–111.
47. Chen, 237; Fairfax Harrison, *Southern Railway System, 1911–1920: A Record of Growth* (Washington, D. C.: Southern Railway System, June 15, 1922): 5.
48. Presbrey, 108–109.
49. Roland B. Eutsler, "Transportation Developments and Economic and Industrial Changes," *Annals of the American Academy of Political and Social Science* 153 (January, 1931): 208–209.

COMMENTS

1

Naosuke Takamura
University of Tokyo

I am interested in Professor Oates' report in comparison with the Japanese cotton spinning industry.

She mentioned that southern cotton mills were decentralized and community-sponsored. In Japan, influential persons of a local community promoted building of 2000-spindle scale mills with governmental support during the early 1880s. Their business philosophy rested on "local patriotism." Their aim was to relieve Japan from shortages in foreign currency by decreasing the import of cotton goods, and at the same time to revive declining cotton cultivation in order to recover the local economy. However, since these promoters lacked in efforts for rational management, most of these community-sponsored cotton firms were unsuccessful. I am quite interested in the business philosophy of southern promoters. Why and how did they embark on the foundation of cotton mills? I would be interested in concrete examples of how they supported the foundation of local enterprise. Did community sponsorship put a positive or a negative influence on the development of the southern cotton industry?

The average number of spindles per mill was given as approximately 6,000 in 1890, 11,000 in 1900, and 19,000 in 1920. In Japan, the average number of spindles per mill was approximately 8,000 in 1889, 14,000 in 1900, and 26,000 in 1914. Thus, the average scale of southern cotton mills was smaller and the speed of their expansion was slower than that of Japan's industry. Shortages in the number of managers and engineers was given as the reason for this slow expansion, but I do not think this is persuasive. In the

South, a large number of small cotton mills were dispersed, and such a situation should have required more managers and engineers than in the case where a smaller number of large-scale mills existed. Moreover, as Professor Oates mentioned, engineers were able enough to introduce and handle new machines. Nevertheless, southern cotton mills failed to secure the number of managers and engineers needed for the expansion of factory scale after the 1900s. It is true that the enlargement of a factory requires more managers and engineers, but a twice-enlarged mill does not always call for twice as many as managers and engineers. In Japan one able engineer held the post of engineering director in three factories simultaneously. Therefore, it would be interesting to know more about the shortage of talent in southern cotton mills. Perhaps it is possible that another factor prevented the enlargement of factory scale in the South. May I suggest that managers' business philosophy may have had some effect?

Professor Oates mentioned that northern commission houses charged high commissions and interest to southern mills when functioning as their sales agents for cotton cloth; even in 1920 the southern cotton mills were not big enough to become independent from such commission houses. I would be interested in the influence of northern commission houses on the development of southern cotton mills from the point of management and its nature. In Japan the import of spinning machines and raw cotton and the export of cotton yarn and cloth were controlled by a small number of large trading companies. While big spinning firms which maintained advantageous relations with these large trading companies succeeded in enlarging the scale of enterprise, middle and small-scale cotton firms, which operated in less advantageous conditions, often had difficulty surviving and sometimes went bankrupt or merged with other big spinning firms.

2

Masami Kita
Soka University

Professor Oates is to be complimented for providing us with this fascinating account of the historical progress of the southern cotton industry from 1880 to 1920 as contrasted with its northern counterpart. This has given us a detailed portrait of industrial development in a less advanced economy compared with that of a more developed economy.

So far as the business climate is concerned, this paper suggests that it may be valuable to summarize some of the factors which launch and encourage an industry in certain environments: timing, accumulation of capital (banking and financial facilities), supply and quality of labor, access to resources (material and energy), availability of transport services and the development of technology. Again, we have been shown classical examples of conflict and the process of compromising between powerful areas of the industry and weaker ones, the latter being absorbed later but still flourishing on the national market.

It is quite interesting to compare the United States experience with that of England and Scotland, in particular Manchester and Glasgow. Scotland in the late eighteenth century was very eager to introduce new ventures in the cotton industry from England, although it had enough equipment and technical knowledge of textiles from its own traditional sector of linen which was, by then, a national industry. Entrepreneurs in Scotland bought used machines from old companies in Manchester, although they could have made their own; they had a well experienced labor force from the declining woolen and linen textile industries, and also could have made use of their cultural identity in banking, which had greatly assisted Scotland's industrial progress. While Manchester was showing off its new wealth as a result of success in the cotton industry, Scottish entrepreneurs and "enlightened" landlords might have recognized such an opportunity to offset the sudden depression of their successful tobacco trading business with America which had been caused by the American Revolution. The Glasgow Chamber of Commerce, the first institute of its kind in the country in 1783, also might have materially encouraged them to consider this new type of business.

The cotton industry in Scotland developed rapidly on the national market but by the mid-19th century realized it was unable to compete with Machester's medium and plain cloth products in overseas markets. They had to make a choice—to specialize in fine cloth and fancy goods with their own technology of this traditional industry (although it was becoming more dependent on the unpredictable fluctuation of the market's taste and fashion) or to enter a new venture, the iron industry, which soon became a leading factor in the Scottish economy.

Next I wish to clarify some points in this paper. Firstly, one of the three differences between America's North and South which Professor Oates mentioned is that the mill size and degree of integration within the South varied widely and was different from that of the standardized scale characteristic of New England's cotton industries. Was it lack of competition or something else which caused this?

Secondly, how were the initial mills, which were community sponsored, financially launched and supported?

Thirdly, from the viewpoint of the labor force, how did the southern workers react when faced with the introduction of the ring mill which meant that less skilled labor—even children— could be used? Why did they not react to the difference in wages among mills in the South? What was taking place in the labor movement in the South at that time? Another point I wonder about is why the South's shortage of experienced engineers did not stimulate establishment of some technical schools.

Fourthly, the South specialized in establishing spinning mills rather than cloth mills. Would they have financed the latter if they had had enough financial institutions to do so? Why could they not have done it? Dr. Oates has said that commission houses in

the North not only supplied a sales agent for southern cotton mills
on the national market, but also gave credit for the establishment
of cloth mills in the South. Does this mean that some of the modern
integrated establishments in the South were financially controlled
by the North? Is it possible to tell how much they depended on
this northern power?

Business Climate and Industrialization of the Korean Fiber Industry

Jong-Tae Choi
Seoul National University

I. The Present Situation in the Korean Fiber Industry

In order to understand the present situation of the textile industry in Korea, we must understand the close relationship which exists between the gross national product (GNP), the output of the manufacturing industry and the output and export of the textile industry. Historical trends and variables and the proportion of the latter to the former are all a part of this understanding. The proportion of the product output of manufacturing industry to GNP is shown in Table 1, and the trends since 1953 are traced in Figure 1. As we can see, the percentage of total output for which this industry is responsible has steadily increased over the years. The proportion of output of the textile industry to the total manufacturing industry is shown in Table 2; trends since 1953 are traced in Figure 2. As is obvious, there has been a gradual but steady decline in the role this industry has played in the overall picture.

II. History of the Development of Korean Fiber Industry

1. The Cotton Textile Industry in the Era of the Yi Dynasty[1] (1392–1910)

The spread of cotton in Korea and the invention of spinning and weaving machinery marked a change in the material aspects of the Korean way of life and the history of the Korean economy. This can be realized from the fact that cotton became so important it was used as a substitute for a currency.

It was after the fifteenth century that the real cotton industry

249

TABLE 1 Proportion of Product Output of Manufacturing Industry to GNP (%).

Year	Proportion (%)	Year	Proportion (%)	Year	Proportion (%)	Year	Proportion (%)	Year	Proportion (%)
1953	*8.9	1958	12.7	1963	14.5	1968	19.8	1973	25.0
	**4.8		7.5		9.7		15.0		23.7
1954	11.6	1959	14.0	1964	15.5	1969	20.1	1974	26.2
	5.3		7.9		9.7		16.0		25.5
1955	11.4	1960	13.7	1965	17.9	1970	20.9	1975	26.9
	6.1		8.4		11.1		17.9		26.9
1956	11.4	1961	13.5	1966	18.4	1971	21.1	1976	28.1
	7.2		8.3		11.5		19.6		28.8
1957	11.1	1962	14.3	1967	18.8	1972	22.4	1977	27.6
	7.2		9.1		13.1		12.1		39.8

*   At current market prices.
** At 1975 constant market prices.

FIG. 1 Trends in Proportion of Output of Manufacturing Industry to GNP.

TABLE 2 Proportion of Output of Textile Industry to Total Output of Manufacturing Industry.

Year	Proportion (%)	Year	Proportion (%)	Year	Proportion (%)	Year	Proportion (%)	Year	Proportion (%)
	*22.6		23.3		18.2		17.1		20.2
1953		1958		1963		1968		1973	
	**20.1		22.9		16.3		12.9		15.8
	25.7		21.9		18.4		17.1		15.6
1954		1959		1964		1969		1974	
	21.1		21.7		14.8		13.1		14.8
	23.0		21.1		19.3		16.9		15.6
1955		1960		1965		1970		1975	
	21.2		19.5		14.5		13.2		15.6
	23.9		19.5		17.9		17.6		15.4
1956		1961		1966		1971		1976	
	22.5		17.6		13.7		14.1		15.1
	24.0		19.7		18.3		20.8		13.5
1957		1962		1967		1972		1977	
	24.7		17.3		13.4		16.0		13.4

* At current market prices.
** At 1975 constant market prices.

came into being and became productive in Korea. Although the development of the industry was ascribed to the tax system of the Yi dynasty, there were two factors that promoted its progress. The demand for cotton fabric was increasing as an important export item to Japan, and such fabric was also being demanded as a financial resource for the military.

Since textile fabrics were then used as a means of tax payment, their demand also increased, causing an increase in production. However, after the 17th century the cotton industry in Korea began to wither, and we shall examine the main causes of the decline. First, the level of production technology was very low and was being handled by ordinary farmers. Its management structure and systems were thus very weak, and this fact made it difficult to expand cotton agriculture to a large enough scale for commercialization. Second, since the cotton industry had reached its

FIG. 2   Trends in Proportion of Textile Industry to Total Manufacturing
         Output.

position because of its use as a tax payment, it was not only demanded by taxpayers in the form of cotton textiles but was also the
subject of a high tax levy by the government. Third, during the
Russo-Japanese War Japan imposed her political control system
upon Korea; to assure its acquisition of raw materials, the capital
of the Japanese textile industry controlled Korea's developing
cotton agriculture. The cotton industry therefore became the
main supplier of raw materials to the Japanese spinning industry
and lost its own industrial field, the textile industry. With the
control of its textile industry in Japanese hands, the basic separation
process of agriculture and industry, which was essential to Korea's
modern economic development, was interrupted.

In addition to the development of the textile industry, there arose the question of whether the cotton industry had a modern production style of organization. It was considered important whether or not there was an actual manufacturing system. From historical data it seems that in the cotton textile industry of the late 19th century such a system did exist, though not a strong one. However, even more important than the existence of a manufacturing system was that from a historical economic viewpoint, the production relationship could never be advanced to a fully modern style. Some reasons for this were the paucity of accumulated technology, the limited availability of capital, complete lack of modern entrepreneurial spirit, and inferiority of management technique. But above all, the advancement was primarily denied because of the invasion of Japanese imperialism. The local market was looted of all raw cotton and textiles of higher quality were exported. Accordingly, the demand for traditional cotton fabrics in Korea diminished.

2. The Generation of the Modern Cotton Textile Industry[2] (1910–1919)

During the domination of Korea by Japanese capitalism, Japan proclaimed the Company Law which suppressed the accumulation of Korean national capital. Therefore, Korean enterprises could not free themselves from oppressive industrial conditions despite steady increase in their number. Korean enterprise activity was not allowed by order of Japanese colonial policies. Such suppression consequently affected not only the number of companies but also the national capital.

3. Establishment of the Modern Cotton Textile Industry[3] (1920–1929)

Around the period when the 1919 Samil Independence Movement took place, modern spinning and weaving companies were founded, such as the Kyungsung Spinning and Weaving Company, which were managed by national entrepreneurs. This was not accomplished by chance; there were many direct and indirect factors that caused the foundation of the Kyungsung Co. Many of these were associated with the social and political factors of the Samil Independence Movement which provoked the nation's spirit. But the direct factors that stimulated the birth of such national enterprises were a number of economic conditions.

First, increased investment in the Korean economy had been made by Japanese enterprises; Korean entrepreneurs were shocked by this fact. Secondly, the increased feasibility of the mobilization of national capital by large national landowners (who accumulated such capital by executing government policy to increase the yield of rice) also played a critical role. Third, there was optimism for broadening the country's share of the market. Fourth, as a result of the greater availability of modern education, qualified technicians and engineers were being produced. Fifth, there existed individuals who were equipped with a modern knowledge of management and its operation. These political, economic and social conditions made it possible to quicken the evolution of the modern national textile industry by such means as introducing spinning and weaving to the cotton companies.

In 1911 the Kyungsung Co. Ltd. was established; it was organized as a limited company for the first time in the history of Korea's national textile industry. Its foundation was accomplished by mustering capital and work forces from small textile makers. But the management of this company was not handled well and around 1916 it was on the verge of bankruptcy. At that time control was assumed by Kim Sung-Soo, who had a strong national spirit and a modern education. He changed and diversified the products of the company, intending to develop it on the model of a large-scale modern national textile company using national capital. The later company, Kyungsung Spinning and Weaving Company, actually was established in October 1919 through the participation of large landowners and leading figures of various social strata.[4] Although this was founded as a national company, its development and foundation as a profit-making industry was only achieved after Kim Nyun-Soo actively took part in its management. He was the younger brother of Kim Sung-Soo and made the company profitable, extending its size and scope.

The managerial aspects of Kyungsung during its foundation

and development process are of interest. First as previously mentioned, the foundation philosophy of Kyungsung was nationalism. How did nationalism evolve in the business development process? Second, Kyungsung was a rare case where success was achieved as a national enterprise even under Japanese imperialism. Which factors made Kyungsung succeed? Third, as Kyungsung progressed, what characteristic changes were adopted in its managerial staff and capital structure?

Nationalism, the philosophy on which Kyungsung had been founded, had been a definite business ideal.[5] Founder Kim Sung-Soo had the support of people all over the country. Kyungsung was managed entirely by national technology and capital. At that time, it was almost impossible to manage a business without any assistance from the ruling colonial government. In an underdeveloped country it was generally accepted that foreigners were to be used as managerial and technical staff, but Kyungsung avoided this. Employment applications were accepted only from Koreans. In its operating enterprise, Kyungsung made full use of its nationalism. In marketing, an advertisement displayed the mottos "Korean fabrics for Koreans" and "Developing national enterprise." Additionally, the founder erected an educational institute, ran a newspaper and awarded scholarships to Korean pupils.

The element which made Kyungsung succeed was the management's rational and creative thinking. When Kim Sung-Soo took over the textile company, it was on the verge of bankruptcy. He installed new machinery and changed production methods, thereby achieving a profit. From 1925 the net profit ratio increased, while the Cho-Sun Silk Producing Company, which was owned by Japanese businessmen, incurred a loss. Kyungsung's management policy was to produce products suitable for Korean taste, and to produce fast fabric to ease penetration into the rural market. The top management of Kyungsung exercised frugal and calculative thinking; if additional capital was needed, it was obtained by self-financing from stockowners or from other assets.

The third matter concerns changes in the structure of the managerial staff. The foundation capital of Kyungsung was 1,000,000 won; a single share of stock was 50 won and 20,000 shares were issued. At the beginning, major stockholders held less than one-half of the total stocks; one hundred and eighty-two persons from all over the country were minor stockholders. The management staff was composed of major stockholders and other capable men. But the structure of distribution of stocks changed rapidly. Soon the proportion owned by major stockholders was three-fourths of the total amount. This was mainly due to Kim Sung-Soo and Kim Nyun-Soo's positive attitudes toward management; they invested their own assets in the company in preparation for redeeming the company's debts due to Kyungsung, since at that time it became a nepotic company largely owned by Kim's family. Such a nepotic company is not unusual in underdeveloped countries. In Western capitalistic countries, an originally nepotic company would later change into a joint stock company, reflecting just the opposite order of development. At this point, reviewing Kyungsung's developmental process, we are aware of its being a model case of national enterprise under colonialism. It started as a national company to compete with a Japanese firm, but later became a nepotic company.

4. Development of the Cotton-Weaving Industry[6] (1930-1945)

During this time, one of the important Japanese economic policies affecting Korea was the Japanese amendment of the Control Law of Key Industries, which was to be enforced in Korea. As a result, Korea lost her economic independence, and with the 1937 advent of the China-Japan war, her industries were completely merged into the structure of a controlled economy in war, followed by the establishment of policy regarding high national dependence. Accordingly, the economy became the base for war supplies and provided a source of food and clothes to the front line. It also played a role as an independent production base for new weapons.

After the war began, even more Japanese monopolistic capital was invested in Korea; the military reorganization of industry in the Korean economy eventually also exploited industrial resources, raw materials, manpower and so on. Being the base for war supplies brought about the industrialization of the Korean economy and an increase in the heavy chemical industry. In the late 1930s, during the period of preparation for war, the growth rates of the various light industries differed greatly. Industries such as spinning, weaving and ceramics related to munitions production and the building industry took long strides, but consumer goods industries were relatively tied up, although a spinning plant located near a munitions plant grew rapidly in the 1930s.

The rapid growth in the number of factories and workers in the spinning and weaving industry is noteworthy: in 1939 factories numbered 608 and workers 47,000. The concentration of production and manpower was high. Large factories, although representing only 7% of the total number of firms, employed 67% of the total work force and accounted for 86% of all production. Despite having been completely under the domination and financial control of Japan since the 1930s, the spinning and weaving industry made great strides toward becoming a modern factory-manufacturing industry.

Traditionally in Korea textile products have been able to sustain themselves as a home industry, but once a factory-manufacturing industry had been set up, the products became dependent on the demand. In the textile industry of 1939, private factories accounted for 77.5% of the total products, government enterprise 0.2% and domestic industry 22.3%.

In brief, since the 1930s the spinning and weaving industries in Korea have grown rapidly, particularly in the cotton industry, and have gradually attained self-sufficiency. In other cloth, however, thise self-sufficiency is still far from being realized, and Korea is still very dependent on Japan.

5. War and the Period of Disturbances[7] (1946–1961)

Following the general pattern of industrial growth, the fiber industry of Korea increased its production and employment and rapidly substituted for the import of fiber products. After the Korean War, the characteristic of the fiber industry, complemented by a sufficiency of equipment, raw material and low-paid labor, enabled Korea to develop in this area. Because of this, the natural fiber industry was able to become completely self-supplying by

1956. In the chemical fiber industry, however, there was only slow development in spite of the increase in demand. Following Korea's liberation in 1945 and the establishment of a new government, the fiber industry continued to expand, and there was good growth in the development of woolen fabrics. However, its equipment was destroyed during the Korean War, which began in 1950.

There was a great increase in production capacity between 1953 and 1957, Korea's reconstruction period, and the industry had completed its quantitative enlargement by 1957 when importation was prohibited. But the rapid development in equipment and the increase in demand of the chemical fiber industry yielded an over-supply, producing new problems; old equipment was replaced with new and the qualitative progress of textile goods became important. By the end of the 1950s fiber products had not increased, but through improvements in equipment, the quality and the productivity were enhanced, and thus greater efforts were made to create a larger demand. The first step was also taken to provide equipment for the production of chemical textiles.

The war had not interrupted silk spinning and weaving, however, and this had developed steadily with constant access to raw materials. Demand increased and support from the government helped the industry to realize greater sales than any other industry.

Since the establishment of the First Republic in 1948, people had recognized the importance of the cotton spinning and weaving industry and strove to make it a normal operation. Raw materials and equipment changes were promoted by Economic Cooperation and Administration aid. The destruction wrought by the Korean War on this industry was so great that it was forced to start over again. Government statistics showed that 70% of the industry's existing facilities and 69% of its buildings were destroyed during the war. Damage totalled $23 million. A plan for reconstruction of the industry was established with help from the United Nations; Korea began to import reconstruction equipment and started stocking raw materials with funds from United Nations Korea Reconstruction Agency, Civil Relief in Korea and ECA. Its emphasis shifted from imports to domestic products. Since 1953 the industry has further enlarged by importing raw materials with Korea Foreign Exchange funds. By the 1960s Korea was able to supply herself and also export cotton fabrics. But as she depended completely upon U.S. raw materials for her cotton spinning and weaving, she could not keep a balance of supply and demand, and this resulted in financial difficulties.

After 1947 raw silk production began to decrease year by year. In 1949 it was 540 tons, just 31% of what it had been in 1940. In 1956 Korea exported 145 tons of raw silk, 24% of all exported products, with the help of equipment reconstruction funds and foreign aid; international prices went up. Since 1956 raw silk production has remained stationary because of the decrease in export prices. Annually, however, the ability to produce this item has increased. After the Korean War, with the products of the domestic silk spinning and weaving industry tied up, the supply of raw silk was completely dependent on foreign demand. Stocking raw materials and enlarging the equipment were only a subsidiary task. The growth of the spinning industry was due to the regular export of raw silk in the 1960s. From 1954 to 1961 the silk and artificial silk spinning and weaving industries were both tied up, which reflected their relative weakness in contrast to the chemical textiles industry.

Since the country's liberation in 1945, the wool spinning and weaving industry has made the greatest progress. Because it was situated in the southern district, it was not destroyed during the war and developed rapidly and without interruption during the postwar years. All the equipment was very old and there were no pieces for combing and spinning, however; because of this, the modernization plan of this industry began with such equipment as its emphasis. With equipment modernization and sufficient raw materials, the woolen spinning and weaving industry was able to develop in earnest. From having had no production equipment in 1945, this industry accounted for 4.4% of total manufactured products and 17.6% of textile products in 1960. It replaced imports with domestic products and greatly aided the development of the domestic apparel industry.

Synthetic fiber goods were introduced into Korea during the

Korean War. In the 1950s the country produced nylon textiles only. At the end of the 1950s stretch nylon yarn and P.V.A. (polyvinyl alcohol) yarn were produced. Lack of production equipment for synthetic fiber yarn caused this industry to remain undeveloped in equipment and productivity, thus causing an imbalance in supply and demand. After 1961 the demand for synthetic fiber became very strong. The wool spinning and weaving industries switched over in part to synthetic fiber production, and in the 1960s this was the basis for the rapid progress in the synthetic fiber industry.

6. The Turning Point[8] (1962–1966)

The 1960s were important in Korean economic development. Up to then the economic development plan, which had been only partially achieved, was carried out systematically as a part of a middle and long-term plan.

The government's first five-year economic development plan began in 1962. Its objectives were the improvement of the ailing industrial structure and construction of a self-sustaining economic system with the help of the industrial foundation. It contributed little to the cotton and spinning and weaving industry but much to the artificial textile industry. The development of the latter, which was completely dependent on imports, was well planned and thus a balance of supply and demand was achieved.

In October of 1962 the government announced a basic ploy regarding cotton spinning and weaving equipment which included such things as prohibition of new equipment construction. The government intended to import raw materials for the purpose of exporting.

In that foreign and domestic economic environment, funds for buying raw cotton had been assured by the International Cooperation Administration aid fund and the Public Law 480 aid fund (Agricultural Development and Assistance Act, 1954) since 1962. Under the terms the U.S. insisted that Korea should import raw cotton from them since that was an important American export.

To export more cotton spinning and weaving products, an export responsibility system and a self-compensation system for deficits were planned and implemented. Through these effective export development policies, Korea exported $15,690,000 worth of cotton products in 1966, which was 20% more than in 1965.

7. The Growth Period[9] (1967–1971)

The cotton spinning and weaving industry of Korea built a foundation for keeping pace with the world during 1967–1971. As the government's economic development plan was successfully carried out, this industry developed greatly. The goal of the government's second five-year economic development plan, beginning in 1967, was to develop positive growth in the chemical, steel and machinery industries, and then to build in the potential for high industrial development. Because of this shift in emphasis, the cotton spinning and weaving industries decreased greatly in efficacy.

The demand for raw cotton was the principal factor determining annual expansion of cotton spinning and weaving products, and as foreign and domestic demand increased for cotton products, equipment size was enlarged to handle this demand. The majority of raw cotton used was furnished by the aid plan of the U.S. and large surpluses accrued, but the development of the national economy and a change in that foreign aid policy caused alteration in the supply structure.

The supply of and demand for cotton textiles fluctuate according to the increase in national income and foreign demand. Between 1967 and 1971, the increase in foreign demand altered the direction of the production system of cotton spinning and weaving industries from domestic demand to export. The quantitative supply of cotton textiles increased in proportion to the increase in equipment but the managerial environment of the cotton spinning and weaving industry, as a result of the continuous price rise of raw cotton and the import regulations of developed countries, became worse. Since the objective of the government's economic policy was continuous growth through export enlargement, however, the cotton spinning and weaving industry practiced this policy. Thus, since 1966 the industry has operated under this export responsibility and self-compensation system without outside help.

8. The "Take-off" Period[10] (1972–1976)

During 1971–76, the government's third five-year economic development plan was successfully carried out. Korea was severely tried by the oil shock in 1973, an unstable international monetary system and a sudden change in the international economic environment. Still, by coping with these problems rapidly, the country exported $10 billion of goods in 1977. During this growth trend in the national economy, the cotton spinning and weaving industry developed more rapidly than during any other period. As cotton spinning and weaving equipment increased, the consumption of raw cotton also increased commensurately.

9. The Maturity Period[11] (1977–present)

The total scale of supply and demand of the fiber industry in 1977 was ten times greater than in 1961. After the government's concentrated economic development of Korea, the production of fiber goods was accelerated. The growth of the fiber industry was attributed primarily to the increase of exports and the substitutions for imports by the increasing production of chemical fiber. The ratio of export to demand for all fiber increased from 2.4% in 1961 to 61.1% in 1977, and the dependence on imports decreased from 85.3% to 46.9%. The supply of fiber in Korea was greatly improved with the increase in production of chemical fiber which began in the 1960s. Taking into consideration the various ways in which it is used, the present situation with alternate chemical fibers is one of continued optimism.

Recently the economic situation has allowed old equipment to be replaced and more units to be acquired, and automation has been introduced; these factors contribute to the growth of productivity and improved international competitiveness. The equipment of the Korean cotton spinning industry was a mere 430,000 spindles in 1953, increasing to 961,900 in 1971, and in late 1977, 2,542,684 spindles were in use, just behind the U.S., China, Japan, India, West Germany, France and Brazil. The cotton spinning industry was second only to the chemical fiber industry for its economy of scale.

The chemical fiber industry made rapid progress in a short period after equipment for PVA fiber production 2MT was introduced from Japan.[12] Such chemical fibers as Nylon Fiber, Viscose Fiber, PVA Staple Fiber had only 20.8MT, and almost all such items were being produced by late 1976.

III. The Business Climate of the Korean Fiber Industry

It may be said that the style of top management plays the most important role in formulation of the business climate. The fiber industry offers an interesting opportunity to examine the development process of the business climate in Korea and how this affected one industry.

I will divide the process of development of the business climate on this industry into two periods: pre-modern (before 1900) and modern (after 1900). The latter will be further divided into four stages: the formulation period (1900–1945), the transition period (1946–1961), the growth period (1962–1977), and the maturity period (1978–present) (see Figure 3).

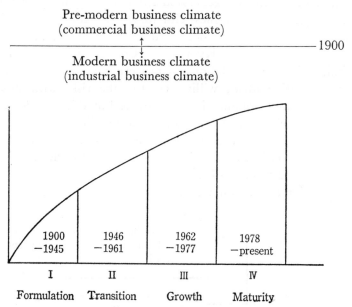

FIG. 3   Business Climate Life Cycle in the Modern Korean Textile Industry.

In the modern Korean textile industry, the formulation period of the business climate took place during the time of Japanese colonialism and the transition period during the Korean War, being influenced by American domination. The growth period was achieved during the First, Second and Third Economic Development Plans for independent economic growth which were carried out following the May 16th Revolution in 1961, and the maturity period began during the Fourth Economic Development Plan, running into trouble over the increasing problems of the high-growth policy.

1. Business Climate in the Formulation Stage

The management style of the entrepreneur, who was a type of business agent, had four possible requisites, depending on his management philosophy and strategy: innovative ideas, risk-taking, financing, and staffing and organizing. Among these, the former two are understood as "upper concepts" and the latter two, as "lower concepts."

Although supposedly generated from the beginning of the 20th century, the modern business climate in the Korean fiber industry actually appeared to have been formulated from 1920. At that time entrepreneurs like the Kyungsung Co., relying upon national capital, built the foundations of modern management combining their innovative ideas, willingness to take risks with financing, and staffing and organizational abilities. But this was done under the pressure of Japanese colonialism, so the climate was greatly influenced not only by the technical and economic environment but also by the political and social environment. In addition, modern scientific management still could not be established in the areas of compensation and organization.

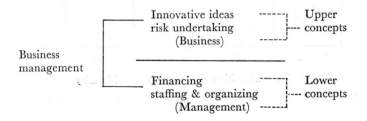

2. Business Climate in the Transition Stage

The transition period was an unstable period which saw the occupation under the military administration of the U.S., the First Republic, the Korean War, and the April 19th Movement, all of which lasted from 1945 to 1960. The Korean War had the greatest impact.

The war lasted for three years and destroyed nearly all production facilities; it also caused a great change in the value system of the Korean people. During this period the Korean military attempted to modernize by patterning itself after the U.S. military forces. The receiving of military assistance and long exposure to the American culture inevitably influenced postwar enterprises to imitate the American technology and management climate. At that turning point, a rapid transition took place in Korea's traditional business climate, and the philosophy of competition and ideology of the bourgeoisie infiltrated business in the Korean fiber industry. It can certainly be said that the Korean War provoked the business climate of Korea to take continuous steps toward industrialization.

3. Business Climate in the Growth Stage

After the May 16th Revolution in 1961, the management system of the Korean military forces was adapted to fit governmental and other institutional systems. The Korean military had accepted U.S. military ways, which were based on an advanced management system. As a result of this, government and business were introduced to a truly scientific system.

The First Five-Year Economic Development Plan paved the way for independent economic development in Korea. Through the positive policy of industrialization the textile industry also made rapid progress. Advanced technologies and management systems were introduced from abroad. Growth-oriented production became important, and a business climate based on innovative ideas and risk-taking had been established.

Through the high-growth policies of the First, Second and Third Five-Year Plans, the textile industry's progress was possible because of the low cost and good quality of labor. The chemical

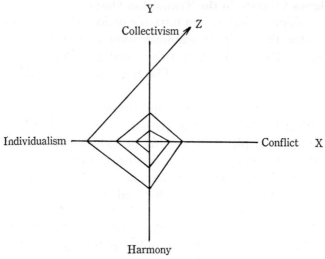

Fig. 4.

textile industry was among those heavy and chemical industries able to step-up production with government aid.

Business enterprises emphasized a production-technology system under growth-oriented management policies and strategies. So the important thing that we are interested in is the risk-taking ability and innovative ideas based on the vitality of top management. They had accepted rationalism and endeavored to establish a dynamic and unique management style. Though lagging behind, the production-technology approach was able to produce an advanced kind of system, an "underdeveloped country-forward type." As a result, a dynamic management system through unprogrammed decision-making had been created. It was an "organic" management style unique to Korea, and combining the advantages of both the Western (U.S.) ways of handling "conflict," and the Eastern (Japanese) way of "consensus"—a Z-dimensional management style (Figure 4).

In some fields a major change in management culture from production-oriented to market-oriented had taken place. For instance, the D-Nylon Co. had produced only nylon since its founding in 1965, but in 1968, recognizing the limitations of the market, management began producing items of polyester, and diversified to such popular goods as tirecords, tents and fishing nets, in addition to expanding the supply of fabric items.[14] Thus the company was able to keep its share of the market in spite of strong competition.

4. Business Climate in the Maturity Stage

The world experienced inflation, making it difficult for the growth-oriented economic policy of the Third Economic Development Plan, which had been aimed at the heavy and chemical industries. Many problems had emerged from business climates that had been dependent on the idea of innovativeness and risk-taking, and those of production and high-growth-oriented management strategies. Hereafter a new dimension of business climate and management system was required:

(1) Excessive desire to accomplish high growth had given rise to business instability.

(2) Accumulation of technology in the areas of marketing and business administration required coping with international competition.

(3) Lack of marketing technology set limits to the development of the textile industry.

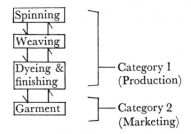

Although there was great progress in Category 1, more production technology was needed. Category 2 could not develop because of the shortage of expert fashion designers or marketing experts.

(4) Lack of understanding of a business administration system connecting production with marketing was an obstacle to the development of the textile industry. In the personnel and organizational areas particularly, employee-employer co-

operation and motivation had become very important. Unprogrammed decision-making combining the stylistic advantages of both the U.S. and Japan was expected to develop
during the growth stage, but what Korea experienced were
the disadvantages of both. Accordingly, the necessity of establishing a better view of management is still keenly required.

(5)   A new dimensional business climate should be formulated
in the maturity stage of the life cycle. To do something for
the development of the Korean textile industry, we should
first of all establish a stable business climate which can cope
with competition under a low-growth policy, giving up the
high-growth policy. Next, we should change the style of management from a "dependent-on-government" type to an
"independent" type through the accumulation of administra-
tive and operational technology cost-cutting know-how. Finally,
we should establish a management system based on the "principle of community" through renewed employee-employer
cooperation.

NOTES

1.   Park, J. E., "The Historical Study of the Korean Cotton Textile
     Industry, "Ph.D. Thesis, Kyung Hee University, Seoul, 1980,
     pp. 17–67.
2.   *Ibid.*, pp. 68–114.
3.   *Ibid.*, pp. 115–159.
4.   Joe, K. J., The History of the Korean Entrepreneurs, Bak Young
     Sa, Seoul, 1973, pp. 239–267.
5.   Kyung Sung Spinning and Weaving Co. Ltd., "The Fifty-year
     History of Kyung Sung Spinning and Weaving Co. Ltd.," Seoul,
     1969, pp. 48–53.
6.   Park, J. E., op. cit., pp. 160–197.
7.   Kim, Y. B., The Production Structure and Growth Process of
     Korean Fiber Industry, Research Report Vol. No. 75–21, Korean
     Development Institute, Seoul, 1975, pp. 46–55.
8.   Korean Textile Association, "The Thirty-year History of the
     Korean Textile Association," "Seoul, 1977, pp. 108–122.
9.   *Ibid.*, pp. 123–141.

10. *Ibid.*, pp. 146–183.
11. Kim, Y. B., The Characteristics and Demand-Supply Structure of the Textile and Electronic Industry, Research Report Vol. 28., Korea Development Institute, Seoul, 1977, pp. 24–39.
12. Kolon Co. Ltd., "The Twenty-year History of Kolon Co. Ltd.," Seoul, 1977, pp. 218–260.
13. Dong-Yang Nylon Co. Ltd., "The Ten-year History of Dong Yang Nylon Co. Ltd.," Seoul, 1976, pp. 59–69.
14. *Ibid.*, pp. 132–147.

COMMENTS

1

Gerhard Adelmann
University of Bonn

I have written these comments on the paper of my colleague, Professor Choi, with a certain uneasiness. On the one hand, I hold the Japanese colleagues here to be more experienced than me, a European from far away, to comment on the development of the Korean textile industry which has been influenced to a great extent by Japan. On the other hand, I am pleased that Professor Choi placed the "business climate" in the center of his paper, just as I did. Yet his definition differs in some aspects from my understanding of the term.

In chapter II, "The Historical Domination of the Development of Korean Fiber Industry," Professor Choi points out the socio-economic and political environment under which the firms are managed. This business environment I understand to be in accordance with the outline given by Professor Yonekawa, i.e., the business climate of any industry, textile or cotton industry. Business management or business structure, as Professor Choi describes them in chapter III, are not the "business climate" itself, but "they and their behaviors reflect the business climate" or, at most, influence it.

At the beginning of his paper Professor Choi shows clearly the present situation of the Korean fiber industry by presenting two tables and figures for the period 1953 (the end of the Korean War) —1977. If we put the trends of manufacturing output to GNP and of textile industry output to total manufacturing industry output into historical perspective, we can see that between 1953 and 1977 the Korean industry was at a stage of development which might be compared with the English industry of the seventeenth, eighteenth and beginning nineteenth centuries.

The proportional share of the German industry's net inland production also amounted to 20% in 1850, the earliest year for which we have rather reliable data and was 29.8% in 1886. In the period 1953–1977 the importance of the Korean textile industry in the total industry, if the output is taken, was just about equal to that of the British textile industry around 1907. After its industrialization the German cotton industry never had such a high proportional share (1859: 5.2%, 1913: 2.4% of the net value added) of the total output of industry. The importance of the Korean textile industry declined in the period researched, a development which is typical for the process of industrialization; yet, and this is typical once more, the relative decline of the importance of the textile industry has progressed faster in the late-comer Korea than in Great Britain or Germany, where the industrialization began earlier.

Now I shall turn to the historical development of the Korean textile industry, especially the cotton industry. In early modern times the Korean cotton industry was by no means underdeveloped. It exported substantial amounts of cotton cloth to Japan, as we know. According to Professor Choi the decline of the old Korean cotton industry began at the end of the seventeenth century, i.e., much earlier than the effects of the English industrial revolution. He mentions interior Korean factors as reasons: first the fiscal factor, an overcharged taxation of cotton products, second the economic factors, and here the agrarian production system seems very important to me.

As far as I could see in the literature I had at hand, the old Korean cotton industry was an old house industry for the rural self-sufficiency or organized in the putting-out system. According to Professor Choi this Korean house industry could never advance to the modern production style at the end of the nineteenth century. He mentions interior reasons and foreign Japanese political influences. Of the interior economic reasons, i.e., among others, lack of capital and missing entrepreneurial spirit, I cannot accept the "low level of the endogenous technology accumulated" as a reason. None of the cotton industries which had been industrialized at an earlier stage based on the "endogenous technology accumulated," but got the necessary technology from abroad, for instance Germany from England. In my opinion the rural state of the Korean economy and especially the feudal system continuing under Japanese rule hindered an earlier industrialization of Korea.

To what extent the "invasion of Japanese imperialism" was the main reason for the delayed industrialization or mechanization of the Korean industry, as Professor Choi and other Korean authors like Sung-Jae Koh* and Sung-Jo Park**, think, could only be shown in a closer study than Professor Choi much less I could offer. Yet it seems to me, after reading the paper, that the "Company Law" of the Japanese colonial policy did not have such oppressive effects as are often attributed to it, as otherwise the founding of a national Korean enterprise in 1911, even before the politically successful Samil Independence Movement in 1919 which led to a certain readjustment of the Japanese administration policy, could not be explained. Taking the example of the Kyung-sung Spinning and Weaving Company, Professor Choi impressively describes the national emotions as a foundation philosophy of the few Korean enterprises. But according to Sung-Jo Park they got subsidies from the Japanese colonial government later on too, because of their unsatisfactory development.

How difficult it was to overcome the emotional barriers between Korea and Japan we have known from the history of their relations after the end of World War II and the end of the Korean War. Professor Choi has pointed out the rather successful reconstruction of the Korean textile industry which was damaged badly during the Korean War; this was done with the help of government plans and foreign aid, especially from the United Nations and the U.S.A. I would only like to add one more aspect and that concerns the Japanese share in the reconstruction after 1963 and after the Japanese-Korean Normalization Treaty. The Japanese contribution

---

* Koh, Sung Jae, *Stages of Industrial Development in Asia. A Comparative History of the Cotton Industry in Japan, India, China and Korea*, Philadelphia, 1966.

** Park, Sung-Jo, *Die Wirtschaftsbeziehungen zwischen Japan and Korea 1910–1968*, Wiesbaden, 1969 (Schriften des Instituts für Asienkunde in Hamburg, Bd. 24).

was first given in an indirect way by reparation payments, then by private investments, mainly in the way of private loans and less in the way of straight private investments in Korean counterparts, especially in the synthetic fiber industry (as especially C. Itoh, Mitsui and Mitsubishi did). The last-named firms had been extensively investing in colonial Korea before World War II (Park, pp. 194 f.).

Looking at the immediate past, people have tried to discredit the growing Japanese economic influence in Korea as a new Japanese neo-colonialism. But looking at the earlier colonial economic ties one can also detect further-reaching forces which might form a model for an international division of labor, for a necessary international economic cooperation of partners.

Although I regard management style or strategy as a topic of its own, I am sure that Professor Choi and I do agree on the fact that the business climate/business environment has influenced the management style. When Professor Choi points out that U.S.A.-style and Japanese style had been combined in a new Korean view of management he is obviously aware of certain different national mentalities standing behind those styles. Perhaps they may be labeled by the sociological categories of individualistic and group spirit.

2

Eisuke Daito
Tohoku University

Professor Choi analyzed the process of development of the Korean textile industry by dividing it into several stages. The main characteristics of and the changes in the "business climate" were clearly described. It would seem safe, however, to say that he focused his analysis on the development of the industry as a whole, not on the growth of individual firms. I am therefore raising some questions concerning the internal structure and managerial aspects of the industry.

First of all, I found it very interesting that the Kyungsung Co., the first modern cotton textile firm in Korea, could prosper only after it became a family business. The reason why I am interested in this story is that it seems to form a marked contrast to the Indian experience explained by Professor Tripathi. It may be argued that industrial late-comers have to develop a more powerful institution, such as the management agency system, from the outset of industrialization, in order to gulf the gap between themselves and advanced countries. Although Professor Choi wrote that "such a nepotic company generally appears in developing countries," this generalization may not apply to some nations. In any case, the relationship between the family system and the business system provides us with an important clue in understanding the "business climate" of a society. What can be said about the relationship between these two basic social institutions in the subsequent stages of development of Korean industry?

Second, I would like to know about labor management in Korean firms. In the 1930s, as was shown by Professor Choi, Japanese firms built factories in Korea. I think that one of the main factors which motivated them to do so was the Factory Act which prohibited late-night work in Japan. This had been an integral element of their labor management practices. It is well known that more than 80% the workers in the Japanese cotton textile industry were young girls who worked for a few years before their marriage and lived in dormitories attached to factories. According to the company history of the Toyo Cotton Spinning Company, the Japanese transplanted not only late-night work but also other elements of their labor practices in Korea. Did Korean firms follow Japanese practices or develop their own?

Third, I would like Professor Choi to clarify the highly abstract concepts in the third section of his paper. He should elucidate more concretely the concepts of "the growth-oriented management policies and strategies" and "the production-oriented management culture." In every country, with the exception of a few major firms which handle the entire manufacturing process from spinning to finishing, most firms sell their woven products in the gray. They think it is too risky to venture into the finishing phase of the industry. Moreover, there are many advantages in this strategy of partial integration. On the one hand, it provides them with a much wider market, which makes it possible for them to realize economies of scale. On the other hand, they are able to avoid the inherent risks of dealing with finished products by utilizing such middlemen as converters, which allows them to direct their efforts toward the expansion and rationalization of the production process of gray goods. Since complete integration is a highly risky venture, this growth-oriented, risk-avoiding policy is natural and justifiable as well. I regard this as the essence of "the growth-oriented management policies and strategies" and "the production-oriented management culture." It therefore can be argued that in spite of Professor Choi's insistence that a "business climate based on innovative ideas and risk-taking abilities had been established," the business climate of the growth stage was based more on financing and "staffing and organization." Needless to say, innovative ideas always play vital roles in industrial development. However, the growth of an industry depends not only on innovators, but also on imitators who quickly follow them.

Japanese Cotton Spinning Industry during the Pre-World War I Period

Naosuke Takamura
University of Tokyo

I. Market

1. Cotton Yarn and Cotton Cloth

Cotton cloth was the cloth most in demand among the Japanese people during the Edo Era (1603–1867). The production of cotton cloth relied on hand spinning and hand weaving, using domestic raw cotton which grew extensively in the western part of Japan, and it was for commercial purposes as well as for home use. After the opening of the ports in 1859, cotton cloth and cotton yarn were imported from England. Their import continued to increase even after the first cotton mill started operation in 1867. The demand for cotton cloth in 1880 was estimated as 23% for imported cotton cloth, 41% for cotton cloth made from imported yarn, 35% for that made from hand-spun yarn, and 1% for that made from domestic machine-made yarn.

In the latter half of the 1880s, however, spinning mills of over 10,000 spindle size were built one after another, and by 1890 the domestic production of machine-made yarn exceeded the imports from England and India. In the 1890s, the export of cotton yarn to Asian countries including China increased, and finally exports of this material exceeded imports in 1897 (Figure 1). Domestic production was concentrated on the production of coarse yarn such as 16s and 20s both for export and domestic use, and such coarse yarn was used for hand weaving. During the 1900s, a third of the cotton yarn was exported, and Japan displaced India from the top position in the amount of cotton yarn imported into China in 1914.

Also during the 1900s, spinning firms competed to import power

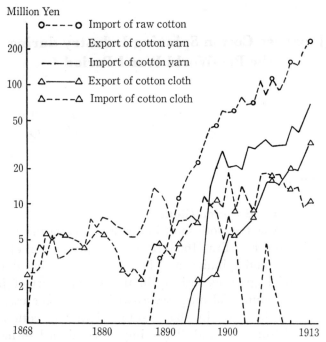

Million Yen

FIG. 1   Trends in Cotton Trade of Japan.

Source: Tōyō Keizai Shinpō-sha, *Foreign Trade of Japan: A Statistical Survey.*

looms and to produce cotton cloth as well as cotton yarn. These were coarse goods such as sheeting made from low count yarn. Though the homemade cotton cloth was too coarse to be used in Japan, it was used in China and Korea because of low prices. Thus, the export of cotton cloth increased and exceeded the import from England and other countries in 1909. In 1911, Japan exceeded the United States in the amount of cotton cloth imported into China, moving up to the second position after England, and its share became about 20%.

Japanese spinning firms were eager to export. About half of the homemade cotton yarn was exported as yarn or cloth just before World War I. There were two important factors which encouraged this. First was the contribution of trading companies, including

TABLE 1 Growth of the Spinning Industry in the World.

Country	No. of Spindles (thousand)				Estimated consumption			
	1877	1900	Aug. 1913	% of Ring Spindles	Bales (Sept. 1912–Aug. 1913)	American %	Indian %	Egyptian %
England	41,881	45,500	55,653	18.7	3,825 thousand	85.8	1.2	9.2
U.S.A.	9,600	19,472	31,505	86.9	5,786	96.0	—	3.5
Germany	4,650	8,000	11,186	54.2	1,580	79.7	11.1	6.5
Russia	2,500	7,500	9,123	58.7	1,942	19.4	0.8	3.5
France	5,000	5,500	7,400	45.7	987	79.8	9.4	7.9
India	1,287*	4,945	6,084	72.5	1,698	4.3	95.6	0.1
Austria-Hungary	1,555	3,300	4,909	49.0	837	74.9	18.4	3.9
Italy	800	1,940	4,600	75.3	744	72.3	22.2	2.4
Japan	8	1,274	2,300	97.7	1,581	26.8	62.5	1.0
Spain	1,750	2,615	2,000	60.0	329	79.5	9.5	5.7
Belgium	800	920	1,492	66.8	257	66.4	32.0	0.3
Switzerland	1,850	1,550	1,398	18.0	89	65.9	3.6	29.4
Total	70,921	105,681	143,453	50.5	20,277	67.9	16.7	4.5
China	—	497	823	—	—	—	—	—

* Figure is for 1878.

Sources: Bureau of Agriculture and Bureau of Commerce, *Report of Competitive Exhibition on Cotton and Sugar, No. 2,* Japan Cotton Spinners' Association, *Reference Books for Cotton Spinning.*

TABLE 2   Estimated Consumption in the Settsu Spinning Company.

Year	Average Count	% Chinese	% Indian	% American	% Others
1903 first half	......	44.5	29.2	13.5	12.8
second half	16.5	27.9	57.0	7.8	7.3
1904 ————	16.9	38.0	42.0	20.0	—
	16.0	46.1	38.9	10.4	4.6
1905 ————	16.0	35.0	35.0	30.0	—
	16.8	40.0	40.0	20.0	—
1906 ————	15.8	50.0	30.0	20.0	—
	15.9	32.0	23.0	45.0	—
1907 ————	15.7	32.0	38.0	25.0	5.0
	16.2	25.0	52.0	18.0	5.0
1908 ————	16.2	31.0	47.0	18.0	4.0
	15.8	20.0	59.0	17.0	4.0
1909 ————	16.5	8.1	76.6	15.0	0.3
	16.7	10.8	74.5	13.4	1.3
1910 ————	16.5	10.5	80.5	9.0	—
	16.5	18.3	80.8	0.1	0.8
1911 ————	16.5	32.4	66.4	1.2	—
	16.5	21.3	6.0	72.6	0.1
1912 ————	16.2	9.3	72.2	17.1	1.4
	16.1	9.0	72.1	15.7	3.2
1913 ————	16.2	12.1	70.0	16.2	1.6
	16.3	8.2	82.6	4.8	4.4
1914 first half	16.2	5.2	83.9	8.1	2.8

Source: Japan Cotton Spinners' Association, *Reference Books for Cotton Spinning.*

the Mitsui Bussan Company. They exported cotton yarn and cloth on consignment of spinning firms in the beginning and then later by purchasing from the firms. Unlike Western commercial companies, they did not rely on compradors in the Chinese market but traded directly with Chinese merchants. Second was the contribution of the Spinners' Association, which was organized among spinning firms in 1882 and had often tried to prevent the decline in prices since 1900 by reducing operations. This association encouraged export by excluding the production of cotton goods for export from the object of output reduction or by offering subvention for production for export.

2. Raw Cotton

Domestic raw cotton was used in Japanese spinning mills in the early stage, but it was displaced by inexpensive Chinese raw cotton, and in the 1890s Indian and American cotton was used. In the 1900s, Indian cotton took the greater portion, and American and Chinese cotton followed (Table 1), while domestic raw cotton was little used. Spinning mills developed a special art of mixing various kinds of raw cotton. The growth in mixing technique made it possible for spinning firms to spin a fixed count yarn by mixing different kinds of raw cotton which were available at lower prices on occasion, and to reduce the cost. As shown by the example of the Settsu Spinning Company, the average count of yarn was almost constant, though the kind of raw cotton varied (Table 2).

There were two reasons why foreign raw cotton was available at low prices. First was because of the activities of trading companies. These companies, which imported raw cotton under the consignment of spinning firms in the beginning and later to sell it to spinning firms, began to purchase raw cotton in cotton-growing areas in India and the United States after 1905. Thus, good quality raw cotton became available at lower prices. Moreover, trading companies tried to supply the cheapest cotton of the time to spinning firms by collecting information through cotton trading centers in various countries. Second was the contribution of the Spinners' Association. With the increase in the import of Indian cotton, the Nippon Yūsen Company inaugurated a regular service line between Japan and Bombay in 1893. Taking this opportunity, the Spinners' Association, trading companies, and the Nippon Yūsen Company signed a contract, agreeing that spinning firms and trading companies should entrust the Nippon Yūsen Company with conveyance of cotton, and, in return, the Nippon Yūsen Company gave a discount on freight charges. This contract made it possible to supply Indian cotton economically to spinning firms.

II. Capital

1. Integration

Spinning mills, which produced only cotton yarn in the early

TABLE 3   Equipment Fund (major firms).

		1889	1894	1899	1904	1909	1914(g)
Total of 5 firms (thousand yen)	Fixed assets	2,526	5,881	10,410	15,945	36,936	55,565
	Depreciation on fixed assets	2	41	614	1,710	7,725	17,896
	Internal reserve(a)	453	911	1,532	3,833	15,602	26,529
	Paid-up capital	2,527	4,954	7,600	11,553	21,709	35,538
	Liabilities(b) (long-term)	468	1,006	832	1,989	2,984	10,716
	Surplus from owned capital(c)	454	−16	−1,273	−559	375	6,501
	Surplus from long-term fund(d)	921	990	−447	1,430	3,359	17,217
	Name of company						
% Fixed asset ratio(e)	Osaka	81.5	124.7	119.6	124.3	102.6	102.7
	Mie	88.9	96.1	90.1	94.9	87.2	87.7
	Kanegafuchi	88.5	78.0	134.5	118.0	113.7	103.6
	Amagasaki		146.6	113.4	57.5	64.5	61.6
	Settsu		87.6	86.5	83.4	98.6	66.2
	Total	84.8	100.3	114.0	103.6	99.0	89.5
% Internal capital ratio(f)	Osaka	32.1	11.1	22.9	19.8	39.8	52.6
	Mie	6.8	34.5	27.0	32.7	53.8	64.0
	Kanagafuchi	0.2	3.4	7.7	17.5	43.3	47.2
	Amagasaki		10.1	24.8	96.0	117.1	80.2
	Settsu		28.1	48.1	58.0	70.7	92.4
	Total	18.0	16.1	19.5	31.4	52.2	60.5

(a) Reserves and balances carried forward. (b) Debentures and loans. (c) Internal reserve and paid-up capital minus fixed assets. (d) Internal reserves, paid-up capital, long-term liabilities minus fixed assets. (e) Fixed assets divided by owned capital. (f) Internal capital (internal reserve and depreciation on fixed assets) divided by fixed assets and depreciation on fixed assets. (g) The Osaka and the Mie figures are as of June, 1914.

Sources: Kazuo Yamaguchi, *History of Industrial Finance in Japan, volume on Finance in the Cotton Industry.*

period, began to produce cotton cloth as well as cotton yarn during the 1900s through the use of power looms introduced from foreign countries. In 1913, spinning mills consumed 18% of the cotton yarn which they had produced themselves in the production of cotton cloth. In Japan, however, the rate of integration was quite limited, only 31% in 1928. Spinning firms believed that it was safer and more efficient to treat yarn and cloth from the point of management, because market conditions varied between yarn and cloth.

2.   Legal Form of Business and Fixed Capital

It was in 1893 that the Corporation Law was enforced, but most of the firms which were founded before that time were actually organized as joint stock companies. They were founded by collecting funds from several hundred stockholders, including merchants of major cities. It was not common in this period for one stockholder to hold more than half of the stocks, but about ten highly ranked stockholders generally shared 30–50% of the stocks. In this period, fixed capital was furnished mainly by share-capital (Table 3). The payment for stocks was usually made in installments. Banks indirectly supported spinning firms by financing stockholders on security of their stocks. As their internal reserve increased, spinning firms tended to appropriate it for fixed capital. While the capital increase was generally carried out by allotment to stockholders, some spinning companies offered stocks for public subscription at a premium.

3.   Working Capital

On the occasion of purchasing raw cotton, spinning firms usually advanced to trading companies a promissory note, which was to be discounted by city banks and rediscounted by the Bank of Japan. On the other hand, the marketing of cotton yarn with trading companies and wholesale dealers was usually based on cash payment. Therefore, spinning firms were favored with working capital. With the repletion of internal reserve, spinning firms began to purchase raw cotton at lower prices with cash payment.

III. Technique and Labor Forces

1. Technique

In the early period, spinning firms employed foreign machines such as the mule, ring, and throstle. In the latter half of the 1880s, these firms became careful about the selection of machines, and sent technical advisors to England in order to investigate various kinds before purchasing. As a result, ring frames were considered best for spinning coarse yarn; these exceeded mule frames in the number of spindles in 1890 and continued to increase. In the later period, ring spinning frames were also used for spinning high count yarn such as 60s and 80s, and took 98% of the spindles in 1913 (Table 1).

Among spinning frames imported from England, Platt Brothers' Company frames, which were imported by the Mitsui Bussan Company, were regarded as most efficient. Though water power was used as motive power in the beginning, it was later displaced by the steam engine, which was usually imported from England.

2. Labor Forces

A major part of the labor force were young female operatives. With the growth in ring spinning, the ratio of female workers increased to more than 80%. Most of them were daughters from poor farms and they entered spinning mills obtaining some advance payment, and lived in a dormitory. In spinning mills, operation was a day and night two-shift system. It was in 1929, when the factory law was enforced, though it was established in 1911, that night labor of female workers was prohibited by law. The Spinners' Association took effective measures for labor management. For example, spinning firms were united against strikes and picking out of workers.

III. Technique and Labor Forces

1. Technique

2. Labor Forces

CONCLUDING REMARKS

Shin-ichi Yonekawa

I shall mention several topics that I think the participants were deeply interested in through the conference.

First of all, I must start from the title of the conference, which is "the textile industry and business climate." As I had expected, many or almost all of the participants spoke of what they understood by the words "business climate," and quite naturally they differed subtly from each other. Fortunately, I do not think that this became a barrier to our having a fruitful discussion. As far as the top management is concerned, as M. J. Oates, H. V. Wortzel and others said, "business climate" includes problems both internal and external to firms, although the latter looks more challenging to management. At the same time we scholars have to take an interest in what H. Watanabe called "subjective factors" as well as the "objective conditions." In this respect D. Tripathi provided us with a helpful chart in his comment paper, which will certainly be useful to all of us. Moreover K. Nakagawa gave us an excellent explanation in the concluding discussion of the importance of cultural factors in understanding the business climate. In J.-T. Choi's paper, "business climate" seemed to imply a fairly short-term variable, while a large number of the attendants perceived it as a long-term variable. In reference to business climate I wrote in my paper that "above all he (the business historian) will take interest in the human elements: in the entrepreneur more than in capital and in the worker more than in wages, including their motives, behavior and the underlying social values." I think there is nothing novel in my emphasis, but in Japan a *homo economica*-oriented explanation of economic history is still dominant. As a matter of fact, I could not explain the differences of growth in firms without consideration of the social and cultural elements which stemmed from management and labor.

The next problem is the content of the textile industry. As expected, many papers started from the cotton spinning section of the industry. It was also natural that J.-T. Choi's paper was mainly concerned with both natural and synthetic fibers, because the industry has a short history in Korea. As business historians we tend to pay attention to the spinning sector of the industry, where comparatively large firms were predominant. On the other hand, H. Watanabe's comment was impressive in that it reminded us of the strategic importance in this century of the finishing sections, that is, bleaching, dyeing and printing. The Japanese textile industry has been suffering these days mainly because of these fragile sections, in contrast with Germany where they are most competitive. D. A. Farnie lamented in his paper that the small size and short life of the firms in England caused a lack of good enterprise history. This is especially true in the finishing sections of the industry, even in Japan where voluminous company histories of spinning firms are most available.

The participants took a common interest in the following items of the cotton spinning industry in the course of discussion.

The remarkable contrasts in the growth of firms in the four countries discussed in my paper interested them. The exposition of these contrasts would not be enough without the broad insights into every aspect of business climate in each country. In addition to what I wrote I should have referred to the difference among firms' financing power. This was just what M. Miyamoto referred to in his comment on T. Kuwabara's paper. However, all the participants agreed with G. Adelmann that production factors would not be enough to explain such contrasts. As far as Lancashire is concerned, D. A. Farnie put emphasis on "first experience" and "localism." Tripathi also mentioned the managing agents' unique ideology of mill management. On the other hand, it was quite natural that English spinners' behavior sounded strange to N. Takamura, who asked D. A. Farnie why they stopped their growth at their initial stages and why horizontal combinations overcame vertical ones there. Japanese scholars have tended to consider a stereotyped model of growth of firms as European reality. However, looking at the tables shown in my paper, it was striking that the growth of Japanese cotton spinning firms seemed to deviate less from the usually presumed model of growth.

N. Takamura also asked a question on M. J. Oates' remark that the smallness of mill scale resulted from the shortage in the number of managers and engineers available in the southern states. His question stemmed from the Japanese experience that sometimes professional managers and engineers did business in two firms. In this regard she answered that what mattered was the type of managers and engineers.

Non-profit motivation in building spinning mills was often mentioned. It has been confirmed that employment-oriented mill buildings were fairly common regardless of nationality. In her paper, M. J. Oates called the southern firms "community-sponsored" where the prime motive was the use of cotton cultivated in the area. Needless to say, cooperative mills in Lancashire can be called "community-sponsored." In Japan also we can easily find a number of cases based on local patriotism and nationalism.

The problem of commission merchants raised hot discussions among the participants. It has been confirmed that their roles were crucial in shaping the industrial features in each country. How high were their commissions in the four countries? What were their roles in the flotation of firms and in the formation of integrated firms? H. V. Wortzel supplied us with a good case study on the Lowell spinning industry. In Japan's case trading companies (*shosha*) were dominant in every aspect of the industry, but with the coming of this century large spinning firms became independent from them for their financing while remaining dependent upon them for the export of goods and the import of cotton. In this regard N. Takamura suggested that their commission generally was not high (around 2%). I might say that this is one of the reasons why the integration did not go down to the selling function in Japan as it did in the U.S.A. It is also deplorable that little is known with regard to English commission houses. D. A. Farnie's remark mentioned before holds truest in this section of the industry. A deeper understanding would be most fruitful considering their strategic roles in the industry. As T. Yuzawa commented on H. V. Wortzel's paper, we take common interest in the typology of merchants in each country.

In reference to my paper D. Tripathi cast doubt on Schumpeter's key words of "innovators" and "followers." I am afraid that there was some misunderstanding among us with regard to this terminology. I presumed that each country had an innovative and influential firm even if it used imported technologies. Although it is true, as D. Tripathi mentioned, that the circumstances of firms differ even within one country, the degree of difference comes into question. The high localization of the cotton industry and the phenomenon of the "imitation effect," mentioned by M. J. Oates and observed in many spinning centers of the world, seem to demonstrate that this hypothesis was more useful in this industry than in other industries.

As far as political circumstances are concerned, colonial and tariff systems were discussed. To what extent was the British colonial system hostile to the growth of the Indian cotton industry? J.-T. Choi's paper asserted that Japanese imperialism surpressed the infant cotton industry in Korea. Was there any basic difference between the two colonial systems? T. Kuwahara was concerned with the various attitudes of Japanese management towards mill-building in China. It was properly pointed out that although Japanese management expertly handled the internal problems of each firm, Japanese political advantages in China must be considered in this case.

The effect of tariff was another topic. The underlying implication in D. A. Farnie's paper was that the English traditional belief in free trade did fatal damage to the Lancashire cotton industry. This roused a sharp comment from H. V. Wortzel. I think L. G. Sandburg's argument, on which D. A. Farnie depended, seems fragile, to say nothing of Lazonick's recent persuasive opposition. As business historians we seem to still have a lot of work to do on the managerial problems of the English cotton industry. As G. Adelmann described, the depressed period of the industry in Germany was a good chance to restore competitiveness to individual

TABLE 1 The Cotton Textile Industry around the Turn of the Century.

	Market			Capital		Technology & labor	
	Raw cotton market	Cotton goods marketing	Integration or specialization	Family business or corporation	Working capital	Ring or mule	Male or female
Germany	Bremen Cotton Exchange 1867	Export to Europe, Latin America; domestic	Partly integrated	Family business; corporation	Own (short-term); capital loans	Mule; ring	Even
India	Bombay Cotton Exchange	Export to China; domestic	Partly integrated	Family-dominated corporation	Public deposits; loans	Mule; ring	M
Japan	Sogoshosha	Export; coarse cloth to Asia; domestic-(kimono)	Partly integrated	Corporation	Promissory note; own capital; trading co.; bank	Ring	F
Korea after World War II	Seoul Daegu	Export; domestic	Partly integrated	Family-dominated corporation	Trading co.; bank	Ring	F
U.K.	Liverpool Cotton Exchange	Export to Europe, Asia; domestic	Specialization	Family business; corporation	Bill of exchange	Mule	F
U.S.A.	New York Cotton Exchange	Export to China (by large mills); domestic	Integrated	Corporation	Selling agent; bank	Ring	Even

firms. This was true in Japan. The replacement of mules by rings proceeded there in the depression years.

One of the most undeniably important political circumstances would be associated with the government assistance during the formative years of the industry, although a great number of the participants did not regard it as almighty. There were delicate shades of difference among the opinions in terms of appraisal of governmental support in the Japanese cotton industry. Compared with those of other countries, I drew attention to the indirect support maintained by the Japanese government besides its direct financial assistance for transplanting modern mills. On the other hand, K. Nakagawa declared the governmental support negligible, generally comparable with those of other industries in Japan, and D. Tripathi agreed with him. In any case it was confirmed that it was not a panacea.

N. Takamura also gave us a most useful macro-approach outline of the development of the Japanese cotton industry from a macro-economic standpoint. I think this was especially useful to foreign participants.

To our regret, among the various elements of the business climate discussed, the topic of intra-firm organizations (about which K. Nakagawa commented on my paper) was left unexplored. It has been said that the All Japan Spinners' Association was a very rare case of a successful attempt to reduce the operating spindleage of member firms. Lancashire was barren of trade associations, as D. A. Farnie said. In the U.S.A. there have always been a number of strong outsiders against trade agreements.

In the concluding discussion of the conference the participants worked together to compile strategic facts concerning each country's cotton textile industry. The result is Table 1.

I was deeply impressed with the number of stimulating questions and discerning answers at the conference, which enabled us to see a new possibility in treating the business history of this industry. At the same time, however, I have to confess that a lot of questions were left unexplored or even untouched. I think that historial works on managerial problems have a bright future, and this conference has given us an opportunity to collaborate in one common field of endeavor.

INDEX

A. & A. Lawrence Co.   205, 211, 212, 216, 217
Ahmedabad (India)   175, 178, 185, 187, 195, 196
Alabama, *see* Piedmont states
All-Japan Spinners' Association   29, 292
Alsace-Lorraine   94, 101, 106, 108–110, 113, 114, 115, 128, 131, 137
Amagasaki Cotton Spinning Company   141, 146, 147, 151–154, 170–171
amalgamation   22, 25, 29, 77, 90
   (*see also* merger movement)
Amalgamation Movement of 1898–1900   76
Amoskeag Manufacturing Co.   234
ancillary industries   57, 59, 60, 87
Anglo-American War of 1812–14   50
Appleton, Nathan   202, 203, 205–206, 215
April 19th Movement (Korea)   265
Ashton Brothers (Co.)   19
Ashton-under-Lyne (England)   62
Asian markets   ix, 11, 22, 54, 88
Augsburg (Germany)   108, 131
Ayer, James C.   201, 208–209, 212–218, 224

Baden   94, 108, 112, 115, 131
balance of trade   130
Bank of Japan   29, 284
banking   75, 83, 90, 102, 185, 203, 224, 284
Barlow & Jones (Co.)   19
Baumwoll-Spinnerei (Co.)   116
Bavaria   102, 108, 112–113, 136
Bayerisch-Schwaben region (Germany)   94
Belgium   101, 128
bimetalism   81
Blackburn district (England)   63, 68

Bolton (England)   26, 60–61, 67, 74
Bombay   20, 21, 175, 178, 183–184, 190, 195
Bombay Dyeing Co.   20, 196
Boston Associates   202–203, 224
Boxer Rebellion   147–148
Bremer Baumwollbörse (cotton exchange)
Britain, *see* England
British Textile Employers' Association   72
Brügelmann, J. G.   130
building societies   55
Burnley (England)   68, 70
business climate   41, 93, 101, 108, 126, 135, 137, 168, 179, 181, 270; and business decisions, 39; and business environment, 93, 126, 135–136; and business strategy, 42–43; definition of, 3, 39, 41, 126, 127, 136, 171–172, 246, 270, 274–275, 287; in Fall River, 25; in Germany, 93–94, 98–99, 100, 104, 108, 109, 111, 115, 117; in India, 27, 44, 197; in Japan, 29, 44, 159, 167; in Korea, 249, 263, 264, 265, 267, 268, 273; in Piedmont states, 227, 237; in U. K., 44; in U.S., 224
business ideology   151, 245
business strategy   42–43, 167

C. Itoh Co.   273
Calcutta   46
calico machines   113
Calico Printers' Association   69
Canada   202
capital   55, 90, 93, 181, 184, 186, 229, 284; fixed, 101, 284; founding, 255; loan, 55, 65
Centralverband deutscher Industrieller   118
chamber of commerce   107, 114

Chandler's paradigm 199, 200, 201, 202,
    206, 208, 219, 222, 223
chemical fiber industry 258, 259
chemical industry 58, 128, 257
child labor 100, 235
China 51, 52, 54: customs autonomy in,
    146, 149; domestic textile industry in,
    23, 89, 158; markets in, 28, 139, 140,
    155, 156, 157, 158, 159, 167, 187, 280
China-Japan War of 1937, *see* Sino-Japa-
    nese War
Cho-Sun Silk Producing Company 255
Civil Relief (Korea) 258
Civil War (U.S.) 51, 109, 111, 201, 213,
    228
coal mining industry 57
coarse yarn 112, 153, 154, 155, 156, 157
Coats Archibald 79
colonial environment 169, 175, 176
Columbia Water Power Co. (South Caro-
    lina) 237
commission 289; of Indian managing
    agents, 27, 185, 222–223; of Japanese
    trading firms, 30, 223; of Lowell sales
    agents, 201, 208, 212, 215, 216, 217,
    222; of New England commission
    houses, 225; of Northern U.S. commis-
    sion houses, 231
commission houses 231, 245, 247
communication facilities 39, 70, 107
Companies Acts (England) 196
company law 179, 180, 258
competition 76, 93, 109, 148, 262, 265,
    268
competitive bidding 178, 218
Control Law of Key Industries (Korea)
    256
Coolidge, T. Jefferson 234
cooperative society 26, 27, 31
"co-partnership" 178
Corporation Law (Japan) 284
cotton: blending, 140; exports, 278; con-
    sumption, 46, 47; cultivation, 244;
    supply, 72
    (*see also* raw cotton)
Cotton Board (England) 72
Cotton Famine, 1861–65 45, 46, 58, 63,
    65, 67, 111, 112, 113, 124
cotton spinning firms 1, 4–5, 6–7, 8–9,

12–13, 14–15, 95, 141, 169, 261, 262,
    288

Dainippon (Cotton Spinning Co.) 146,
    147, 153, 154, 157, 159
Dairen (Talien) 156
Daniels, G. W. 49
Davar, Cowasjee Nanabhoy 177, 182,
    188
deposit system (India) 184, 185, 186
depression 70; of 1837, 206; of 1857,
    208, 210; "Great Depression," 98, 115,
    117, 126
direct foreign investment 141, 146–147,
    149, 151, 153, 159
directors 205, 207
    (*see also* shareholders)
diversification 2, 11, 23, 25, 71
dividends 78, 207
D-Nylon Co. 266
Draper Co. 232

E. D. Sassoon United Mills Ltd. 20
East India Company 51
Economic Cooperation and Administra-
    tion (ECA) 258
Economic Development Plans (Korea)
    264
education 39; technical, 67
Ellison, Thomas 48
embroidery 129
employer-employee relations, *see* labor
    relations
Empress Mills 176, 177
engineers 70, 233, 245
England 81, 94, 101, 119, 122, 123, 128,
    175, 180, 189–190, 194
English Sewing Cotton Company 80, 83
Enquiry on the State of the Cotton and
    Linen Industry of 1878 114
entrepreneurial pattern 201, 207
entrepreneurs 127, 136, 154, 157, 159,
    170, 229, 287: American, 202, 203,
    208; English, 26, 34, 71; German, 93,
    99, 107, 108, 113–114, 117, 118, 124,
    129, 130, 137, 138; Indian, 27, 175,
    176, 195; Japanese, 27, 139, 167, 168;
    Korean, 253, 264; Scottish, 246, 247.
    (*See also* family business)

entrepreneurship 71, 82, 116, 150, 151, 153, 154, 157, 159, 168, 194, 199, 201, 206, 219, 221, 238
export responsibility system (Korea) 260
export strategy 80, 87, 128, 129, 130–131, 140, 152, 158, 167
external economies 59, 70, 74

factory legislation 54, 285
fair trade 81
Fall River, Mass. 19, 24, 221
Fall River Iron Works 25, 222
family business 42, 71, 182, 183, 194, 203, 211
fiber industry 257, 262
financial factors 168, 170, 171, 173, 185, 248, 288
Fine Cotton Spinners' and Doublers' Association 26, 69, 77
fine grade cloth production 233
finishing processes 19, 23, 24, 94, 128, 129, 288
First Republic (Korea) 178
First World War 141, 159, 167, 175, 177, 178
flax 45, 47
floating boom 29, 197, 222
"follower" firms 3, 41, 155, 159, 290
(*see also* "innovator" firms)
foreign subsidiaries, *see* overseas operations
France 60, 113, 114
Franken (Germany) 94, 107
free trade 81
Fuji Gasu (Cotton Spinning Co.) 150, 151, 152, 153, 154, 155, 157, 159, 171
Fukushima Cotton Spinning Co. 154, 156, 159, 170

G. A. Clark 79
Gandhi, Mahatma 187
Georgia, *see* Piedmont states
German cotton industry 93–94, 103, 117, 124, 126, 127, 128, 271: division of labor in, 115; domestic market in, 100; regionalization of, 130, 131; export orientation of, 127; market for, 113; yarn production in, 113, 119
German Custom Union 127, 128, 131
German Empire 127, 128, 131

German-French War of 1870–71 109, 113
German Reich 100, 114
Germany 94, 95, 99, 109, 122, 123; North German states, 109; southern Germany, 100, 102, 106, 107, 108, 114, 117
Gerrit van Delden & Co. 103
Gladbach Stock Company 100, 103, 136
Glasgow 246, 247
government, assistance to cotton industry 18, 29, 44, 125, 292
gray goods 275
Great Britain, *see* England
Great Exhibition of 1851 58
Gregory, Frances 202
Gronau (Germany) 103
growth of firms 23, 28, 288
growth-oriented management policies 266, 275

Hamilton Company 204, 207, 215
haulage industry 59
Hof (Germany) 108
horizontal reorganization 19, 42, 89, 90, 203
Horrockers (Co.) 19
Horrockses of Preston (Co.) 77
hosiery 119, 129
hydroelectric power 237

imitation, *see* "follower" firms
"imitation effect" 236, 290
imperialistic approach 169
import substitution 140, 146
Independent Labour Party 54
India 20, 21, 27, 28, 41, 51, 54, 175, 177, 179–184, 194: cotton duties, 72; exports, 141; industry in, 175, 181, 183; mills in, 185; social structure, 183; textile manufacturers in, 178, 187
Indian Company Act of 1850 180
individualism, *see* entrepreneurship
Industrial and Provident Act of 1852 26
industrial relations 186, 187
(*see also* labor relations)
Industrial Revolution 175
industrial welfare policy 107
industrialization 39, 94, 95, 99, 131,

167, 181, 249; rate of, 104
innovation 177, 184, 188, 265, 266, 267;
    "adaptive," 175, 197; primary, 176
"innovator" firms 3, 41, 290
    (*see also* "follower" firms)
insurance 55, 179
integration 3, 11, 18, 19, 22, 23, 24, 25,
    30, 31, 32, 103, 104, 150, 151, 213,
    221, 275, 284; forward, 211, 225
internal expansion 19, 25
International Cooperation Administra-
    tion aid fund 260
international division of labor 273
international monetary system 262
investors 93, 101, 116, 199, 200, 203,
    204
    (*see also* shareholders)
iron and steel industry 55, 107, 117

J. & P. Coats Co. 49, 58, 75, 77, 79
J. Hoyle (Co.) 19
J. N. Tata Co. 176, 177
J. Ryland (Co.) 19
J. W. Paige & Company 205, 215, 224
Japan 21–23, 28–30, 41, 74, 79: in Chi-
    na, 141, 146, 148, 149, 151, 152, 153,
    154, 155, 156, 157, 159, 167, 172; co-
    lonialism of, 264, 272; cotton industry
    of, 1, 127, 139, 167, 252, 277, 292;
    economy of, 127; export trade of, 89,
    149; in Korea, 252, 253, 254, 256,
    271, 273, 289
Japanese Cotton Spinners' Association
    44
Japanese-Korean Normalization Treaty
    273
joint stock companies 55, 56, 61, 74,
    102, 104, 178, 179, 180, 181, 194, 256,
    284
jute 46

Kanegafuchi Cotton Spinning Company
    2, 22, 23, 30, 141, 149, 151, 152, 153,
    154, 156, 159, 171
Kikuchi, K. 147, 152, 154, 157
Kim Nyum-Soo 254
Kim Sung-Soo 254, 255
Kishiwada Co. 154, 156, 157, 159, 170
knitting 128, 129

Kondratieff long waves 50
Korea: cotton industry in, 252, 253,
    261, 271; economic development in,
    260, 261, 265; fiber industry in, 249,
    265, 270; Foreign Exchange funds in,
    259; market in, 169; textile industry
    in, 270, 271
Korean War 257, 258, 264, 265
Kurashiki (Co.) 154, 156, 159, 170
Kyungsung Spinning and Weaving Com-
    pany 253, 254, 255, 264, 272, 274

labor costs 232, 234, 235, 238
labor market 54, 93, 104, 107, 125
labor productivity 171, 173, 177
labor relations 28, 72, 100, 121, 171,
    186, 187, 195, 246, 247, 267, 268, 274,
    285
lace 129
Lancashire Cotton Corporation 69
Lancashire cotton industry 11, 18, 24,
    27, 43, 47, 49, 54, 55, 63, 75, 94, 175,
    176, 177, 181, 184, 185
land availability 239
Laskari, Bechardas 185
Latin America 51, 59
Lee, H. 224
Lees & Wrigley (Co.) 84
Leipziger Baumwollspinnerei AG 103
limited companies 196, 254
limited liability 178, 179
linen 56, 131
Liverpool 49, 70, 72, 81
Lloyd's Packing Warehouses 57
loan system 26, 31, 196, 197
localization 236, 239, 288
Lokanathan, P.S. 197
London Stock Exchange 74
looms: hand, 58, 59, 125; narrow, 22;
    Northrop, 102, 232; power, 22, 95,
    102, 112, 113, 125, 202, 277, 281;
    wide, 22
low-growth policy 268
Lowell (Carpet) Company 212, 214, 216
Lowell, Francis Cabot 202
Lowell, Massachusetts 19, 199, 200, 201,
    204, 214, 219, 221, 223, 224
Lower Silesia region 131

machine making 48, 58, 62
macro-economic approach 49
management 73, 136, 158, 187, 188, 199, 200, 201, 203, 207, 209, 213, 245, 255, 264, 268, 270; cooperative, 26, 222
management style 30, 31, 156, 159, 187, 266
managerial problems 206, 292
managerial skills 29, 181, 233, 239
managers, professional 29, 32, 43, 199, 209, 210, 221, 225, 245
managing agency system (India) 20, 27, 28, 31, 42, 179, 181, 183, 184, 188, 189, 190, 194, 196, 222, 223, 274
Manchester 26, 56, 60, 63, 66, 67, 70, 73, 75, 77, 81, 176, 246
Manchester Chamber of Commerce 81
Manchester Cotton Association 72
Manchester Exchange 76
Manchester Liners 72
Manchester Ship Canal 55, 72
market conditions 43, 99, 172, 199, 219; response to, 154, 157, 159
market mechanism 24, 250, 268
marketing 205, 208, 212, 267
Marshall, Alfred 59, 72, 80
Marxist historians 49, 55
Mason and Lawrence (Co.) 224
Massachusetts State Legislative Committee on Manufactures 210
Masters' associations 72
McGouldrick, P. F. 225
mechanization 92, 95
medium and small-scale firms 130
Meiji government 28
merger movement 19, 21, 22, 29, 42, 43 (*see also* amalgamation)
Merrimack Manufacturing Company 203, 207, 221
Merwanji Framji & Company 183
Middlesex Woollen Company 208, 209, 210
Mie Cotton Spinning Co. 141, 148
mill: agent 204, 205, 222; combined, 102; decline of small-sized, 124; location 22, 107, 227, 228, 237, 238; settlement patterns 234, 235, 238; size 247
Mitsubishi group 273
Mitsui Bussan Company 280, 285

Mitsui group 141, 273
Miyajima, K. 155, 157
Mönchengladbach (Germany) 107, 112, 131
money lenders 179
Montgomery, J. 223
Moody, Paul 202
mule spinning technology 87, 88, 112, 285
Muto, S. 149, 155, 157

Nagasaki (Cotton Spinning Co.) 154
Nagpur (India) 176
Naigaiwata Co. 141, 158
national capital 253, 254, 264
national goals 160, 167
national landowners 254
nepotism 217, 256
Netherlands 101, 106
New Bedford (Mass.) 221
New England 19, 201, 227, 247
Nippon Yūsen Company 281
Nisshin Cotton Spinning Co. 154, 155, 157, 159
North Carolina, *see* Piedmont states
Northrop looms 102, 232

Ohara (president of Kurashiki Co.) 156, 157
oil shock 262
Oldham (England) 21, 24, 26, 55, 57, 60, 62–68, 70, 196
Oldham Limited 26
Osaka Cotton Spinning Co. 21, 29, 147, 148, 197
Osaka Godo (Cotton Spinning Co.) 151, 152, 153, 154, 157, 159, 170, 171
Oriental Mills 183
overall frame structures 101
overseas operations 79, 140, 147, 160, 169; *see also* direct foreign investment

packing industry 56
Paige, James W. 205 (*see also* J. W. Paige & Company)
papermaking industry 57
partnership 178, 179, 180, 181, 182, 202, 224
Pender, John 73

Pepperell Mills   221
Philadelphia   24
Piedmont states   227, 229, 232, 237
Piedmont, South Carolina   236
Platt Brothers (Co.)   58, 63–64, 66, 67,
   177, 194, 285
population growth   99
product market structures   150, 151, 152,
   153, 157, 159, 168, 170
production orientation   168, 253, 266,
   275
production technology   251, 266, 267
productivity   137, 262
profit margins   47, 73
"proto-economic space"   131
proxy voting reform   214, 215
Prussia   100, 131
Prussian-Austrian War of 1866   109
public companies   11, 18, 21, 26, 28, 31,
   222

Rabbeth ring spindles   176
railways   55, 100, 107, 108
rate discrimination   238
rationalization   74, 107
raw cotton   50, 60, 107, 111, 112, 117,
   122, 127, 128, 235, 285
raw silk production   259
rayon   23
Redlich, F.   127
reflotation boom of 1919–20   74
regionalization   71, 94, 115, 130, 131
reserve rate   166
Rhedyt (Germany)   107, 112
Rhenish cotton industry   137
Rhineland   94, 95, 102, 103, 107, 112,
   114
ring frame   47, 177, 285
ring spindles   88, 102, 176, 195
risk-taking   265, 266, 267
Rochdale (England)   26, 67, 196
Rossendale (England)   68
Royton (England)   27
Russo-Japanese War   141

sales agents   200, 201, 204, 207, 216, 217,
   218, 224
Samil Independence Movement   253,
   254, 272

Saxony   94, 95, 107, 109, 112, 113, 114
scale of enterprise   74, 103, 231, 244
Schumpeter, J.   41, 127, 222
Scotland   247
self-compensation   261
self-sufficiency   119, 131, 135, 138 257
Settsu Spinning Co.   147, 170, 171, 281
sewing machine   56, 79
Shanghai Cotton Spinning Co.   140
shareholders   179, 182, 184, 188, 189,
   190, 207, 211, 215, 217, 221, 256
Shaw (England)   27
Shimonoseki Treaty   140
Shirley Institute   72
Silesia (Germany)   94, 112, 131
silk weaving   112
Sino-Japanese War   146, 256
Smith, Adam   69
sole proprietorship   178, 179, 182
South Carolina, *see* Piedmont states
Southern Railway System   238
southern states (U.S.)   19; mills in, 227,
   235
spindleage   11, 20, 21, 25, 26, 47, 54, 60,
   95–98, 101, 113, 114, 194, 230, 231
Spinners' Association   280, 281, 285
spinning and weaving   16, 68, 76, 94
   126, 127, 128, 257, 259, 279
steam power   101, 237, 285
stock companies   90, 100
stock exchanges   102
subsidiary industries, *see* ancillary industries
Suez Canal   46, 55
Sun Mill   67, 197
surplus production   115
Switzerland   47, 101, 106, 119, 128
synthetic fibers   259, 260

Taniguchi, F.   154, 157
tariff reform of 1879   118, 136
tariffs   79, 81, 82, 89, 93, 100, 101, 108,
   111, 113, 115, 117, 119, 125, 137, 139,
   147, 149, 170, 290
tax system   251
technicians, English   106
technology   41, 47, 93, 101, 128, 175,
   176, 177, 188, 265, 268; development
   of, 101–2

terms of trade 99
Textile Institute 72
thread trade 76
Tientsin (Tianjin) 156
Tokyo Cotton Spinning Co. 155
Tootal, Broadhurst, Lee & Co. 19, 69
Towka Cotton Spinning and Weaving
  Co. 140
Toyo Cotton Spinning Co. 30, 147, 148,
  151, 154, 155, 159, 171
trade press 73
trade unions, *see* labor relations
trademarks 80
trading companies 23, 30, 90, 246, 278,
  281, 284, 289
transport facilities 70, 128, 235, 238
treasurers 204, 205, 211, 218, 225
Tremont and Suffolk Companies 218
tulle 130
two-shift system 285

U. K. (United Kingdom) 11, 18, 19,
  25, 119
  (*see also* England)
U.S.A. 19, 20, 24, 25, 50, 51, 60, 74,
  79, 119, 272; cotton textile industry,
  202, 227
Union Bank of Calcutta 179
United Nations 258, 272

von Juraschek, F. 194

Wada, Toyoharu 152, 155, 157
Wadsworth, A. P. & J. de L. Mann 49

wages 54, 141, 234
Waltham Company 203, 205
Ward and Company 203
Ware, C. F. 225
water power 95, 107, 236, 285
weaving 94, 103, 128, 129; half-cotton,
  112; hand, 20, 24, 95, 109, 112;
  (*see also* spinning and weaving)
weaving capacity 147, 148, 152, 155,
  156, 157, 159, 170
Weberei-Augsburg 116
Westphalia 94, 106, 108, 136
wool 45, 47, 258
wool spinning and weaving industry 56,
  81, 112, 259
workers: female, 285; unskilled, 106
Worrall's Cotton Spinners' and Manufacturers' Directory 50
Württemberg 94, 108

yarn 63; agents for, 61, 68; consumption of, 150–51; cotton, 141, 146, 277;
  epxort of, 152–54; fine-count type, 146,
  153, 155, 159; gas-burned, 147; medi-
  um-count, 146, 147, 155, 157; milling,
  231, 238
Yashiro (president, Fukushima Cotton
  Spinning Co.) 156, 157
Yi Dynasty 249

zaibatsu 28
Zollverein 99, 100, 109
Zorn, W. 127